BLACK

Parm Sandhu joined the p ___ough
the ranks to become the hig...st ranking female Asian officer in
the Met. Among many honours, Parm has been awarded Asian
Woman of the Year, the Vasakhi Award (Mayor of London)
and the Sikh Women of Distinction Award (Sikh Women's
Alliance).

Stuart Prebble was for many years a leading television journalist,
notably on ITV's *World in Action* programme, and later became
CEO of ITV. He is now a successful producer and writer.

'Inspiring... Sandhu's account of her ascent through the ranks
of the Met is testament to her extraordinary tenacity and
ambition... Shines an important light on the Met's failure to
understand and represent the diverse community it serves.'
Observer

'Parm Sandhu's story is an inspiration to anyone who has found
themselves struggling against adversity. It's also a page-turner
which everyone who cares about policing and justice in Britain
should read.' Meera Syal

'A captivating exhibition of courage and conviction, Sandhu's
story is an inspiration for those facing prejudice and a revelation
for those in the dark.' David Lammy MP

'A brilliant book full of nail-biting tension and shocking statistics that make it hard to put down. It made me simultaneously angry and tearful. Parm's story leaps off the page and makes you want to walk every step of the way with her, to be her friend, to stand shoulder to shoulder with her.' Andi Oliver

'*Black and Blue* is a profoundly moving account of life as a senior police officer. It is essential reading for anyone who wants to understand our police service.' Rob Rinder

'A powerful, page-turning – and often shocking – story of courage. It's essential reading for those interested in the state of policing Britain, and for readers who enjoy memoirs with inspirational bite.' Joanne Owen, LoveReading

BLACK
AND
BLUE

One woman's story of policing and prejudice

PARM SANDHU

With STUART PREBBLE

Atlantic Books
London

First published in Great Britain in 2021 by Atlantic Books,
an imprint of Atlantic Books Ltd.

This paperback edition first published in Great Britain
in 2023 by Atlantic Books.

1 2 3 4 5 6 7 8 9

A CIP catalogue record for this book is available from
the British Library.

Paperback ISBN: 978-1-83895-267-9
E-book ISBN: 978-1-83895-266-2

Design and typesetting benstudios.co.uk

Printed in Great Britain by Clays Ltd, Elcograf S.p.A.

Atlantic Books
An Imprint of Atlantic Books Ltd
Ormond House
26–27 Boswell Street
London
WC1N 3JZ

www.atlantic-books.co.uk

For Satnam

Authors' note

Victims of crime and abuse are entitled to privacy and so, in some cases, are the perpetrators. For this reason we have made some minor amendments of detail, in order to protect identities where necessary.

Contents

Prologue

These days, the Eleanor Street district of Bow in the East End of London isn't somewhere you'd want to visit at night. Small industrial units line up on one side, and a railway bridge at the junction with Tidworth Road provides shelter for all manner of nefarious activities. And it certainly wasn't somewhere you wanted to spend time in the dark winter months of the 1990s. All sorts of street crime, drug abuse, prostitution and burglaries were rife in the area, and little in the way of street lights made it feel like a dangerous place to be.

One freezing cold night in February 1990, at a point just below the railway bridge, the designated Metropolitan Police Area Driver for the borough pulled his car over to the side of the road. Area Cars ferry firearms officers or local patrol officers, and are kept on standby in major cities and large urban counties for moments when emergency help is needed. The cars are always high performance, and the men who drive them are high-performance officers – specially trained in tactical pursuit, advanced driving and stopping fleeing offenders – their status frequently the envy of fellow officers.

On that February evening, however, this particular Area Driver wasn't feeling very revered. Rather the reverse, because – before leaving the police station at the start of his shift – he'd had an altercation with his superior officer. The argument was over the question of who would accompany him on his patrol that night. His usual partner was not available, and so his inspector asked him to take a new recruit along with him instead.

Area Drivers are so exalted they're usually allowed to choose their own partner, and this one informed his superior officer that he didn't want to babysit some rookie. However, when the exact identity of his new partner was revealed, his objections multiplied. If it wasn't bad enough that the officer in question was fresh out of Hendon, she was also female, she was young, and she was Asian.

She was me. At the time, I was just 25 years old and the only young female Asian officer based at Limehouse station, and one of the small number of black, Asian and minority ethnic (BAME) officers who made up less than 1 per cent of the entire 28,000-strong Metropolitan Police Service (MPS).

After a heated dispute with our inspector, the Area Driver was eventually ordered to allow me to get into the passenger side of the car. He slammed shut his own door, put his foot down hard, and we set off on our patrol of the neighbourhood. He hardly spoke to me at all after we left the station, and I did my best not to irritate him any further by asking questions. I remember hunching myself up as far away from him as possible, pressing myself back against the seat to keep out of his eyeline.

Our patrol continued in silence around the main highways of Bow and Limehouse but then, without warning or explanation, we turned off the A11 at Mornington Grove and headed towards some of the unlit side-streets. I was curious but didn't dare ask what the Area Driver had in mind. A few minutes later, he stopped the car under the railway bridge in Eleanor Street.

It was a moonless night, and the grimy, graffiti-covered brick of the bridge made for dark and dingy surroundings. I had no idea why we'd stopped, but there was another car parked on the side of the road.

'That motor over there,' the driver said. 'Looks like it might have been nicked. Check out the number plate.' I told him there wasn't enough light to be able to see from our distance, but he wasn't having it. 'Go over and take a closer look,' he ordered.

I was reluctant at first, but he was very much the boss so I thought I'd better do as I was told. I opened the door, got out and started walking.

I was already feeling ill at ease, heading away from the light of the car and into the gloom, but suddenly I heard a powerful engine roaring into life behind me, and turned to see the Area Car setting off at high speed. Within a moment, I was alone in the middle of nowhere, plunged into almost total darkness, unable to see more than a few yards, in an area well known to be a crime spot. Just a few yards further along was a site designated for the travelling community, many of whom, at that time, lived as much outside the law as within it. I was terrified.

Unable to believe what was happening, I reached for my personal radio and pressed the switch to broadcast an emergency message, but there was no response. Now my concern was rising fast, so I tried again – nothing, but as I looked around it became clear that the bridge overhead was obliterating any chance of a signal. I was checking my bearings to determine which direction I should walk in when I heard footsteps approaching from out of the darkness. Within a few seconds, I could see two men coming towards me from the direction of the travellers' site. Both were smiling, but their smiles didn't look friendly.

'Hey, are you on the game?' said one, laughing.

I was, of course, in full police uniform, so the question was hardly a serious one.

'How much will it cost us?' asked the other.

I mustered my courage and told the pair to back off, but felt my voice catch in my throat. At only 5 foot 3 ½ inches tall, and of slight build, I felt very vulnerable in a dark street with no access to back-up, and no way to raise the alarm if I were attacked. My fingers closed around the grip of what seemed to be a very flimsy truncheon. I tried to summon up my most authoritative voice.

'Don't be stupid now,' I said. 'Just step away.'

The men were not impressed.

'We could certainly have some fun with you,' said one, and once again the two men exchanged looks and laughed.

I truly believed I was going to be assaulted or raped, and suddenly I had a visceral recall of the moment nine years earlier, when the man I'd only just met but been forced to marry, overwhelmed and raped me on our wedding night. I was just 16 years old. Now, here I was again. New on the job, new on this beat, unfamiliar with the area, and completely powerless and out of my depth. I turned and started running, and I ran and ran and ran, almost all the way back to Limehouse, with the peal of the men's laughter echoing around my head.

The incident was only the latest – and most serious – in several months of my life as a probationary WPC (woman police constable), in which I had already been frequently punched and kicked during demos, abused in the street, and subject to everyday racism and discrimination at work. That same night I telephoned my friend Shabnam Chaudhri. 'I've finally had enough,' I told her. 'I'm going to quit.'

'No, you're not.' Her tone left no room for doubt. Then Shab reminded me of the agreement we'd made just a few months earlier as new recruits training at Hendon. 'Don't let the bastards grind you down!'

Next morning, still feeling shaken and upset, I went to find the inspector and told him what had happened. He was unsympathetic. 'You could make a formal complaint if you like, but then again he's the Area Driver and you're just a nobody.' Junior and inexperienced though I was, I already knew enough about the Met to understand that, no matter what injustice you might experience, you must never complain. Anyone who did could be ostracized, made the victim of dirty tricks or, worse still, denied back-up in case of emergency.

All that was thirty years ago, and by October 2019, when I resigned from the Met, I was a chief superintendent – making history as the first non-white female to rise through the ranks and achieve that status in the 189 years of the London force.

My time in the Met was full of incident – some of it positive, even comic, much of it disappointing – and I have had more than my share of tragedy. It's been an extraordinary career in many ways, and as I began to see the end of it looming up ahead, several people told me I should write my life story. Kind friends pointed out that my journey from a family of immigrants who spoke no English to becoming the highest-ranking BAME female in the Metropolitan Police would be an inspiration to some and a revelation to many. I always shrugged off the suggestion – excusing myself by saying I didn't have the time, had signed the Official Secrets Act, and anyway I didn't think I was all that special.

There the matter might have rested, but what I didn't know was that I had already made the mistake that would turn my career, and my life, upside down. It was a mistake I should have learned not to make all those years earlier – a mistake I'd warned others against making many times since. Nonetheless, it was a mistake that a number of black, Asian or minority ethnic police officers had made in recent years. Sick and tired of being bypassed, bulldozed or ignored, I had finally confronted a white senior officer about what I suspected was a breach of regulations, and from the moment the complaint was made, my professional life would never be the same again.

Suddenly, having broken through more glass ceilings than any other BAME woman in the Met, and having upheld the law the best way I knew how for nearly thirty years, I found myself accused of a series of charges of misconduct, gross misconduct, and even of breaking the law. False and malicious allegations were leaked to newspapers, and the force to which I had given loyal service above and beyond the call of duty turned its fire on me in a manner which seems so vindictive that it defies understanding.

But as incomprehensible as the story is, what happened to me follows a familiar pattern. When a black or Asian officer in the Metropolitan Police toes the line, keeps their head down and suffers racial and/or gender discrimination in silence, we are tolerated and can even thrive – up to a point. If and when any of us stands up and says, 'I'm not having this,' we instantly become subject to a systematic campaign of smears and persecution more fitted to the pages of Kafka. At the time of writing, no fewer than five of the six BAME officers of chief superintendent rank or above in the MPS are under investigation for alleged misconduct.

It didn't have to be so. In London, 43 per cent of people are from a BAME background, and yet the police force seeking to serve this population contains only 14 per cent BAME officers. Given how under-represented black, Asian and minority ethnic communities are in its ranks, the Met could so easily have used my story as an example to encourage recruitment from among these groups. Instead, I found myself compelled to end my career by resorting to what would inevitably be a highly public and damaging employment tribunal, citing evidence of systematic and long-term discrimination on grounds of race and gender. To any black or Asian youth considering

joining the Metropolitan Police Service, the message would
be clear: Don't.

My eventual decision to take my case to an employment
tribunal didn't come easily. It was the culmination of thirty years
of enduring regular episodes of discrimination – many relatively
slight and many breathtaking. Incidents have ranged from low-
level sexual and racial abuse, which was so commonplace that
it became part of my daily routine, to finding myself in the
crosshairs of forces which seemed determined to thwart any
promotion, or even to drive me from the service altogether.
It's a story which many people might find unsettling, but it
should not be surprising, because my life in the police has been
conducted against a background of seemingly never-ending
reports from public inquiries, parliamentary select committees,
the Commission for Racial Equality (CRE) and the Equality
and Human Rights Commission, among others – all of them
highly critical of racism in the Met and exhorting the force to
do better. More than two decades after the Macpherson report
into the murder of black teenager Stephen Lawrence branded
the Metropolitan Police Service as institutionally racist, most
of the data and most of the experience demonstrate that little
or nothing has been learned.

The evidence is stark. A young black man on the streets of
England and Wales today is forty times more likely to be stopped
and searched than his white counterpart. Officers in the Met
are four times as likely to use force against a black person than
against a white person. A black person driving a car is twice as
likely to be pulled over and required to produce documents.

In the event that someone from the BAME community should choose to join a force which many regard as the enemy, they are less likely than their white colleagues to stay the course. If they do stay, they are less likely than their white colleagues to achieve promotion to the higher ranks. They are twice as likely to be accused of misconduct and, once accused, are more likely to be found culpable. If accused, their names are more likely to be leaked to the media, which will highlight the charges alleged against them in bold headlines. If found guilty, they will receive more serious disciplinary sanctions than white officers. A higher proportion of BAME officers, sick and tired of the perpetual struggle, will give up and retire early. Or our careers will end with a rancorous employment tribunal.

All this means that, when the Met's first female commissioner Cressida Dick claims that the force is no longer institutionally racist, as she did on the twenty-fifth anniversary of the murder of Stephen Lawrence, the facts very clearly say otherwise. The Chair of the House of Commons Home Affairs Committee, Yvette Cooper, described progress in dealing with the criticisms made by the Macpherson report as 'glacial'. In light of the most recent discriminatory treatment of BAME officers, such as myself, even that depressing metaphor might seem to be over-optimistic.

I hope that the story of my early life, in a family whose customs were formed in a very different time and place, contributes to a wider understanding of the struggle undergone by hundreds of thousands of second-generation immigrants into Britain. I also hope that my account of the daily life of a police officer will encourage people to consider the price paid by any ordinary copper who dedicates themselves to serving the public. Most of all, though, I believe that my experience of finding myself on the wrong side of a police service still riddled to the core with institutionalized racism should make every one of us feel ashamed.

My story – and the stories of so many of my fellow BAME officers – is of a struggle against adverse odds. A good place to begin this particular tale is in the Punjab area of northern India nearly twenty years before I was born.

CHAPTER ONE

A Difficult Child

Both my parents, Malkit and Gurmaj, were born in the small village of Rurka Kalan in the Tehsil Phillaur area of Jalandhar in the Punjab. One day, sometime in 1951, a group of strangers arrived in the village carrying a message for the young men of the community. Any man willing to travel to the land of the former colonial ruler, they promised, would find work and would prosper, so that he would be in a position to send money back home to support his family. Since supporting the extended family was seen to be one of the main duties of the men of the Sikh community, there were plenty of volunteers.

My dad, Malkit, always told us he was chosen to come to Britain over any of his four brothers because he was known to be the hardest worker. He and my mum, Gurmaj, had been married by arrangement between their families when she was just 10 years old, and she'd given birth to their first child – my eldest sister – Jindo, while still in her teens.

Being an entirely rural community where everyone lived off the land, life was very hard. These were the years before investment in agricultural technology and developments in seed fertilizers boosted the production of wheat and rice in the region, and tilling the soil and the constant need for irrigation called for heavy manual labour. A woman bearing a son added a useful pair of hands to the joint effort, whereas a woman bearing a daughter simply introduced an extra mouth to feed. If that was not bad enough, there would later be the potentially huge expense of getting together a dowry, which must be provided when the girl came to be married. This would inevitably include a set of clothes, gifts for all the husband's family, and something in gold – nothing less than 24 carats would do. Unfortunately for Gurmaj, she had two more children in quick succession, but one of them was another girl, Balbiro. The family of farmers had already experienced one of the deprivations of poverty in a land recently partitioned following independence from Britain; Jindo suffered from an eye infection as a child, and the failure to have it treated led to permanent blindness.

All of this was such a serious disappointment that some members of her community told Gurmaj she was worthless, and that the best service she could perform for her hard-pressed family would be to commit suicide. Taking her two daughters with her would reduce the hungry mouths by three. So great was the pressure on her that, one day, she took Jindo and Balbiro to the edge of the well in her village, and was at the point of throwing my two sisters and herself down. Just in time, she stopped and thought, 'No, we are worth more than this,' and decided to spare her own life and that of her two girls. It was a story from the past which she told me many times as a child growing up years later in Handsworth, and which I would have many occasions to bring to mind way into the future.

My dad was one of approximately 7,000 Sikhs from the region who came to Britain that year. No-one from the family today is quite sure how he managed it, but he travelled on an illegal passport in the name of Amar Nath, with a made-up date of birth. The village all contributed to the cost of the air fare on the understanding that they would be repaid from his future earnings, which eventually they were. Dad was immediately shipped to the Smethwick area of Birmingham, where he quickly got a job as a labourer at Birmid Industries. Birmid was an iron, aluminium and magnesium foundry, one of the largest employers in Smethwick, providing jobs to thousands of local people. It was hard, hot and dirty work, involving long hours and sometimes dangerous conditions – a million miles away from Dad's harsh but essentially rustic life back in the Punjab. These young men worked six or seven days per week in fourteen-hour shifts. If, and when, they did take any time off, there was nowhere for them to go for relaxation or to practise their religion. They felt themselves abandoned in a country where they couldn't speak to anyone other than fellow Indians, and they also couldn't speak freely to each other at work because safety requirements meant they had to wear ear protectors.

It was tough to find somewhere to live because many of the local people didn't want to rent rooms to immigrants. Signs on pubs and lodgings featured variations of 'No blacks, no Irish, no dogs', and Dad used to say that the British treated dogs better. Eventually he got a place in a shared house where he 'hot-bedded' with other shift workers. It was not unusual in those days for twenty-five young men to share a house, with those working on the night shift sleeping by day and those on the day shift sleeping by night. After a while, groups of men circumvented the system by pooling their resources to buy a house for one of them, who would then assist the others to buy the next house, and so on.

Conscious that his status as an immigrant might not stand up to the closest scrutiny, Dad was always terrified of authority. He'd been advised by others in the community that he should never look a white person in the eye, and always seemed to lower his head when he spoke to outsiders. That didn't save him from encountering racism on his way to and from work, and in later years he told me that he and his friends were regularly kicked, punched and beaten by gangs of white youths, as well as by the police. One time he was knocked off his bike by a car and he apologized to the driver. It turned out that he had broken his leg, but Dad was afraid of doctors so wouldn't go to hospital. The leg healed itself after a time but after that he always walked with a limp.

Despite having to shoulder the burden of taking financial care of a family he now never saw, Malkit made a decent wage for the times, and tried to make the best of his new life in a strange country. For the first time, he was independent and living far away from the tight religious observance of his homeland. Heavy consumption of alcohol became normalized within the community, especially among manual labourers, and local publicans eventually saw the opportunity to stage cabaret acts targeting the needs of young men living a long way from home. Within limits, my father became 'one of the boys', enjoying drinking beer and other freedoms. This went on for eleven years – until 1962, when the imminent prospect of new restrictions in the form of the Commonwealth Immigration Act meant it might well be 'now or never', and he was finally ready to send for his wife and children.

When Gurmaj arrived in Britain to join my father, Jindo was 15, my brother Faljinder was 13 and Balbiro was 11. None of them spoke any English, but by then Dad had managed to save enough money to put down a deposit on a small house in Tiverton Road, Smethwick.

Due to the shortage of manpower after the Second World War, Smethwick had already attracted a large number of immigrants from Commonwealth countries, and Sikhs from the Punjab were the biggest ethnic group. These minority communities were unpopular with many in the white British population of the borough, which had become home to a higher percentage of recent immigrants than anywhere else in England. The boom in job vacancies had proven to be short-lived, and in the same year that my mother and my older sisters and brother arrived from India, a series of factory closures and a growing waiting list for social housing caused race riots in the town. Just two years after that, in the 1964 general election, the Labour MP, shadow Foreign Secretary Patrick Gordon

Walker, lost his seat on a 7 per cent swing to the Conservatives. His defeat followed a campaign in which the slogan 'If you want a n————— for a neighbour, vote Labour' had been used in support of the winning candidate, Peter Griffiths. In his maiden speech in the Commons, Griffiths drew attention to the fact that 4,000 families in his constituency were in the queue for local authority accommodation.

Notwithstanding the prejudice prevalent in parts of the wider white society, my mum and dad lived in an area where all their friends and neighbours were from the same region of India, so they saw no reason to integrate with the host community, or indeed to learn to speak English. They also experienced no pressures to conform to the ways of their adopted country, so their thoughts quickly turned to arranging a marriage for their eldest daughter Jindo. The problem was that her blindness meant that making an advantageous match was not going to be a simple matter. Eventually the couple agreed that 16-year-old Jindo should be married to an older man from West Bromwich.

It was into this culture and mindset that Malkit and Gurmaj's first child to be born in Britain arrived on 5 December 1963 in St Chad's Hospital, Birmingham. They named me Parmjit but always called me Pummy, although my Western name was Parm as I got older. All my life, I've been told what a difficult child I was. My mother later described me as 'the most miserable child ever' and regularly said she wished she'd killed me at birth. Even today, I'm not completely sure whether or not she was serious.

I was followed by my younger sister Sarj in 1965, and my younger brother Satnam in 1966. With Jindo no longer living with the family, my parents and their other five children squashed into the two-up two-down house in Tiverton Road. The congestion was made worse because my dad, being the head of the family and still working shifts at Birmid, slept alone in one of the two bedrooms. This left my mother and the children to sleep together in the other, which had so many beds squeezed together that you had to jump from one to another. I remember that several of the beds were second-hand from hospitals, and there were no gaps to walk in between so the whole room looked and felt like a giant trampoline. The overcrowding was made still more difficult because we were seldom allowed to go into one of the downstairs rooms because it was 'for best'. Despite the best efforts of my mum and dad, there were constant infestations of rats and mice. There were no carpets on the floors, which were covered instead with linoleum. The kitchen had stone flags and they used to drag in a tin tub from the back yard, fill it with hot water boiled on the stove, and all of us children would have baths on Friday nights.

There was no dining table, so all of us sat cross-legged on the floor to eat our food. Most of the plates had hotel names on them and were mismatched with enamel cups and bowls that had been bought second hand from the local market. Nothing in our house was new; there were no toys for any children and no celebrations for Christmas or for birthdays. Birthdays were said to be 'for gurus' (disciples of god), which we certainly were not.

I have a memory that everything was covered in brightly covered fabric which made it seem happy. My mum used to buy material at the local market, and she would knit or crochet covers for the furniture. She also had an old Singer hand-operated sewing machine, and so very little of our clothing was shop-bought, and was either homemade or handed down from siblings or neighbours. Four yards of multi-coloured material would be enough to make a complete outfit, consisting of a long dress, with matching trousers and a headscarf. Often, she would unravel jumpers and then reknit them for us, which was as close as we got to wearing new clothing.

The family had brought very few possessions from India other than a few old quilts. What they *had* brought with them was a strong culture which put the family at the centre of all aspects of life. Having lived as a Sikh minority in a region long dominated by Muslims, loyalty to the family was considered to be not so much a matter of social convenience, but more one of survival. A family's esteem within our community was measured by its prestige and honour, or *behzti*, which in turn were a function of the family members' *izzat* – their ability to garner wealth, especially land, but also the obedience and chastity of the daughters, for whom advantageous marriages must be procured.

Our house was separated from next door by a narrow alleyway, and on the other side of the divide was another family from the same area of India. Two of our neighbours' children, known to us kids as Bubby and Juggi, were more or less my age, and so were natural playmates. No-one from the

Indian community was given individual surnames at the time – all the men added 'Singh', meaning lion, to their names, and the women 'Kaur', meaning princess. As children, we'd play hopscotch and games of chase, but mostly we would ride our bikes around the block. Dad was always pretty useful at mechanical things, and made my bike himself from spare parts he'd managed to collect.

One day, the people next door had a telephone installed, which was a rare and amazing thing, so there was even more traffic across the alleyway. Family members were constantly going back and forth, making and taking calls with friends and relatives from the locality or sometimes from the sub-continent.

I also remember that Dad brought home an old black-and-white television which was propped up high on a cabinet. Needless to say, there was no remote control, so the children had to climb up if we wanted to change the channel. I enjoyed *The Man from U.N.C.L.E.*, *Blue Peter* and cop shows like *Starsky & Hutch*, but I wondered why the programmes featured so few people who looked like me, unless of course they were criminals. We could never find the right place for the aerial, and so my younger sister Sarj would be required to stand and hold it in position above her head –a grievance I don't think she's forgiven to this day.

Dad was still working long hours and incredibly hard, and occasionally we'd go to visit him at the foundry at the weekend. We were mesmerized as we watched our father wearing a protective mask and goggles, while hot sparks flew all around him and molten metal was poured nearby. On

Sundays, we would pick the fragments of metal out of his work-clothes.

Apart from cutting his hair and shaving his beard for reasons of safety at work, Dad's only real concession to integration was to abandon the turban which was so emblematic of the Sikh faith of his forefathers. Many of his contemporaries preferred not to follow suit, and in August 1967, just down the road in Wolverhampton, a bus driver named Tarsem Singh Sandhu (no relation) returned to work after a period of sick leave wearing a turban. He was sacked for failing to observe rules on uniform, and subsequently some 6,000 Sikhs marched through the streets in his support. There were significant signs of a white backlash, and a letter appeared in the local paper in which the correspondent claimed, 'It is time they [the Sikhs] realized this is England, not India.' After two further marches, the leader of the local Sikh community, Sohan Singh, declared his intention to set fire to himself on 13 April if the Wolverhampton Transport Committee did not change its policy. Four days before the deadline, the Mayor of Wolverhampton, describing the threat as blackmail, reluctantly gave in, having been 'forced to have regard to the wider implications'.

Meanwhile, our dad still liked a drink and loved music, playing the radio for much of the time, and also kept a reel-to-reel tape recorder with Indian music for special occasions. I suspect he was 'a bit of a lad' during his time in England alone, but once our mum and his children and responsibilities arrived, he struggled with depression. Later, as I was growing up, he was in and out of a number of mental institutions, and I vividly recall the trauma of standing outside a treatment room as he underwent various rather primitive 'electro-therapies'. For the moment, though, his wage was steady, and so our parents began to allow themselves a few luxuries. Mum's pride and joy was a highly ornate tea-set with gold detailing, bought at the market for £20, which was a week's wages. It was kept in a display cabinet and only used once or twice a year for special occasions.

It was soon very clear to the family that I wasn't conforming with the quiet, unassuming and almost invisible role traditionally played by young girls from the Sikh community. I would speak without waiting to be spoken to, and would not readily merge into the background, allowing my brothers to take centre stage. I was always wanting things, and continuously getting into trouble. (A prized china dog which was kept on a window-ledge was mysteriously broken and the culprit has never been identified to this day.) Nonetheless, I was entrusted to walk to the off-licence on the corner of the road carrying a two-pint glass jug which would be filled with mild ale and carried home for my dad. Mum used to manage all the money, and on Friday nights she would give Dad a small amount for beer at the pub, and then he would bring back a bag of chips.

On Saturday mornings, Dad would walk me down to Smethwick library. Although he still spoke no English himself, and the whole family spoke only Punjabi at home, he ensured that all three of his British-born children had learned the English alphabet before we started at primary school.

Later, the house in Tiverton Road was the subject of a compulsory purchase order and our family moved a mile and a half to 22 Paddington Road, Handsworth. Another tiny terraced house, but this one had three steps from garden gate to front door, and three upstairs bedrooms. Still, every Saturday, Dad would walk me, and later also my sister and brother, to the library. He would never come in with us, preferring to wait outside whatever the weather, feeling that his working clothes were not suitable. The librarian once said to me that he could come in and wait. I went out and told my dad, but he said that people like him couldn't go into places like that. He didn't complain, even if we took a long time choosing books.

I spoke some limited English when I first went to school at Parkside Infants in Smethwick, but it hardly mattered because most of the community was Indian. Although the lessons were in English, all of us children spoke Punjabi to each other. Gradually, as we learned more English, my younger brother and sister and I began to speak it among ourselves, but our mother would tell us off – believing, often correctly, that we were talking about her. Since almost everyone around us was Indian, and since we girls in particular were being raised to be obedient wives and mothers and seamstresses, what need of English?

Looking back on it now, I think my dad feared and revered education at the same time. He loved books and, despite his own lack of formal schooling, always made us wash our hands before reading and never allowed us to put them on the floor or bend back the spines. He knew that it was his own lack of education which had led to him being at the lowest strata of society. He also respected the one good English speaker in the row of houses who knew enough to deal with official correspondence on behalf of all the neighbours. Most streets would also nominate one person who'd go to register things like births and deaths, and would fill out any forms in English.

In some ways, it seemed as though a whole community of people with the same culture, language and religion had been lifted up wholesale and transplanted to the heart of industrial Britain. Apart from the dramatic change of weather and the regular work in factories, shops and offices, very little about their personal and family lives had changed. The reluctance of the immigrant community to integrate, coupled with the racism which accompanied shortages of jobs and housing, were jointly the cause of the often poor relationships between the local indigenous people and the new arrivals.

It was this tension and disquiet among the local population which gave rise to one of the most notorious episodes in the history of race relations in Britain. In April 1968 – the same year that I was starting school just down the road in Smethwick – Tory MP and shadow cabinet member Enoch Powell made a speech to the local Conservative Party in Birmingham. In it, Powell was strongly critical of the recent bouts of mass immigration, especially from the Commonwealth. Always a melodramatic orator, Powell quoted a line from Virgil's *Aeneid*: 'As I look ahead, I am filled with foreboding; like the Roman, I seem to see the River Tiber foaming with much blood.' His address became universally known as the 'Rivers of Blood' speech. Powell's argument caused a storm of controversy, and Tory party leader Edward Heath reacted strongly to the accusations of racism and dismissed Powell from his shadow cabinet.

It was 1968. Students in Paris were rioting in favour of academic reform and civil rights activists in America were following Martin Luther King just ahead of his assassination. In Britain, anti-war demonstrators were clashing with police in front of the American Embassy in Grosvenor Square over Vietnam, but the biggest marches were by East End dockworkers taking part in spontaneous demonstrations in support of Enoch Powell. Some people believed that the popularity of Powell's doom-laden prophecies was a major contributor to the Tories' surprise win in the 1970 general election.

Even though I was only 5 years old, I have a hazy memory of the controversy and concern caused in our community by Powell's speech. At the time, though, I had more important things on my young mind because I was beginning to enjoy my education at Parkside Infants. I loved school from the first day and was good at every subject: books, sums and sport, especially cross-country. My first reports were positive about my work in class, but would say things like 'wilful and forceful'. As one of six children, I had to be those things if I was to have any chance of being heard.

Already I was showing more and more signs of being unwilling to conform to the culture and manners my parents had brought with them from India. One of my friends was a girl from a lower caste, a chamar. Chamars were traditionally considered to be leather-workers, and (worse still) landless –

outside of the Hindu ritual ranking system of castes, so-called 'untouchables'. It's widely believed that Sikhs don't observe the caste system, but they absolutely do, and many of them also discriminate based on the lightness of your skin and how tall you are. One day some of our relatives living a few streets away saw me speaking to my friend and reported the scandal to my parents. Later that day, I was severely chastised for bringing shame on the family. Needless to say, I defied them and kept my friendship.

I remember one day feeling curious about the reason my father had signs of piercing in both ears. He explained that when he was a child, during the partition of India in 1947, small boys from his community would be taken and murdered by Muslims, but girls were left alone as being hardly worth the effort. His parents disguised him as a girl to keep him safe, piercing both ears as part of the subterfuge. The underlying message, that girls were seen as so insignificant that it wasn't even worth the effort it took to murder one, didn't go unnoticed. All his life, my dad told me to 'stay away from Muslims', which was another warning I cheerfully ignored.

The fear of persecution, which had haunted my mum and dad's lives as children, continued to be fed by events in the wider world. In early August 1972, the President of Uganda, Idi Amin, ordered the expulsion of his country's Asian minority, giving them ninety days to leave. Many of those expelled had links to Britain, and more than 27,000 arrived here in the UK, leading to further public disquiet and sometimes violent demonstrations on the streets of major cities. Whenever something happened in politics or an immigrant was threatened, beaten or killed, everyone would gather at one of the houses to decide what they should do and how to stay safe and away from trouble.

My parents were never allowed to forget that this was not truly our home, and that we were not welcome. They believed that the British would also kick them out when they no longer needed the workers or when they got too old to work. My dad and the community felt that if one of you had a British passport you could fight for the right to stay, but if you were both Indians you would be deported. They did not want to end up stateless so my mum always kept her Indian passport.

They felt they had to own their own home to make sure they had a place to stay, where they were relatively safe, but their houses were always in rundown areas and in a poor state of repair. We had locks on all the exterior and interior doors, which made the rooms feel a bit like panic rooms. Even the staircase had doors fitted at the top and bottom, and both were bolted from the inside in case anyone got in. They had to protect themselves, because they would not call the police under any circumstances.

My mum always had a packed suitcase at the ready in case we were obliged to leave quickly. She told me that Asian women living alone could not and should not own a house because they might have to move suddenly, and anyway they were likely to have their windows broken. I remember feeling angry and resentful – it didn't seem right or fair that I should have to live under such a cloud. I'd been born here, I hadn't hurt anyone; why should I feel afraid just because my skin was a different colour?

Growing up in this environment, I worked out quickly that if I didn't do something for myself, no-one was going to do it for me. One of the things I realized pretty soon was that the education I was getting was second rate, and that other kids from better-off families were getting superior opportunities. The 11+ was still operating in my area, and I found out that if you passed you could get to King Edward VI High School for Girls, which was well known to be the best in the area. I understood enough to know that this was likely to be a fork in the road ahead, but then was dismayed to discover that pupils from my school weren't even going to be entered for the exam. I tried to speak to my teachers about it, but none was interested, so I went to the library, found out where I could get entry forms, filled them in and applied to take the test. Then on the day I had to get myself on a bus to a test centre in Handsworth Wood, where I sat among a whole group of children I'd never met and took my 11+. I waited and waited for the results, and I remember tearing open the envelope when it arrived. The good news was that I'd passed, but the bad news was that my mark wasn't quite high enough to get me into King Edward. Instead, I attended the newly built Holyhead Comprehensive. It was a big school, almost all the kids were black or Asian, and I remember that there were only four white girls in my year.

It was only once we attended secondary school that we children needed a surname for the first time. Although my surname was Kaur, the school had refused to allow registration for exams unless you had a 'proper' surname, as the school was full of

Singhs and Kaurs and they couldn't differentiate between us all. The family adopted Sandhu, which was the area in northern India that Mum and Dad had originally come from.

Even at that young age, I was acutely aware that I was a member of a community which was set apart from, and seen as being inferior to, the mainstream of life in Britain. We lived in a ghetto, and the school was a ghetto. The teaching was second rate, and no-one thought it important to educate Asian girls in particular. I was good at maths but the teacher, Mr Twyman, used to open the windows and say, 'You lot stink' and 'Why don't you lot ever wash?' This was not my first experience of racism. Two friends and I had been chased down the street by young white boys yelling abuse at us, and we'd had to hide in one of those old-fashioned red telephone boxes. We were terrified and I remember that we looked around to see if anyone might rescue us. The phone box was next to a pub, but it was full of white people and it didn't even occur to us that they might be willing to give us any help.

I remember the chemistry teacher, Mr Christie, was good, and he eventually married the biology teacher, who was also good. There was one teacher who favoured me, referring to me as 'Brown eyes' and uttering inappropriate endearments, which caused my school friends to taunt me as 'Teacher's pet', although nothing untoward ever happened.

I needed to be self-motivated because Mum and Dad never attended parents' evenings because they couldn't understand what was being said, and were unable to read my school reports. When I occasionally played truant, I could just go home – there was no problem because my mum had no idea what was expected. If I was ill, I had to write my own sick notes. I was my own keeper, and also the keeper of my younger siblings, writing sick notes for them too when necessary, and encouraging them with their schoolwork.

I flatly refused to wear one of the multi-coloured suits which my mum had so carefully made for me to go to school in, and I was beaten when I threw the clothes away. However, I eventually reached an age where the school required us to wear a uniform – it was a huge relief when my parents succumbed and bought me a pair of school trousers.

When I was 10 or 11, Satnam, Sarj and I decided we'd like to celebrate Christmas the way we'd seen it on TV, so we told our parents we would take over and organize everything. The trouble was that none of us had the first idea how anything should be prepared or what to cook. We bought a frozen turkey from the supermarket and put it in the oven, expecting it to take about an hour. Needless to say it was still raw and stone cold when we were ready to eat it, and I was dismayed to find a plastic bag full of unidentifiable body parts still inside. That year I think we ended up with chapattis.

My continuing reluctance to behave as the demure and timid young Asian woman was rapidly making my parents despair. Instead of enjoying the traditional Indian music favoured by my father and staying close to neighbours from the sub-continent, my friends were mostly West Indians who were much more laid back and enjoyed pop and reggae. There were constant arguments at home because I wasn't allowed to go to any youth clubs or discos, on the grounds that a girl who went out in the evening damaged her chances of getting married. I remember having to lie in order to go to the school disco, even though it was on in the afternoon.

Photographs from my childhood and early teens invariably show me dressed in modest and sober clothes, with my hair parted in the centre and falling in two long plaits. In most, I seem to be sombre and serious, staring into the camera with an expression which says, 'Let's get this over with.' Above all, I considered all the restrictions keeping me from wider society – white society – a consequence of me being an Indian. Like every kid that age, I just wanted to be like everyone else, and so Indian was the last thing I wanted to be.

All things considered, however, my early schooldays were happy and unexceptional, and my disputes with my mum and dad were probably not very different from those faced by most teenagers at that stage of their lives. Not far away over the horizon, though, an event was coming which was to traumatize me for decades to come.

One day in September 1979, when I was still just 15, I came home from school to find Jindo's father-in-law at the house. I was aware of a strange atmosphere, as if there was serious business to be discussed but no-one knew how to start. Mum and Dad were looking at each other as though deciding who should speak first. Eventually our visitor seemed to summon up courage and told me the reason he'd come. He had found me a husband. He said it like it was an achievement; like it was some kind of good news.

Needless to say, I was shocked and horrified. I'd been a tiny child when my older sisters had left home, so I had no direct experience of anything like this happening before. I was also terrified. The tight restrictions of my upbringing meant I'd had no experience whatsoever of boys, and now I was to be married. I learned on that day that the husband chosen for me was to be a 21-year-old man whose family originally came from the same region in the Punjab as ours. He'd been brought up a strict Sikh by highly orthodox parents. A man six years older than me whom I'd not even met.

Of course, I said straight away that I didn't want to be married at all, and that even if I did, I'd want it to be to a man I'd chosen myself. My parents were outraged by my ingratitude and a noisy row developed. When I continued to object, they threatened to throw me out of the house. Still, I would not stay silent, and in the end I was beaten by my father and sent upstairs. That night I could not sleep and spent the long hours trying to picture the person I was supposed to be spending the rest of my life with, and searching my mind for some way out of my fate.

I considered running away from home, but as I was part of an Indian community which expected obedience above all things, there was nowhere I could go. Over the coming months, as all the arrangements were being made, I continued to plead with my parents not to force me, but they would not be budged. A daughter's failure to comply with her parents' wishes would bring shame on the family, which could not be countenanced. One day, my mother took the quilt off the bed and threatened to throw me out at night. Eventually, my parents told me that, if I disgraced them by failing to obey, they would kill me.

In an effort to make me 'go quietly' and not disgrace them, it had been agreed that I could take my O levels if I went through with the religious part of the ceremony. So on 15 March 1980, I was driven the two and a half miles from my home in Paddington Road to Sandwell Register Office, a white-fronted building off the main road in West Bromwich. There, for the first time, I met Maninder Singh, the man I was about to marry. My first impressions were that he was far taller than me, he seemed much older with a long beard, and wearing a turban. Terrifying. His three brothers were also there, wearing full Sikh dress – characterized as 'the five Ks': these are *kesh* (unshorn hair and beards), *kacha* (cotton underwear), *kirpan* (a sword or steel dagger), *kara* (an iron bangle) and *kanga* (a wooden comb). All of them were wearing bright blue Indian *kameezes* and carrying these intimidating swords strapped to their waists, as well as these round and sharp-edged metal weapons called *chakkaer* around their turbans. Needless to say, I was petrified.

Although we'd always kept up the traditions of family life from the Punjab, my family had not been particularly observant of the Sikh religion, and so I felt completely estranged from the culture and community that was forcing me into a life I had not chosen. I was experiencing some kind of personal nightmare from which there seemed to be no possibility of escape. Both sets of parents were also present, but this English civil ceremony was to be a formality, and not the real wedding so far as the families were concerned, which was to take place in the summer.

That single hour at the civil ceremony was the only time I would see my new husband for several weeks. Directly after it, I returned to my parents' home and on the following Monday I went back to school. I felt ashamed and embarrassed that I was married, so I took off my wedding ring during the day and kept it a secret. Already, I had a notion that perhaps getting an education was my only possible escape route from the life being laid out before me, so while school policy was for students to take five O levels, I found a way to take ten.

As soon as the exams were over, it was time for the religious part of the marriage ceremony. When I woke up on the morning of 5 July, I felt sick at heart and refused breakfast. My mum said, 'You've got to eat something or you'll feel faint during the day,' but I still refused. She tried to reassure me by saying, 'It's just a formality. You'll be back home again by this evening,' but it all just seemed unreal to me. Like it was happening to someone else and I was seeing it in a film. I remember being dressed by my mother and sister in a traditional Indian ceremonial sari in red with gold embellishments, and taken to the Guru Nanak Gurdwara temple in Smethwick, which had been converted from its previous incarnation as the Congregational chapel. There, I was married in front of a gathering of some 300–400 Sikhs from the local community. In the Sikh tradition, the marriage service, *anand karaj*, is described as a ceremony of bliss signifying the union of two souls who become one, leading to the ultimate union with the Divine.

That's not quite how I experienced it, and while the events of the day have merged into a blur of noise and colour, I well remember that the only thing saving my sanity was the thought that custom spared me the prospect of returning to my new husband's home and bed that same night.

A week later, however, I was obliged to move into his family home. I was only 16, had had no boyfriends or life experience, and so on our first night together the only way I can describe what happened to me was that I was raped. Perhaps that's not how it felt to him, I don't know, but for me it was an experience which would remain with me forever, and would poignantly inform what would become my lifelong mission to help women who find themselves victims of honour-based or domestic violence.

CHAPTER TWO

Hostage

My husband's family lived in two houses, much like the one I had come from, but alongside each other in a street in West Bromwich. The houses were shared by Maninder's parents as well as his three brothers, two of whom were also married with three children each. Maninder had a job as a warehouse operator during the week, but at weekends he helped his parents and brothers in a textile business. All the women of the family were seamstresses, labouring for long hours at home on sewing machines, and producing a range of colourful garments which they sold in street markets in Birmingham and more distant towns and cities.

Just as with my own family, none of my new relatives spoke English, but unlike my mum and dad, they were strict in their religious observance. All the men wore turbans. None ate meat. The three older brothers were religious elders, and the women seemed to me to be there exclusively to serve the needs of the men.

If I'd already felt that the restrictions of my earlier life were difficult and frustrating, I now felt as if I'd been taken prisoner and was being held hostage. And if my new life was not shocking enough, worse was to come. I quickly learned that if I irritated my husband in any way, he felt quite at liberty to beat me. A meal which was unsatisfactory or perhaps not ready on time would result in me being punched or kicked. Any response which was less than complete obedience and acquiescence would result in a harsh telling-off.

And not only was it common practice for my husband to beat me for any perceived misdemeanour, but his brothers were also allowed to do so. Sometimes, they would come home from a day at the market at 1 a.m. and demand to be served a freshly cooked meal. Any reluctance or perceived failure on my part could lead to me being punched or kicked by any of them.

There's no way to describe what it feels like to be cornered in that way. You know you have to escape, but wherever you turn for help there's a barrier rather than an exit. Everyone is telling you this is 'normal', and you'll eventually get used to it. I was effectively being held against my will, and at that time I had no idea how I was ever going to be allowed to be free. After only a week of my new life, I feared that the stress might be threatening my sanity, so I went to see my GP, Dr Singh, and poured my heart out about my situation, including that I felt I was on the brink of a breakdown. He listened very carefully to all my complaints, and the next day he came to the house to see my father-in-law and husband and told them everything I had told him in confidence. I was prescribed anti-depressants, which I carefully flushed down the lavatory.

I could now clearly see that my only possible escape route was to try to continue my education, otherwise I'd end up like my sisters-in-law, running up traditional Indian garments for the rest of my life. The only concession I'd been able to ring out of my parents in return for going along with the wedding, was that I'd be allowed to take some exams, so my father had included it as a condition as part of my marriage contract. Now I begged and pleaded with my husband and his father to allow me to take A levels, and to my complete surprise, and probably only to shut me up, they agreed. So, in September 1980, I began a course in English, maths and biology at Warley College of Technology in Crocketts Lane, Smethwick.

It was made clear to me that the demands of the coursework could only be met after my household duties had been taken care of. This involved cooking, cleaning and looking after my husband and his extended family. I would frequently find myself trying to complete my homework at midnight after everyone's needs had been taken care of, but still, anyone felt able to interrupt my studies at any time with a demand to prepare food, and casual violence was commonplace.

My only allies in the house were my two sisters-in-law, neither of whom spoke any English, which made me useful as an interpreter to ease the general running of the household. I would translate their shopping needs for the grocer, but once the family's order had been delivered, our father-in-law would ration provisions between the three of us. He might easily decide that one of us was using too much sugar or too much bread, and would cut our allocation. His favourite was Daljit, who was married to the oldest of the brothers, because she had the palest skin, and her children were also favoured for the same reason. Jaspal, who was married to the younger brother, had darker skin and so received less preferential treatment within the family. I was treated with particular contempt because I was thought in some way to be 'English'.

My new family were Sikh fanatics who were involved with the fight for Sikh Independence and the establishment of a separate Sikh nation in the Punjab region, called Khalistan. They would quite often go to Handsworth to damage property belonging to the Indian state, such as the Bank of India, and to other rallies and demonstrations. They had no wish to blend or integrate into British society.

The tension I felt inside the house was echoed by tension outside in the wider community. Relationships between the police and the local ethnic population had been poor for many years, and in 1981, when I was 18 years old, rioting broke out close to where we lived. The trouble in Handsworth coincided with larger-scale disturbances in Brixton in London, Toxteth in Liverpool, and Moss-side in Manchester. Each of these areas saw ferocious confrontations between the largely West Indian and Asian youths of the area on one side, and the police on the other.

Rioting on the streets of mainland Britain was, and is, a rare occurrence, which leaves a powerful and lasting impression on those caught up in it. These were the days when police tactics lacked some of the relative sophistication and subtlety they adopted in later years. TV news reports of the thin blue line in Liverpool and Manchester showed organized phalanxes of officers beating their truncheons against the backs of their shields in rhythm, and chanting in a way they might have witnessed with the warlike African tribes in the 1960s cinema hit *Zulu*. The effect was intended to be intimidating and terrifying, and it was.

I attended college with a number of the other girls I'd gone to school with, and thoroughly enjoyed the escape it offered. However, some of the other students eventually found out I was married and I became subject to bullying. Whenever I walked past groups of students, they used to sing or hum the Specials song: 'You've done too much, much too young, Now you're married. . .'

Despite the inauspicious background to my studies, I passed my A levels in June 1982 with a C in English, a D in biology and an O in maths. A final report from my course tutor, Mrs Cockburn, described me as: 'A determined student with a clear idea of what she wished to do. Her written and spoken English are both excellent and she has considerable powers of expression.' Whatever I'd managed to learn in my time at Warley College would stand me in good stead in years to come.

I applied for and got a place at Wolverhampton Polytechnic to start a degree in English, but by now my luck had run out. Despite the agreement that had been reached with my father, my new father-in-law insisted that he'd humoured me enough. No-one else in the family had an education, so why should I be any different? He refused to allow me any further studies, and so it was with a very heavy heart that I had to inform the poly that I wasn't able to attend.

My next challenge was to persuade Maninder and his family that my qualifications would enable me to get a more lucrative job outside of the home. They may already have begun to realize that life would be easier if they let their daughter-in-law have some of her own way, and I was hugely relieved when I was allowed to apply for a job as a cashier in the West Bromwich Building Society. My A levels were already providing the possibility of an alternative to life as a seamstress. Despite the fact that fewer than one in twenty of the local ethnic population leaving school that summer had found employment, I was interviewed and given the job. I was thrilled.

The prospect of being able to work and have some money of my own gave me hope that I might be able to achieve a small measure of independence, but it was quickly made clear that this was not to be the case. I was told I had to hand the whole of my wages immediately and directly to my father-in-law, who would then allow me a few pounds for bus fares and the like. The remainder would be put into the family kitty as my contribution towards bills for the entire household. The arrangement was not untypical of the communal living that was the custom in the Sikh community but, at 18 years old, all I wanted was to be able to manage and spend my own money as I saw fit. I was permitted to travel from the house to work and to return directly home at the end of the day, but I was allowed no socializing outside of the home, no alcohol, no dancing, no life at all – other than that provided for me by my 'family', who spoke no English and made no attempt to integrate with any world outside of the strict bounds of the Sikh community to which they belonged.

The pressure I felt was made worse by the fact that Maninder and his parents were looking forward to the prospect of children. This was the last thing I wanted, so I secretly visited a family planning clinic where I was prescribed the pill. Each month I'd be asked if I was pregnant, and each month I had to pretend to be disappointed when I answered. I managed to get away with this for three years, but then I must have become complacent or careless because in the summer of 1983 I discovered I was indeed pregnant. I was horrified. It was bad enough having to endure this way of life for myself, but at least my job got me out of the house and gave me the opportunity to interact with people who spoke English. I didn't think I could endure the isolation and confinement I'd inevitably face bringing up a child in my husband's family home.

Fortunately, it was not unusual in our community for a pregnant woman to return to her parents' home for a period before childbirth, and so I begged my mum and dad and they agreed to allow me to stay, at least until the child was born. After that I'd have to return to my husband.

I was 21 when my son was born in the Queen Elizabeth Hospital in Edgbaston on the morning of Sunday 11 March 1984. Despite all my earlier misgivings about having a child in my circumstances, from the moment I saw him I felt the deep and intimate bond of a mother's love. At the same moment, though, I felt a strong sense of duty to protect him from the life I was being forced to live. Straight away I knew I would do whatever I could to give him the freedom that I was being denied. My husband Maninder was present at the birth, but when the newborn boy was handed to him he immediately fainted, dropping the child on the floor. The medical team scooped up the baby and mercifully he was unharmed.

After the delivery, I was allowed to return with my baby to my parents' home, which is also not so unusual in the Sikh community. However, I was soon being urged by my mother to return to my husband. 'If he has to come to fetch you,' she complained, 'it will bring shame upon the family.' Bringing shame on the family was the ultimate crime, and if it was necessary for their daughter to endure harsh words and physical abuse to avoid it, then so be it. When I continued to refuse to obey, my mother eventually summoned my older brother Faljinder to the house. He duly beat me and forced me to return with my new baby to my husband's family.

I remember those few months nursing my son in my husband's house as among the most miserable of my life. I was hardly ever allowed to go out, there was scarcely anyone with whom I could speak English, and I continued to have to look after my husband and his brothers, as well as my new baby son.

The strain of living in a situation where I felt totally out of place and under threat was taking its toll on me, and I suffered from depression. Every time I was on the receiving end of violence from my husband or his brothers, I felt myself on the brink of making a break for it, and more and more I was concerned about the effect such an environment would be having on my baby. I felt I must do anything I could to avoid having him brought up in a situation where women were treated in this way.

The decisive moment came one day in the summer of 1984, when Maninder and his brothers came home after a day selling clothes at the market and demanded I cook for them, but my son was screaming across the room, also in need of attention and feeding. I asked if I could be allowed to take care of my baby before cooking for the brothers, but one of them cornered and beat me. He stood between me and my son and would not let me go to him. I was forced to take care of the brothers before I attended to my child, and that was the final straw.

Next day, I took my son in my arms and fled back to my parents' home, pleading to be allowed to stay. Initially, they refused. It was the role of the woman to remain subservient to her husband, and to tolerate beatings if her disobedience made such things necessary. The shame on the family of a broken marriage was too great to be borne. Still I refused to return to the marital home, and so, once again, my older brother Faljinder was sent for. He came round and shouted at me, ordering me to be an obedient wife to my husband, and daughter to our parents. When I still refused, he beat me again.

With no other options available to me, I told my parents that, even if they forced me to leave their home, I still would not return to live with my husband. I had no idea what I would do, or where I could go instead, but nothing would make me go back. Eventually, my mother decided that they might still salvage some reputation if at least I remained within the family, so she agreed that I could stay for a while.

After six months, I again begged to be allowed to go to work, pointing out that the extra money I could bring in would be helpful to the family. Eventually, I was allowed to apply for a short contract working for the Department of Health and Social Security (DHSS). I got the job, and the contract was made permanent after a few months, so now I was an administrative assistant with the chance to move quickly up the civil service career ladder towards promotion to an executive officer. The work opened up a window onto the world – encountering all sorts of ways of life I hadn't come across before, and giving me the opportunity to make new friends from outside my own community. Among them, a young woman whose friendship and family were soon to provide me with a lifeline in my hour of greatest need. Her name was Daisy Reid.

Daisy's parents had come to Britain from Jamaica and the family lived for the first fourteen years of her life at 79 Holly Road, Handsworth. When her father died, her mother Cyriline moved to a house in Maxwell Avenue, which is the family home to this day. There were four children, Carol, Daisy, Devon and Marvyn, each of them born a year apart. Daisy attended Handsworth Girls School and wanted to be a chef, but quickly realized she would have to spend what seemed to be a small fortune on a set of knives, which her mum couldn't afford. So, after a couple of casual jobs, at age 20, she went to work at the DHSS in Soho Road as an admin assistant dealing with sickness benefit. That's where she and I met.

Daisy was shocked when I confided in her about the circumstances of my life at home. The local West Indian community, and her own family in particular, were generally open and easy-going. She found the idea of enforced marriage and my stories of the regular violence from my husband and his brothers incredible and horrifying.

It's amazing when I look back on it to recall what it's possible to get used to as normal. This was how it was, and compared with most women in the community, the regime I was forced to live under in my parents' home was relatively relaxed. But even then, I knew that this wasn't how things should be, and there was a part of me looking for a way to be free.

CHAPTER THREE

Escape

One day in September 1985, I was sitting in my office in the DHSS in Soho Road when I became aware of a disturbance outside. Feelings had been running high in the area for some days, and there'd been more rioting in other towns and cities. When I looked out the window, I could see people running in the streets carrying TVs and valuables.

As in the riots of four years earlier, the trouble had been caused by clashes between the local West Indian and Asian populations and the police. A local man had been arrested and hundreds of people attacked police and property, looting and setting off fire bombs. A post office had been set alight in an arson attack and two brothers, Kassamali and Amirali Moledina, were burned to death inside. Thirty-five others were injured during the disturbances and more than 1,500 police officers were drafted into the area. Some forty-five shops were looted and burned out, resulting in damage running into hundreds of thousands of pounds.

Although united in their opposition to the police, the incident also led in turn to conflict between the West Indian and Asian communities, because of course the looted and burned-out shops mostly belonged to the latter.

All of us at the DHSS wondered whether, being government offices, we might find ourselves the target of the rioters. Then someone pointed out that many of the rioters would be receiving benefits, and therefore were unlikely to want to disrupt the work of the people who administered them. Our offices remained undamaged.

The feelings of tension in the wider community were reflected in my own life. My parents were still doing everything they could to force me to return to my husband, but I felt that nothing they could do to me would be worse than going back to his family's house. Day after day I was pressured to take my son and return to them, and day by day I resisted. As days turned into weeks, word reached me that my husband and his family were so outraged and offended by my disobedience that they were making no further efforts to force me to return. As far as Maninder was concerned, he'd have nothing to do with me unless I went back on bended knees and begged for forgiveness. As far as my parents were concerned, my shame was complete.

The tense atmosphere at my parents' home forced me to seek whatever outlets I could, and I found myself spending time whenever possible at Daisy's home. Her mother, Cyriline, was a wonderful Mother Earth character, who loved to have her house filled with her children and their friends. Whenever

I visited, I'd be greeted with a warmth and affection which was quite unlike anything I'd experienced before. My sense of alienation from my own background and culture grew, and so did my feeling that I would need to find a way out of my current life.

Meanwhile, though, my friendship with Daisy was providing some badly needed respite, and our work at the DHSS was at the centre of what little social life I had. At lunchtime, whoever was in the office would go across the road to the pub, the Ivy House. We would head back just before 2 p.m. and pass the queue of claimants waiting to be dealt with.

Above all, we loved music, and one day Daisy was scanning the airwaves and came across this amazing pirate radio station, PCRL (People's Community Radio Link). Listening to it one day, the DJ asked for volunteers so she phoned a number and arranged to meet a bloke at a local West Indian record shop. The man didn't turn up, but he did phone later to apologize and to schedule another meeting. The man was Cecil Morris.

Cecil was already a legendary figure in the world of radio, a pioneer of pirate stations when it was impossible for ordinary people who loved music to obtain an official licence to broadcast. He'd initially set up PCRL as a community response to the recent bout of rioting in 1985. Having tried and failed to obtain a licence, the station set out on what was to be a long-running game of cat and mouse with the relevant authorities. Most of the broadcasters were volunteers, who were unable to use their real names on air because what they were doing was against the law.

Daisy started working as a DJ under the name Lady D, doing three or four shows a week. I volunteered soon after, and went on air in the early mornings under the name Princess, the translation of the surname Kaur which was shared by all Sikh girls. It was all quite illegal, and we used to advertise on air for people with vacant flats in tower blocks so we could keep moving, but we had the support of the community. In fact, the local vicar (at Winson Green) allowed us to put a transmitter on the spire of his church.

The team used to have lookouts set up, to check for officials from the Department of Trade and Industry (easy to identify – the only ones in the area wearing business clothes). If one was spotted, they'd alert the DJ who would broadcast an emergency message. Help would come running to evacuate the all-important equipment and records, and we had ways of jamming the lifts to entrap the inspectors, thereby enabling us to make good our escape.

Daisy loved the work so much that she went part time at the DHSS, so she could do more hours at the radio station. Her mum thought she was crazy to give up regular paid employment with the civil service. Daisy was playing reggae, bluebeat and soul. I was playing mostly soul music, lovers' rock reggae and dancehall, such as Pato Banton and Tippa Irie. One of my favourite songs, *Handsworth Revolution*, by local artists Steel Pulse, captured the mood of the recent troubles on the local streets:

Doesn't justice stand for all
Doesn't justice stand for all mankind
We find society putting us down
Crowning us, crowning us, crowning us, crowning us
A place of Evil, OH, OH
Handsworth means us the Black People
Handsworth means us the Black People
We're talking now. Speaking JahJah language!

We were both taking an enormous risk because, if we'd been caught, a conviction for DJing on a pirate station might well have cost us our civil service jobs. One day, a group of local councillors who'd seen us at a fundraising event for PCRL and knew we were attached to the radio station, visited the DHSS offices and recognized us as Lady D and Princess. After that, we kept out of sight, and luckily no-one reported us.

But my only adventure outside of the house was bound to come to an end, and it did so in dramatic style one morning when I was broadcasting alone from a flat in a tower block and there was a raid. Our early-warning system failed this time, and I was caught in the act and my gear and records were confiscated. Receipts were issued detailing the seized equipment, including a DJ board, headphones, thirty-four LPs, two cassettes and a station clock. I gave officers a false name, Parm Kaur, and went home to wait for the summons and the sack. Neither transpired, but that was the end of my days as a pirate radio DJ. One letter from a fan addressed simply to 'Princess' lamented that 'Wednesday and Thursday mornings just aren't the same any more. Come back very soon.'

While my husband and his family had by now more or less written me off as beyond redemption, my parents remained as desperate as ever to restore me to what they believed was my rightful place at his side. The idea of having a single parent for a daughter was unconscionable, and again they sent for my older brother Faljinder. I was given notice that he would arrive the next day, with the intention of beating me once more, and returning me by force if necessary to my husband's home. Finally, I had run out of options. I couldn't stay with my parents and I couldn't go back to my husband. I'd been feeling for a while that, if and when this day came, I'd have no choice but to leave the area altogether, but of course I knew absolutely no-one outside of the small community I'd grown up in, and certainly no-one in London. Once again, as so often in the past, I knew I'd have to dig deep and fall back on my own resources. So, the following morning, I pretended I needed to go to the shops to buy some shoes for my son, but instead I wrapped him in a blanket and fled.

Daisy was at her desk in the radio station when I came in with a small bag and said I was going to London. I told her the pressure was too great and I couldn't go back. I had to leave that day. I asked her to go into town to buy two pairs of trousers and two tops from C&A. She got them and brought them back, and that's all I took with me when I left.

Notwithstanding my suddenly urgent and desperate situation, I called my manager at the DHSS and explained my position.

I was about to leave my home and family and flee with my son, and therefore would not be able to return to work. The boss was understanding and told me to call him again when I arrived in London.

If I was going to make good my escape, I now needed whatever money I could muster, and the only significant item in my possession was an ageing white Ford Cortina, which I'd bought after running away from my husband's home. My one ally within my immediate family was my younger brother Satnam. He and I had always been close, and from time to time I'd told him that, if all else failed, I'd have no choice but to run away. So now I took him into my confidence and asked him to sell the car for me as quickly as he could. He agreed, selling it that same day to a trader, and brought £250 in cash to me at the coach station in Birmingham. Both of us knew that we were at a defining moment in our lives and that one way or another, nothing would ever be quite the same again.

I took my child in my arms and boarded the bus that would take me away from a life of oppression, and towards the possibility of freedom. As the minutes ticked by before the doors closed, as I was waiting for the coach to leave, I feared that my plan would be discovered and I would be apprehended and dragged back to my husband's home. At last, the coach doors sighed shut, the engine revved, and I was on my way towards a new life. It would be a life full of drama and difficulties, but I did not believe it could be worse than the one I was leaving behind.

CHAPTER FOUR

'Managing my shame'

On the long journey by road from Birmingham to London, I felt a mix of terror and exhilaration as I contemplated my circumstances and the life that might await me. First of all, I knew that my husband and his family would be sure to react in anger to the fact that a person they regarded as a chattel had acted so disgracefully. Second, I knew that my own parents would be horrified that I could shame them with such disobedience. Above all else, the duty of a wife in our community was to obey her husband, and my failure to stick around to be abused and beaten had brought dishonour upon my family. But I also knew that staying in my marriage and in my husband's family wasn't going to be possible. I was unable to countenance the prospect of watching my son grow up in such an environment.

As the coach barrelled along the motorway towards the capital city, I looked down on my young boy and wondered how on earth I would be able to bring him up on my own. I knew no-one in London, had nowhere to live and had no access to anything resembling a support system. When I eventually alighted at Victoria Coach Station, with a carrier bag and my son in my arms, I knew I would need all my strength and resources if I was going to survive.

My first step was to find a phone box and call my boss in Handsworth. He'd been as good as his word, and told me to get to the DHSS offices at Woodgrange Park in Forest Gate and to ask for the Welfare Officer called Maureen. I didn't have the first idea how to get there by public transport, but when I eventually arrived, I was hugely relieved to learn that a room had been found for me that night in a hostel in Edmonton. At least I'd have somewhere to rest my head and for my tiny son to sleep. Moves were also under way to secure a transfer to an equivalent job with the DHSS in London.

A helping hand in my hour of greatest need was enormously welcome, but when I arrived at the hostel that night, my heart sank. I was shown into a dingy room with a single bed which looked as though it hadn't been changed in a month. The wallpaper was peeling off and there was damp and mould on all the walls. Nevertheless, my son and I slept there that night, and for the following few days, while I began the search for somewhere more permanent to live. I went to the Homeless Persons Unit in Lea Bridge Road, E10, to apply for emergency housing, but was told I had intentionally made myself homeless and was therefore not eligible. I was offered no assistance of any kind.

I'd been in touch with Daisy and she'd told me that someone from my husband's family had called at their house asking for me, and that the search was on to track me down. She also confirmed what I already knew in my heart – that my parents were utterly appalled and had disowned me completely.

Being taken away from all that was familiar to him was making my young son more fractious than ever, and I thought that perhaps he was picking up on the tension and anxiety I was feeling myself. Sometimes, we would be sleeping in a different place every night, and he would be so distressed and tearful that I found it hard to comfort him. Many times I felt close to desperation. What would become of me? What would become of him? Of us? We were all alone in an unfamiliar city with no friends, no family nearby, no support system.

Deep in my heart I knew, of course, that my son needed his mother, but he also needed some stability and structure, which I was unable to give him. I searched around in my mind for all possible options, but the one thing I didn't consider was returning to the life I had fled. Whatever fate had in store for me and my son, nothing could be worse than living in that way again. Eventually, without choices and feeling something close to total breakdown, I contacted my younger brother Satnam, who'd helped me to escape. I told him that I wasn't able to take care of my son, at least not until I found a way to get on my feet. We agreed that I'd have to return to Birmingham to hand him over, with the idea that he would be looked after in my parents' home, just as I had been. Although I didn't know it then, he would never return to live with me full time.

Sick at heart at being separated from my child, but realizing I had no alternatives, I began work at the DHSS in Gants Hill and rented a single room in a house in Manor Park. I also took a job in the evenings between 6 p.m. and 11 p.m. stacking shelves in the Ilford branch of Sainsbury's. At weekends, when I could, I worked behind the bar at a local nightclub in Romford called Hollywood's. The work wasn't too hard and the pay was poor, but I made more in tips than wages, and it was a rare chance to get out in the evening.

I was saving as hard as I could in the hope of being able to buy a house, but every second weekend I would return by coach to Birmingham to see my son. I'd had no communication with my parents since I'd left home, but I knew from Satnam that they wouldn't allow me back into their home. However, I was welcomed by Daisy's mother at their house in Maxwell Avenue, where Satnam would bring my son to visit me. My parents knew of the arrangement, and described it merely as 'managing her shame'.

It was always emotional for me to be reunited with my son, but as the weeks turned into months and longer, this arrangement was his 'normal' and he was clearly growing into a well-adjusted and happy little boy. He was, after all, living in a family and a culture in which boys are favoured. He would tell me all about the new friends he'd made and what they'd been doing, and, while of course he knew I was his mum, I think to him I was just someone who was always pleased to see him and usually brought him a treat. Even if it had been an option on a practical level, taking him back to London with me would have been an act of selfishness that was clearly not in his interests. So I had to work hard to keep back my goodbye tears until after he was out of sight. On the coach returning south, I would tuck myself into the most hidden corner seat I could find and try my best to renew my resolve to face the week ahead.

My work at the DHSS took on a similar pattern to what I'd become used to in Birmingham. Detecting benefit fraud could be difficult and traumatic, but mostly the clients were from the West Indian, Asian or travelling communities, and so at least I was mostly spared racial abuse. Claimants had to try to get along with the DHSS inspectors if they could.

When it came to my first Christmas away from home, I faced the prospect of spending it alone in my single room in Manor Park, but when Daisy's mother Cyriline heard about the arrangement, she would have none of it. She insisted that I come back to Birmingham to join in their celebrations. At first I was reluctant, feeling that I'd be intruding on what is essentially family time. Again, Cyriline insisted, and then went out shopping so I'd have presents to open, just like her own children. She bought me a scarf, and I bought Cyriline a vase, which was placed on her mantelpiece and was still there on the day she eventually died in 2017.

By having three jobs and living frugally, I eventually managed to save enough money for a deposit on a two-bedroom house at 52 Worcester Road, priced at £43,000. The tiny end-of-terrace was opposite the petrol station and just a few yards from the busy A118, but none of that mattered. I was a homeowner.

The purchase of a first home is a milestone in the lives of most people, but for me – given that my mother had told me it was a bad idea for a woman to own a house – it felt especially significant. At last I was beginning to put down roots of my own in a community which felt so much more integrated than anywhere I had lived before. But now I found myself paying extortionate interest rates on a large mortgage, on top of all my other bills. I had to save hard to pay my utility bills and domestic rates, itemizing everything, from food costs to bus fares. By the time I got to payday at the end of one particular month, I had exactly 50p left over. The discovery of a hole in the roof which was letting in rain caused an immediate crisis, and I was obliged to cash in my civil service pension to fund the repairs – something I've always regretted. I discussed my situation with Satnam, who told me he also felt like getting away from the West Midlands, and that it might be a good idea to have a total change of scene. We agreed that he should come to stay with me, along with his girlfriend Lorna, so we could share the bills.

The sharing of expenses and the extra incomes began to make life easier, and by working and saving hard, I eventually found I could afford a bigger house. So I moved again, to Christie Gardens, opposite Chadwell Heath Academy. This house was smarter, with mock-Tudor beams amid the pebble-dash, and it provided a bit more space and even a small garden. But when Satnam got a job as a caretaker at a Newham housing estate, a small flat went with it, so he moved out. That caused a renewed financial problem, but then my great friend Daisy decided it was time for her to move away from Handsworth to see whether life in London suited her. So she, and another colleague from the DHSS, Pauline Rose, requested transfers to London, and travelled south to share the new house. We three friends were reunited, and we had some happy times together.

While Daisy's job at the DHSS was more or less office-based, mine took me out and about as part of the team investigating people suspected of defrauding the welfare system. We might make an unscheduled visit to a sweatshop where people claiming unemployment benefit were suspected of working illegally. Or we would make a pre-dawn visit to a hostel that was claiming income for housing homeless families, to check they were really in residence. Sometimes, we might arrive at an encampment of travellers where a family was claiming child benefit for a number of children, only to find that the same children were also being claimed by the family next door. I found the work interesting and challenging, and felt I had 'a nose' for people who were living on the wrong side of the rules.

My work in the benefit fraud department meant I frequently found myself in the company of police officers, investigating the same or related matters. One day I met a young PC called Chris Donaldson, whose family had originally come from Jamaica. Chris pointed out that I was effectively doing the same work as a copper, but not being paid the same rate. It was the first time I had given any serious thought to the possibility that I might join the police.

Despite being one of only four non-white recruits when he'd trained at Hendon, Chris reassured me that he'd experienced very little discrimination, and what there was he had taken very much in his stride: 'They picked on you if you were

Scottish, or if you had red hair, or if you were tall, or if you were black.' When asked by the other probationers what he'd done before joining up, Chris had played up to the stereotype. 'I told them I used to steal women's handbags!' Hence he was given the nickname 'Dipper', which stayed with him. Straight out of Hendon, Chris had been posted to Bow Street, where, on his very first day, all the new recruits were gathered in the canteen, mingling with the other officers on duty. Suddenly, at a quiet moment, from the far side of the room someone shouted, 'Oh no, not another fucking n——— at Bow Street.' Chris didn't react at the time and eventually forgot about the incident – until twenty-nine years later, when he received an email from the same man offering an apology. 'He was a DCI [detective chief inspector] and due to retire that day,' Chris told me. 'I think he must have been waiting all that time for me to make a complaint, but I was never going to.'

My opinion of the police up until meeting and talking to Chris had inevitably been moulded by the very poor relationship that existed between its officers and members of my own community as I'd grown up. I'd been vividly aware of the rioting that had taken place in 1981 near to where I lived in Handsworth, as well as in Toxteth, Manchester and Brixton. I was just 18 at the time. Then, four years later in 1985, I witnessed the effects of the further clashes between police and local people, and heard first-hand accounts of the rough treatment handed out to members of the West Indian and Asian communities.

Immediately after the first of these riots in 1981, the Home Secretary Willie Whitelaw had asked a senior judge to investigate the causes. Lord Scarman's findings, published in November of the same year, were highly critical of the racist attitudes of some members of the police force, which had caused 'incalculable damage' to community relations. Among his recommendations were that a whole new dimension should be added to police training to help with policing a multicultural society, and that racial discrimination should be defined as a specific offence in the police disciplinary code:

> The training of police officers must prepare them for policing a multi-racial society . . . the present training arrangements are inadequate. More attention should therefore be devoted . . . to the training of police officers in, for example, the understanding of the cultural background of ethnic minority groups and in the stopping of people in the street.

In July 1983, eighteen months after Lord Scarman's report, the BBC's *Panorama* programme reported on how the Met was responding. Peter Taylor's film went inside the police training academy at Hendon, which I would attend as a cadet if I decided to apply to join the force. The most immediate response, and no doubt also the most televisual, was the increased emphasis on training in riot control. *Panorama*'s cameras witnessed lines of young officers dressed in overalls alighting from semi-military vehicles and crouching behind riot shields as they edged forward, batons at the ready, into a baying mob of rock-throwing demonstrators. This is unlikely to be what Scarman had intended when he recommended a new dimension in training for dealing with a multi-racial society.

Less visually spectacular, and far more alarming, was the insight the programme provided into the attitudes of the young recruits who'd passed through training one year after the Brixton riots, and therefore six months after Scarman's report. A young lecturer had asked the recruits to write an essay on their attitudes to 'Blacks in Britain'. The results were shocking.

'Blacks in Britain are a pest,' wrote one. 'They come over here from some tin-pot banana country where they lived in huts and worked in fields for cultivating rice and bananas, coconuts and tobacco, and take up residence in our already overcrowded country. Quite frankly I don't have any liking for wogs, nig-nogs and Pakis.' Another volunteered: 'It makes me cringe when I see a black bloke going out with a white woman.' A third wrote: 'My general opinion towards blacks is generally very low but has been lowered further still by the trouble they started in Toxteth and Brixton. Just putting it bluntly "kick them out".'

At a loss for an explanation, Taylor asked the lecturer if perhaps he had invited the probationers to put themselves into the mind of a racist, or indeed if there was any other way to explain the extraordinary candour of such comments. On the contrary, said the lecturer, he had written the essay title on the board and there had been no discussion. The man running Hendon at the time, Commander Richard Wells, also could not offer an explanation. 'And what had happened to those recruits?' asked Taylor. The answer was that they had probably gone on to become serving police officers.

Perhaps even more startling than these comments from young recruits was the interview with the much older and more senior chairman of the Police Federation of England and Wales, Les Curtis, who was asked if he thought an officer who calls a black person a 'n————' should be sacked. 'No,' said Curtis indignantly, 'why should he be sacked just for calling him a n————?' He helpfully went on elaborate. 'What about the colours – "n———— brown" – are we going to change the names we use?' When asked what would be his reaction if Scarman's recommendation that racial discrimination should be a disciplinary matter was adopted, he replied that he would be 'disgusted'.

Such attitudes no doubt help to explain why so few members of any ethnic minority were keen to join the police at the time, but not all the hurdles were generated exclusively from the white community. Indeed, the most conspicuous precedent of a woman from the Sikh community joining the police was far from encouraging. Twelve years earlier in 1971, a young woman named Karpal Kaur Sandhu (no relation) had become the first Asian female ever to join the Met. It was the realization of a lifelong ambition, but Karpal's family strongly disapproved of her chosen career. She was a mother of two children, and her husband complained that joining the police was neither Asian nor ladylike. It was simply not a woman's place to assert herself in such a way.

Despite having to cope with opposition from her community and her family, Karpal had initially progressed well as a new recruit and, according to press coverage of the story, her chief superintendent wrote in a report that she was 'proving invaluable with our dealings with the immigrant population . . . and also teaching police officers Asian dialects'. But the job caused a serious rift with her husband, who absconded to India, taking the couple's two children with him. Eventually, Karpal managed to get her children back, but – two years after she joined the police force – Karpal's husband murdered her.

What this meant was that anyone from my background seeking to join the police was likely to face opposition both from the white community, based on racism and ignorance, and from our own community, based on attitudes to women. If I'd needed any further evidence that joining the police was a dangerous career choice, several friends reminded me that it was only five years since WPC Yvonne Fletcher had been shot dead in the street while on patrol outside the Libyan embassy. And only four years since PC Keith Blakelock had been hacked to death during rioting at the Broadwater Farm estate in Tottenham – just a few miles from where I was currently living. It was all a very long way from the demure and retiring life envisaged for me as I'd grown up in Handsworth.

Even against all this depressing and discouraging background, I still felt determined. I'd always been someone who was ready to take a risk, and to try new things, and this seemed like as big a challenge as I'd ever faced. In my application to the Met, I listed my qualifications and relevant experience, concluding that, 'The police force should represent the community it serves and should be proportioned as such, reflecting the sexes and races which are so common in the general public. I have therefore decided that I would enjoy being one of those representatives.'

I was invited for a series of rigorous interviews and tests, including of my health and fitness. I recall that the health check involved turning up at Paddington Green police station on a given afternoon. We were herded into a room, told to change into dressing gowns, and then made to wait around for ages in a draughty corridor. Eventually, the women were given a routine medical examination, which I vividly remember included a requirement to stand naked in front of a male doctor. The men were required to bend over and cough.

The tests seemed to be going well, except that the minimum height for female recruits was 5 foot 4 inches and, no matter how earnestly I tried to stretch, I was just 5 foot 3½. Desperate to be accepted, I fluffed up my hair when being measured and managed to scrape through (a technical breach which was, incidentally, also committed by one Cressida Dick, who went on to be the Met's first female commissioner). Then came another interview in which I was asked whether, while awaiting the results of my application, I would be willing to become a part-time special constable. I replied that my circumstances meant I was already working in several different jobs, and unfortunately I couldn't afford to work for nothing.

Part of the process of selecting recruits into the police in those days included a visit to the applicant's home from the local sergeant. Chris Donaldson told me that he hadn't let his parents know he was applying for the force, so, when a uniformed sergeant knocked on the door, 'my dad immediately assumed I was in trouble with the law. The words "I knew it" were out of his mouth before I could explain.' When eventually the confusion was cleared up, the sergeant was invited in.

'My mum showed him into the room we kept for best,' Chris remembers. 'It was so posh I'd hardly ever been allowed in there myself.' The sergeant was invited to sit, 'and then Mum got out a bone-china tea-set which I'd also never seen used before.' Of course, the sergeant was suitably impressed, but as if all that wasn't enough: 'We had a picture of the Queen on one wall and a picture of Jesus Christ on the other,' says Chris. That was it. His application was cleared.

I had also passed all the tests, but then I was disappointed to have to wait eighteen months before I heard anything further. It wasn't until I was eventually accepted that I learned the reason for the delay. I had, of course, been sharing the house with my younger brother who'd experienced a minor brush with the law sometime earlier. Only after it became known that he'd moved out of my home was the way clear for my application to be progressed.

CHAPTER FIVE

'You've not had your bum stamped!'

So, in August 1989, I reported to the Police Academy at Hendon for training. I was one of one hundred recruits joining at the college on the same day – five classes with twenty in each – and I noticed straight away that I was one of just four women, and that mine was the only non-white face among the recruits. I was given the number 001, and I noted that two other recruits seemed to be marked out for special treatment and given numbers 002 and 003; they were Lynn Owens (née Crew) and Adrian Cree, and both were children of chief constables.

I think I could be forgiven for being surprised to find myself the only non-white face out of a hundred, because I'd recently seen the BBC series *Black in Blue*, produced and presented by Desmond Wilcox. The programmes looked at the efforts being made by the Met to encourage recruits from ethnic minorities, and found no fewer than seven in the intake they were given access to.

The programmes followed the seven black and Asian probationers as they went through training and their first year as probationary officers. As it turned out, five of the seven were so light-skinned that they could easily have blended in with the vast majority of the intake. The featured recruits all start out optimistic and responsible, and the senior officers and tutors are all models of political correctness. However, there's also an excruciating moment in episode one when a cadet of Pakistani origin asks what he should do if he sees a fellow officer beating up a black man. The instructor is unequivocal, 'We have to be whiter than white.'

The series had only just finished being broadcast on the BBC when I embarked on my course at Hendon, and naturally it was a talking point. Several of us reflected that the training was likely to be difficult enough for any candidate, but having cameras and a TV crew following you around the whole time must make it near impossible. By the time the series came to an end, two of the original seven had left the police, but five looked set for promising careers.

Like these and hundreds of other recruits before me, I was allocated a single room on the women's floor of one of three huge tower blocks on the complex. It was sparsely furnished with a bed and chest of drawers and there were communal showers at the end of the corridor. There were two bars in the building, one for instructors and one for probationers. A matron was on hand to look after everyone's needs, and there was a strict 10 p.m. curfew.

Recruits were issued with a Nicholson London Streetfinder

map, a torch complete with two batteries, a light wooden truncheon and a notebook. Useful information printed on the back cover included categories of the 'ident code key', which listed under IC3: 'Negroid types (can be light or dark skinned) (Mulatto, Octaroon or Quadroon come within this category) West Indian, Nigerian, African, Caribbean descent etc.' The terminology smacked of the days of slavery, and we were left to wonder quite how Nigerians were distinct from Africans, or why it mattered. A separate handbook advised that we'd receive basic training in crowd control in preparation for 'demonstrations' and dealing with large numbers of people, 'and also an insight into the role of the police in wartime, particularly nuclear war'. The booklet was illustrated with sketches featuring a total of 120 recruits and trainers in various situations, of whom a few were female but none was anything other than white.

Women were also given a handbag, and all of us were provided with Form 177 which authorizes appearances in court, and Form 29 which licenses the bearer to put down a horse in distress. Most importantly, recruits received a warrant card with their number, which, if everything worked out well, they would keep for the next thirty years or more. My number was 008913.

After a stirring speech and introductory welcome by the Met's chief constable Peter Imbert, I stood to attention alongside the other recruits and took the oath sworn by all new probationers: 'I do solemnly and sincerely declare and affirm that I will well and truly serve our sovereign lady the Queen in the office of constable, without fear or affection, malice or ill will; and that I will to the best of my power cause the peace to be kept and preserved and prevent all offences against the persons and properties of Her Majesty's subjects.' It all felt very exciting.

On the Friday of our first week, we probationers were issued with our uniforms, complete with hats or helmets. I immediately had trouble arranging my very long black hair into and under the hat – something that remained a constant irritation for the next three decades. Then we were transported to various police stations around northeast London for three weeks of familiarization with the real life of a police constable before the formal training would begin. The idea of a period of familiarization was a good one, because recruiters were finding that a worrying proportion of trained graduates from Hendon were dropping out very soon after leaving the college. If we could get an early taste of some of the realities of life as a probationer, it might save wasting time and money on training people who were never going to make it as a copper.

My first surprise when I arrived at Limehouse on the Monday morning was to find that, although the surrounding community had a high proportion of black and Asian people, once again mine was the only non-white face in the station. I was paired with a 19-year-old called Andy and we were put in the charge of one of the street-duty instructors, better known as 'puppy walkers'. The idea was that new recruits would experience as many aspects of the work of a PC as possible, but as observers rather than participants. This included stop and search, attending a crime scene, and the whole procedure of an arrest, including bringing the suspect back to the custody suite and consigning him or her to a cell.

One of the less glamorous aspects of the job was to attend a sudden death, and a call in the small hours one morning led to my first ever sight of a dead body. In this case, the deceased was an old lady who had died in her kitchen and was discovered lying on the floor. There seemed to be no question of suspicious circumstances, and we made a call to the coroner's office requesting that the body should be collected. On this occasion, however, there was an overnight backlog, and we were told to leave the lady where she was on the kitchen floor. She would be collected the following morning.

I felt very uncomfortable about the idea of merely locking the door and leaving the deceased where she was, and my disquiet was made worse by the fact that the woman's nightdress had ridden up, exposing the tops of her legs. She was also lying close to a window and would potentially be visible from the street once the morning came around.

One of the things I learned very quickly is that there is little dignity in death. It was an early opportunity to show a measure of judgement, rather than a slavish adherence to the letter of the law. In this instance, I broke the rules by adjusting her nightdress and placing a blanket over the corpse where it lay. Still, when I eventually got home to my own bed that night, I couldn't sleep for thinking about the poor old woman lying dead and alone on her kitchen floor.

Keen to ensure that recruits were exposed to the full gamut of the delights of the job, one of the further hurdles was to attend our first post-mortem. Naturally, we were nervous at the prospect, and of course the instructors took every opportunity to heighten the tension with ghoulish tales. Andy and I both felt apprehensive as we entered the building where the post-mortem would take place.

As we went in the door, we walked over some weighing scales on the floor and the ground vibrated and shook beneath our feet. Both of us nearly leapt out of our skins with the shock, and poor Andy nearly fainted.

We'd been advised to carry a container of Vicks VapoRub to mask the smells of death, and I was able to survive witnessing the procedure by employing a mind-game which has served me well ever since. I just try to remind myself that what is in front of me is not the person. Their souls have gone, and so I imagine this as a sort of mannequin. Not the real thing. The trick works when it involves an adult, but nothing protects me when the deceased is a child or young person. No matter how many times you see that, you never get used to it. It was a sight I would see too frequently in the coming months and years.

Andy was unusually tall and gangly, and found himself on the wrong end of a lot of the humour from the younger officers. He didn't survive the familiarization period and left the force before the course got under way. Although I'd also found this period tough and challenging, I'd seen enough to convince me that there really was an opportunity to make a difference, so I finished the three weeks feeling completely convinced that this was the career for me.

Back at Hendon, we quickly got into our routine. Breakfast

was at 7.30 a.m., with parade and inspection on two mornings a week at 8.00 a.m. Probationers would stand to attention in a neat row underneath the statue of Sir Robert Peel. I took great care that my shoes and buttons were always shiny, my skirt and jacket neatly pressed, and was acutely aware that my long black hair was usually popping out from beneath my hat.

A typical day was divided into formal lessons, fitness classes and, sometimes, policing exercises, in which teachers would role-play troublemakers while recruits tried their luck at sorting out the situation. Formal lessons were in subjects such as the rules of the road, the Theft Act, and causing criminal damage. In basement rooms, there was a series of crime-scenes complete with dummies representing the dead or injured, and an assortment of forensic clues which had to be carefully preserved and bagged up as evidence.

The total of seven non-white faces in the *Black in Blue* series must have been a lucky aberration, because I felt conspicuous as the only one in my cohort. Then one day, when I was feeling particularly isolated, I walked into the canteen and was amazed to see, sitting at a table in the far corner, another young Asian woman.

'Oh my god!' was also the first thought to occur to Shabnam Chaudhri who, it turned out, had arrived at Hendon in the intake two weeks before me. We gravitated towards each other and introduced ourselves. She was in the Purple intake and I was in Blue.

A comparison of our histories over coffee quickly revealed that Shab had come with her parents from Pakistan when she was just 2 years old. The family had settled in East London and she'd attended Plashet School in East Ham. Unlike me, Shab's parents were Muslims, but she had also been expected to fall in line with their plans for an arranged marriage. She would regularly return home to find that they had invited their latest candidate for her betrothal. 'Most were short, fat, bald and in their forties,' she told me. Fortunately, Shab's parents were less strict than mine had been and, although they were clearly disappointed, didn't try to enforce their will. When she left school at 15, she worked in a series of retail clothing stores and, like me, found she had a nose for detecting wrong-doers. So she'd applied to join the police.

Shab was also the only Asian woman in her intake of 180. There was another Indian man, called Bill Hur. He was a lovely bloke but it was just the two of them.

Neither Shab nor I has any memory of training in anything to do with diversity in our time at Hendon. Perhaps that's not surprising, because only 20 out of 700 classroom hours at the training course were even remotely connected with the subject, and were then described euphemistically as 'human awareness'. Rather than focusing on the complex and myriad issues arising from policing a multicultural society, these were more concerned with the sensitivities felt in different districts of London. We were told that if an officer referred to anyone from the East End as 'sir', he would probably think you were having a laugh. 'Mate', if it was a man, or 'love' if it was a woman, were far more appropriate. In fact, I failed one module because I didn't react when, in a role-play, someone reported to the police that 'This geezer was all tooled up.' Coming as I did from the Midlands, where 'tools' meant 'tools', I wondered how a carpenter or maybe a plumber could be in trouble for carrying a set.

My more vivid recall is that any time the subject of relations between the police and the black and Asian community might come up in passing, I would become the focus of discussion. 'Parm, you're black, tell us how it feels when. . .'. As the only non-white in the whole group, I didn't enjoy having to stand up to explain what it felt like to be victimized for the colour of my skin.

I was determined to make the most of the training and the study, but I felt a separation between the majority of other recruits and myself. Most of the rest were 18 or 19, with time on their hands and no responsibilities. Life in the residential blocks was often more like something out of St Trinian's than a hostel for serious professionals. There were lots of relationships and lots of stupid pranks and practical jokes. Quite often you'd return to your room to find every surface covered in talcum powder or your clothes strewn to the far corners. It all seemed to be a bit of a jolly. But I was 25, I had a son in another city and a mortgage to pay. Indeed, just a month into my training, I was obliged to inform my bosses that I was soon to be involved in legal proceedings of my own in order to obtain maintenance from my husband for my son. The hearing would be at Bow County Court and I undertook to let them know if I would have to attend. If so, I reported, 'I will do so in plain clothes in my own time and at my own expense.'

While most of the other probationers would spend their weekends relaxing and socializing, I was required to return home to check on my house, and I was still returning to Handsworth every second weekend to visit my son, whom I missed terribly. Day by day, my life in London gradually began to become my new normal, but of course the enforced separation from him was a big hole in the heart of it. The passage of time had healed wounds with my parents sufficiently that I could visit him at their home, and I could see that he was growing up in a settled environment where he had friends and a good life. It worried me that he spoke Punjabi most of the time, but now that he was 5 years old and ready to go to school, it seemed best to allow him to remain in the only home he had ever known.

While my parents had gone some way towards reconciling themselves to my disgraceful disobedience, I was nonetheless hurt to find myself omitted from the guest list at my niece's wedding. Also, I dared not tell them that I'd joined the police force: they would have been horrified.

One weekend, while I was still in training at Hendon, I received a phone call from the local police at Chadwell Heath to say that my house had been burgled while Daisy and Pauline were also away. I went home to inspect the damage and then to the local police station to give more details of the losses. When asked about my employment, I replied that I was a trainee policewoman.

'Aha,' said the PC behind the counter, 'you've not had your bum stamped!' I was confused, and so the (middle-aged white male) officer explained that, when female recruits join a new posting, the custom is to turn them upside down and 'brand' them on the bottom with the rubber stamp of the station. I immediately made it very clear that this was never going to happen to me. I could tell from his face that he was already registering 'not one of us', and I knew even then that I was unlikely ever to become 'one of the boys'.

Experiences of racism were seldom overt during our time at Hendon, but the simple fact that Shab and I were the only Asian women among our intakes made us feel conspicuous. There was one instructor from the south of India, Shab recalls, who told the class how relieved he'd been when his wife, who was white, had given birth to babies who also looked completely white. 'Because their lives will be so much easier,' he said. Shab was shocked and made a point of going to him afterwards to tell him he should be proud of his own heritage and skin colour. Many months later, the instructor came to a reunion of Shab's classmates where he took her to one side and said he'd reflected on her words and now saw that what she had said was right.

All recruits had to take an exam every month, and if anyone failed they would be held back to take it again. That happened to a few people in both intakes, but Shab and I both passed all ours with flying colours. And then, twenty weeks after arriving at Hendon, it was time to graduate.

Shab's passing out parade took place a few weeks before mine. Overall, she'd enjoyed her time at Hendon and leaving it was a sad but proud day. She remembers inviting her two sisters to come along, but didn't invite her mother. 'It's something I've regretted all my life,' Shab told me. 'I was going out with a white boy and I knew my mother wouldn't approve. So he came instead of her, and he turned out to be an idiot – pulling stupid faces all through the ceremony. I dumped him two weeks later and was sorry that my mother hadn't seen me graduate.'

I have a vivid memory of wearing a big green frock for the formal ball on the night before my passing-out parade. My younger sister Sarj had recently moved to London, and she was the only member of my family I could invite, because of course my parents were still unaware that I was joining the police. I felt fantastic. I'd overcome many obstacles, endured tough times, but achieved a major goal.

Before Shab and I finally left to take up our first postings, we got together to discuss our experiences so far. We agreed always to be a voice on the other end of the phone when times got tough, and to support each other through thick and thin. It was then that we adopted our mutual *cris de coeur*: don't let the bastards grind you down.

CHAPTER SIX

'A spade in uniform'

With what I presumed were good intentions, both Shab and I were posted first of all to communities where someone thought our backgrounds might be of use. The only trouble was that Shab was Muslim from a Pakistani background and her family had originally spoken Urdu, but she was sent to an area of Tower Hamlets where the minority community were from Bangladesh, and therefore spoke Bengali. My own background was Indian and Sikh, but I was sent back to Limehouse, where there were also quite a few people who had originated from Bangladesh, but precious few Sikhs.

What quickly became clear is that both of us had been landed in the centre of what was, at that time, the main battleground between the burgeoning far right, in the form of the British National Party (BNP) and the National Front (NF), and those organizations who opposed them, such as the Anti-Fascist League and the Anti-Nazi League. Derek Beackon, reported by the BBC to be an unemployed lorry driver, first stood as a

candidate for the BNP in 1990 in the Redcoat ward of Tower
Hamlets. He gained only a derisory 3 per cent share of the
vote, but the relatively large immigrant population made this
ripe territory for the racist policies of the BNP and the NF;
indeed, the leader of the NF, John Tyndall, stood as a candidate
in Bow and Poplar in the April 1992 general election. He also
achieved only 3 per cent of the vote.

The occasions of both elections attracted a mix of political
ideologues, skinheads and assorted thugs, arriving in the area
from far and wide. Some, no doubt, harboured strongly held
beliefs in the supremacy of the white race, while others were
simply happy to turn up for what was very likely to be a mass
punch-up. There were frequent demonstrations and clashes
around Brick Lane, with a focal point at Altab Ali Park, originally
St Mary's, but renamed in memory of a 25-year-old who'd been
murdered by three teenage boys in 1978. The park therefore
provided a particularly sensitive location for the racists to
stage events that were essentially designed to provoke the
ethnic population. Trying to keep order between the warring
factions was dangerous for everyone concerned, and many
officers from every background were attacked and injured by
skinheads and their opponents, some of them seriously.

I was, of course, among the officers routinely assigned to
police the demonstrations, but very quickly I began to notice
that I was a particular target for violence and abuse from both
sides. What might sometimes start out as a contained situation
could quite quickly turn to mayhem, and it's disconcerting to
see yourself being pointed out as a possible target by all manner

of vicious-looking thugs. My colleagues noticed it too, so when crowd-control officers were required to hold each other's belts to maintain their line, few of them wanted to be next to me for fear of being targeted. I was frequently punched, slapped, kicked and spat on as demonstrations got out of hand.

There were only two officers – whom we'll call Frank and Roger – who liked a ruck and would volunteer to be alongside me because a punch-up was more or less guaranteed. The pair had been part of a group of six officers accused of beating up three trade unionists demonstrating at the News International plant at Wapping in 1987. The victims were awarded £89,000 in compensation for their injuries but no charges were ever brought against the officers. They went on to gain some notoriety among our colleagues for being more or less inseparable, and for their penchant for the more physical aspects of policing. This reached such a level that, at one point, Roger was referred to the force's medical officer to check on his mental health. The chief medical officer gave him the all clear, which meant that whenever any of his colleagues questioned his sanity, he would loudly proclaim, 'I'm not mad,' and produce a certificate from his pocket to prove it.

If, on more routine patrols, I was involved in a stop and search of any Bangladeshi youths, they would first of all be outraged to be called to account by a woman – 'You should be at home having babies' – then I'd be accused of being a traitor to my kind.

While racism from within the police force itself was frequently more implied than overt, I found very little support or empathy from senior officers. When victims of crime demanded to speak to a white policeman, my inspector told me: 'They're entitled to speak to one of their own.' Such attitudes were born of a long history in the Met, in which black people were encountered much more frequently in the role of villain rather than colleague. More than a dozen years earlier, a young PC of Jamaican background on his first patrol asked an older officer if everyone felt, as he did, that members of the public were staring at them.

'Yes,' came the reply, 'but in your case they are. You can't blame them, most people haven't seen a spade in uniform before. Or only in a bus conductor's uniform.' The constable, Michael Fuller, went on to be the first black chief constable in Britain, but his road to success was to be nearly as obstacle-strewn as mine. After retirement, he wrote his story in a book with the arresting title of *Kill the Black One First*.

When patrolling PCs came on duty, we'd be given a briefing by an officer known as the 'collator', whose job it was to know and keep notes about local villains. He'd say things like, 'Keep an eye out for Wayne from number 10 – he's been driving around while disqualified. And just up the road at number 17, the husband slaps his wife around.'

Coppers on the beat were given quotas for numbers of arrests or stop and searches, and on cold and wintry nights with few people about, these could be difficult to achieve. Sometimes, my partner and I would pop into the cemetery on the Mile End Road at Bow and copy down some names from the headstones to make up numbers, but we'd be careful to change dates of birth because we needed to avoid awkward questions if the deceased had been well known as a member of the local criminal fraternity.

Quotas for arrests could also be difficult to achieve, and so sometimes we'd find somewhere to hide close to a pub car park and wait for a customer to stagger out and get into the driver's seat. It would be an easy collar, but I didn't feel too proud about it.

The procedure if someone was arrested was that we'd have to call for a van, take the prisoner to the station, stand in line in a custody suite and tell the duty sergeant the reason for the arrest. Then the offender would be put in the cells while a report was written, ready to be presented in court the following morning. All of us were game for as much overtime as we could get, so this was very good news if we were due to clock off at 6 a.m. because we now had to stay until mid-morning or perhaps even lunchtime to give evidence before the magistrates. Sometimes overtime could be earned right up to mid-afternoon, and then the next shift would begin a few hours later at 6 p.m.

One of the jobs we always dreaded was carrying out a search of someone's house or flat, usually looking for drugs or weapons. Sometimes we'd go into the high-rise blocks in Tower Hamlets and be met by conditions you'd scarcely believe people could live in. Before we knocked on the door, we'd often tuck our trousers into our socks, and I always made sure I wore thick gloves. You'd pull open a drawer full of clothes and start rummaging around, only to find cockroaches, sometimes dozens of them, scattering for escape. There would be rats or mice sharing space with cots or beds for infants. Frequently, we were calling on social services to get involved, but basically we couldn't get out fast enough.

In those days, as now, a huge proportion of a young police officer's time was taken up with the drunk and disorderly, but this is one area where I believe that the methods of dealing with the problem were better in the old days than they are today. Most drunks were only a danger to themselves, from throwing up and choking, or dying of hypothermia when sleeping rough outdoors. We'd often gather up people in a helpless condition and bring them back to the station to sleep off the booze in a room with perhaps fourteen beds, which we used to call drunk-tanks. Someone would keep an eye on them, they'd be given a hot meal and then let out in the morning and no harm done. Latterly, though, new rules meant that drunks could only be arrested if they'd committed an offence. If they were brought to the station, they had to be given an individual cell. Pressure on custody suites made this impossible and so police now have no choice but to leave drunks where they are on the street, or to take them to A&E, which is already over-burdened.

Quite frequently, a routine stop and search of a group of young people would reveal a small stash of cannabis. Usually, it was a tiny quantity which was probably just intended for their own use. In such instances, I preferred to confiscate the drugs and throw them into a drain rather than arrest and criminalize people at so young an age. One day, however, my attention was

(Right) My elder sister Jindo holding Sarj on the left, and Satnam on the right. I am standing.

(Below left) My dad, Malkit Singh, and me, aged about 6, at our two-up, two-down in Tiverton Road, Handsworth.

(Below right) My mum, Gurmaj Kaur, in around 1969.

(Left) Satnam, me and Sarj.

(Below) My dad's family in front of his home in the Punjab. My grandfather is on the left. Dad kept the picture as a reminder of the need to send money.

(Right) Tarsem Singh Sandhu, the Sikh bus driver who was suspended by the Wolverhampton Transport Corporation, 1963.

(Below) Enoch Powell electioneering in his Wolverhampton constituency as his wife hands out leaflets, 1970.

(Left) Me aged 12 at
22 Paddington Road.

(Below) Sarj, me and Satnam in
the house on Paddington Road,
1980. The red Choora bangles are
only worn by new brides –
I wouldn't have been allowed to
wear the red nail varnish before
I was married.

(Right) Me in traditional dress with my mum shortly after getting married.

(Below) Sikh men in ceremonial dress, including 'the five Ks'. They look like my first husband's brothers except that they had more weapons, as well as metal discs and beads around their turbans.

My mother and me after I adopted a more Westernized look.
I had cut my hair and my marriage had failed. My husband's family
would not allow cutting of hair as it is against Sikh teachings.

My son and me on his fourth birthday.

Chris Donaldson, who first suggested I should join the police.

Gurpal Virdi.

(Above) Michael Fuller, Britain's first black chief constable.

(Left) Leroy Logan during the formal launch of the Morris Inquiry, 2004.

momentarily distracted and I inadvertently put a small stash of cannabis in my pocket instead of discarding it. Two weeks later, I terrified myself when I discovered it still there. I was horrified. If someone had found it on me, I'd have been accused of stealing. Immediately I threw the cannabis away and thereafter insisted the young people should throw the drugs down a drain themselves so I'd have no need to touch them at all.

One of the other aspects of life in those early days was the rampant homophobia among young officers, which frequently crept into the way trouble was dealt with. Just next to Mile End station was a club called Benjy's, and round the back was another club called Benjy's 2. Benjy's 2 used to have sado-masochism nights once a week, and a gay night on another. The constables used to hate being called down there because, being young and in uniform, they were frequently teased and humiliated. I used to enjoy the banter with the local clientele, and so was perfectly happy to go.

Prejudice also extended among the women, and I was appalled to learn that other female officers were refusing to go into the locker room when the one and only gay WPC was changing her clothes. 'What do they think?' the woman complained. 'That they're so irresistible that I'm going to attack them because they're wearing bras and pants?' In those days, female constables were either a 'bike' or a 'dyke'. You were a 'bike' if you'd sleep with anyone who asked you, and if you wouldn't, you must be a lesbian.

Although much of my daily duty was taken up with relatively minor disturbances and offences, there were also frequent incidents of terrible trauma and tragedy. Sometimes, it seemed as though death and destruction were all around me, and I wondered what horrors the next shift would bring. One day, I was called to the scene of an accident on the A13 involving a motorcycle and a van. When I arrived, I was shocked and horrified to find the motorcyclist's body lying close to his mangled bike, while his head lay several yards away, still strapped inside its crash helmet. At first I couldn't believe what I was seeing – the young man's face was entirely intact, and he was looking back at me through the visor. I kept thinking, 'How are we going to tell his mum?'

When the scene had eventually been cleared up and the remains of the victim taken away, I got back into my car to return to the police station. It was only a short distance, but I kept finding myself getting lost, then finding myself in the wrong place. I even ended up back on the motorway because I couldn't focus or get my mind back onto driving. I lost about thirty minutes, which later I couldn't account for, because all I'd been thinking about was this poor kid's face staring at me.

It was in those first few months of my probationary period that I found myself foisted on the Area Driver for a night patrol around Bow and Limehouse. The senior officer who drove off and left me under a railway bridge in Eleanor Street was a man we'll just call Harry. Harry was part of the team which had already boasted to me that they'd 'got rid of' another one of 'your type' the year before. I found out that a black female officer had indeed been posted there and had resigned within months, due to the treatment she was subjected to. After my conversation with the inspector, however, I knew I'd have no choice but to let the incident pass without making a fuss or formal complaint.

Harry had refused to speak to me since that night, which suited me fine, until one day, shortly after, when he and I were required to give evidence at the trial of a man accused of burglary. While police are not allowed to concoct their evidence, it is of course usual to compare notes to ensure that there are no glaring discrepancies. However, Harry was unwilling to discuss it with me and as a result our evidence in court differed in a number of ways. The accused was acquitted, and the judge admonished us both for giving inconsistent testimony.

Sometime later again, I was surprised to receive a phone call from Harry at home to say I'd stopped a friend of his, a used car dealer from Bethnal Green, and required him to produce documents at the police station. The friend had no insurance, Harry said, but he would 'make it worth my while' to forget about it. He told me not to put in the paperwork – but I was spared having to resist this pressure, because I'd already submitted it. Perhaps Harry was carrying out an officially approved test to discover whether I was potentially corrupt. Perhaps he wasn't. I just mentally added him to the list of officers I had to watch out for.

CHAPTER SEVEN

Zulu

In addition to dealing with dead bodies and attending a post-mortem, an early baptism for a police constable is to deliver what the police call a 'death message'. For most of us, the prospect of having to break to parents or spouses the worst news they will ever hear in their lives is daunting and traumatizing. It's a scene that is frequently depicted in TV dramas, and usually characterized by a sequence along the lines of 'Can we come in?', 'Is there anyone else in the house?', 'Would you mind sitting down?' and 'I'm sorry to have to tell you. . .'. The pattern is so familiar that you'd think it had been learned by rote. However, as a young constable faced with my first experiences of delivering a death message, I'd received no training whatsoever in how best to do so.

I was on night duty when an emergency call came in reporting an incident of domestic violence. The victim was a young midwife who'd been working a late shift and had returned home to find her husband in bed with a female – and the female in question was her own younger sister, aged just 13. The girl had been babysitting her sister's children, who were in the room next door asleep in their beds. They later told us that the 13-year-old regularly slept in their daddy's bed; the girl was later found to be pregnant and underwent an abortion.

Meanwhile, of course, all hell had broken loose at the couple's home, which resulted in the wife sustaining serious injuries and being taken back to the hospital where she worked. Her husband told doctors her injuries were the result of her having fallen over. Staff there immediately realized this was extremely unlikely, and recalled that this was not the first incident of domestic violence she had experienced. The young woman died of her injuries, and her husband was arrested and taken into custody.

Now we were faced with a 13-year-old girl who also needed urgent medical attention, and three small children with no-one to take care of them. Eventually, we ascertained that the children's grandparents lived not far away. We put the children in the back of the patrol car and I drove with another officer to break the news.

I remember it was a lovely Victorian house in a nice neighbourhood. By now, it was the small hours of the morning and I was struggling to find a way to soften the news that would inevitably turn these poor people's lives upside down.

I left my partner in the car to take care of the children and went to the front door. It took a while of knocking and ringing the bell before eventually it was opened and a couple in their sixties appeared wearing night-clothes. I asked to come in and the bewildered grandparents showed me into their living room while they went to fetch their dressing gowns.

I can remember sitting on their sofa, and just above the mantelpiece was a painting of a scene from the Bible. I thought perhaps they were Christians, and wondered if their faith might be of any help to them. I also thought how no-one deserves to hear what they were about to hear. I'll always remember the look on their faces as I broke to them, as gently as I knew how, that their daughter had been killed.

When the couple eventually began to absorb what I'd told them, I raised the subject of their grandchildren, who were still waiting with another officer in the back of my patrol car parked outside. Their immediate reaction was to ask why the children's father couldn't take care of them, so I had to break the further bad news that their son-in-law was in custody, suspected of having murdered their daughter. At first the couple refused to believe it, declaring that the pair had a loving marriage and that he would never do anything to harm her. I knew it was not part of my job to disabuse them of their illusion, but I then had to find a way to impart the circumstances of the violence, and the situation of their other daughter.

It's difficult to even conceive of a set of circumstances more loaded with tragedy than the one that had landed on these good people in the middle of the night. I thought their hearts must break. Eventually, though, I persuaded them to take in their grandchildren so they could go back to sleep, while they tried to absorb the destruction of their immediate family.

It was among the first of what were to become frequent

experiences of giving terrible news to innocent people, and something I've never managed to get used to. We all take for granted that today will be much like yesterday, but then one day something happens completely out of the blue, and everything you thought you knew gets turned inside out. It's a cliché to say 'live every day as though it were your last', but it's a reminder to appreciate what's important.

Not every aspect of my life as a new constable was characterized by tragedy and trauma though. Among the less sombre trials I had to cope with was the constant stream of stunts and tricks which more experienced officers seemed to enjoy inflicting on us younger colleagues.

I was a probationer with a young bloke called Jimmy who'd been a milkman before he joined the force. As the two newcomers, we were the target for all kinds of hazing, as a result of which we tried to stick together for mutual support. We used to have to do night patrols alone on foot, but Jimmy and I would plot a route so we could meet in the small hours of the morning. Quite often, there was very little to be done at 3 a.m., and on one occasion I sat on a park bench while Jimmy lay on the grass beside me, and both of us went to sleep. Next thing we knew it was 6 a.m. and we were overdue back at the station. We brushed ourselves off and hurried back, and it was only when we were about to go in that I noticed his back was covered in grass stains. Luckily, my keen eyes saved us from what would have been the inevitable ridicule.

Less amusing, for Jimmy at least, was an incident that took place when he arrived on his motorbike one evening to start a night shift. He was leaning into a locker to stow his gear when an older officer shoved him from behind so he fell inside, and instantly the door was slammed shut behind him. The next thing Jimmy knew, the locker was being manhandled out of the police station and into the back of a van, and he was bumped about inside as it was driven through the streets. He was still banging and shouting to be released when the vehicle stopped in a disused plot in the Mile End area, and the locker was again hoisted into the air and carried along to where it was eventually dumped. Still shouting pleas for help mixed with abuse and threats of retribution, poor Jimmy heard the sound of heavy boots disappearing into the distance.

Back at the station, Jimmy's shift was starting and his absence was noted by the sergeant. 'He's been called away to deal with an incident,' said another constable. No-one raised the alarm and it was not until four hours later, at 2 p.m., that his colleagues returned to the field, threw the locker back into the van, and brought it back to base. Jimmy was absolutely beside himself with rage. It must have been like being locked in your own coffin, but of course there was nothing to be done about it because the worst thing you could do was rat on your colleagues.

On another occasion from the same period at Limehouse, a different male probationer was instructed to accompany a man who'd been accused of rape for an examination in hospital. Since the penalty for losing a prisoner in your charge in those days was the loss of a week's pay, the usual routine was that the two men should be handcuffed together. Before they left the station, however, other young officers instructed the probationer that he was obliged to wear a set of paper overalls to avoid contamination of forensics. Later, the two men arrived at the hospital handcuffed together, with one of them wearing the familiar rape-suit. Nurses and medical staff therefore assumed that the probationer was the rapist and started treating him as such. The young officer was not amused.

Sometimes, the practical jokes were reasonably harmless, and sometimes they were rather less so. I remember an occasion when a young WPC from nearby Bethnal Green was on patrol when she was suddenly alerted that a burglar had been disturbed in the act and was on the run. She was directed to chase him down through a derelict area and was in full flight when she fell into a ditch, badly twisting her ankle. The story had been invented, but the injury eventually caused the WPC to be invalided out of the force. No formal complaint was ever made.

The rough and tumble of life as a beat copper was not confined to my own borough. I was among some five thousand officers from all over London called upon to police the estimated half a million people who attended the Notting Hill Carnival. It was the 25th anniversary of the event and the crowds were generally in good humour. However, once again, I found myself the target of racial abuse from both sides of the community. People would ostentatiously blow the smoke from weed in my face, knowing that in those circumstances you couldn't do anything about it. At one point, I was called to the scene of a stabbing and in the mêlée that followed I was pushed against a barrier which fell over, and me with it. I got a nasty blow to the head and lost consciousness, waking up several hours later in hospital, where I was checked for concussion but eventually allowed home.

Despite that bad experience, I would go on to help police the Notting Hill Carnival for the next twenty years. On every occasion, rest and refreshment was provided at the same local primary school. Also on every occasion, officers taking a break from policing the carnival were treated to a viewing of the same movie – a 1964 film in which 150 British soldiers, many of whom were sick and wounded patients in a field hospital, hold off a force of 4,000 spear-carrying African warriors – called *Zulu*.

All this time, I was still travelling backwards and forwards to Handsworth to see my son. However, these days the laundry I brought with me to do when I got there mysteriously consisted of a large number of men's white shirts, which then had to be pressed and ironed in a very particular way. Under pressure for an explanation, I eventually revealed to my parents that I'd joined the police. They were horrified; as if it wasn't bad enough that I'd left my husband and was living far away, I now had a job that they imagined would have me rolling around in the mud fighting criminals. It was the last thing they wanted for their daughter, who ought to be at home having babies and sewing.

By now, I was working regular shifts based at Limehouse. My typical work pattern was seven night shifts in a row, finishing at 6 a.m., followed by two late shifts (2 p.m. to 10 p.m.), then two days off, four early shifts (6 a.m. to 2 p.m.), then two more days off. If we were finishing the last of seven night shifts at 6 a.m., but starting again later the same day at 2 p.m., we'd sometimes gather at a pub called the Cart and Horses, known locally as 'the early house', which opened all hours to cater for night-shift or postal workers and market-traders. Among the other regular clientele were the local sex-workers, who were discouraged only to the extent that the landlord would not serve women at the bar. This was therefore the only occasion on which being female meant that I'd be served drinks by the men.

While at Limehouse, I found myself partnered for some patrols with an officer called Steve Reed. Steve was an Area Van driver who shared some of the same status as the Area Car drivers of my recent experience. At that time, he was in the process of separating from his wife and, after they'd parted, he and I started going out together. He was tall and slim and 'a bit of a maverick', which I have to admit I found attractive. We found it easier to socialize with other police officers and gradually I began to feel more at home in the force and in my new community.

Although occasionally violent and always ugly, the everyday racism which arose from policing such a mixed community became part of the fabric of daily life for me and the handful of other BAME officers. However, the combination of mindless prejudice and violent skinhead gangs was increasingly leading to incidents of a far more alarming kind. In our neighbourhood, and in other racially mixed communities all around London, knife attacks between members of rival gangs were becoming all too familiar, and often ended in tragedy.

The eventual Macpherson report into the murder of Stephen Lawrence itemized just a handful of the incidents of racist violence in the Eltham area in the two years before his death in April 1993. In February 1991, a white man named Mark Thornburrow murdered a young 15-year-old black youth named Rolan Adams, in a racist attack at a bus stop after an altercation between rival gangs of white and black youths. Three months later, a black youth called Orville Blair was killed by a white man called Paul Snell. In July of the following year, an Asian boy called Rohit Duggal was stabbed to death by a white youth named Peter Thompson outside a kebab shop. And in March 1993, Gurdeep Banghal, a 22-year-old Asian youth, was stabbed and seriously wounded by a white youth, while serving in a Wimpy Bar. The attacker was reported to have verbally abused his victim, calling him a 'Paki bastard'.

With these and other incidents happening so frequently, and often involving violence between rival gangs, it's perhaps no surprise that some officers developed a lack of sensitivity to them as individual tragedies. When much of the violence is gang-on-gang, it's not hard to see how an attitude of 'they deserve each other' can develop.

So, when police received a series of 999 calls on the evening of 22 April 1993 to say that a young black man had been hurt in an altercation in Eltham, there would sadly have been little reason to think the incident would become the most notorious crime of its type in the history of the Met. The incident took place just twenty minutes across the river from Tower Hamlets, where I was a young WPC. The immediate police response to the brutal and unprovoked murder of Stephen Lawrence by a group of five white youths was careless and disorganized, and quickly drew the criticism that things would have been very different had the victim been white and the attackers black. Later, there were allegations that, rather than putting all their energies into arresting the killers, one corrupt senior officer had actually sought to shield them from blame. And instead of seeking to comfort the bereaved members of the Lawrence family, a secret operation had sought evidence with which to smear their good name. The eventual public inquiry into Stephen Lawrence's murder, headed by Sir William Macpherson, would conclude that the Metropolitan Police was institutionally racist, and that 'the need to re-establish trust between minority ethnic communities and the police is paramount'.

The charge of institutional racism has resonated through the public debate about the state of policing in London from that day to this. Compelling evidence for the prosecution is provided by the stop-and-search figures, which consistently show that black and Asian youths are far more likely than white youths to be targeted. Those arguing in defence of the police point out that our officers are drawn from wider society, and that significant sections of wider society are racist. From my direct experience, I'd say there are plenty of good and hard-working police officers in the Met without a racist bone in their bodies. Unfortunately, there are many more who come with a lot of preconceived ideas about anyone from a different background from their own, which is how the Met has ended up with its appalling reputation for racism then and now.

The depth and degree of racism in the community of Tower Hamlets where I was working was about to be put to the test. Just a few months after the killing of Stephen Lawrence, the resignation of a Labour councillor sparked a local council by-election, and Derek Beackon was chosen again as the BNP candidate. He set about canvassing the area on a platform of 'rights for whites', and ending all immigration from countries other than those in the (then) European Economic Community (EEC).

What seemed to be the distinct possibility that the far right might win their first council seat in Britain brought renewed protests from local people, and a fresh series of clashes between BNP supporters and anti-fascist campaigners. Police were frequently called upon to break up the resulting disorder and, as the only non-white officer in the borough, once again I often found myself the target of both sides.

On 16 September 1993, Derek Beackon won the by-election with a 33.9 per cent share, beating Labour by just seven votes, and thus became the first elected councillor for the BNP in Britain. After the result was announced, Beackon rallied his supporters with a speech in which he said, 'The British people are no longer prepared to be second-class citizens in their own country. The British people have had enough. It's time to take our country back.'

I was on duty that night helping to police the fights between those celebrating and those protesting. It really felt like being on the front line between two warring sides, but instead of being just a neutral arbiter, there to keep the peace and ensure the protesters stayed within the law, it felt like I was a symbol of everything they were disagreeing about. It was all deeply uncomfortable and sometimes far worse than that. I have a vivid memory of a number of skinheads rapping on the window of my patrol car with a beer glass, and being momentarily terrified that one of them was about to smash it in my face.

The following days and weeks brought a whole series of resignations from the council from people who didn't wish to be associated in any way with Beackon, as a result of which some services began to suffer. On the other side of the argument, the racists felt a new spring in their step. 'You won't have a job for long,' was a taunt frequently directed at me as I walked the streets on patrol. 'We'll soon be sending you back where you came from.' (In my case, this was Handsworth.) Although this kind of thing was always irritating, I learned to expect it as an everyday occurrence when I was out on the street. What I was less ready to accept was when it happened in my place of work.

CHAPTER EIGHT

'Prisoners, prostitutes and plonks'

Right from my first days training at Hendon, I'd had a hankering to be a detective. I felt I had a nose for it, seeking out the clues, putting them together, tracking down the bad people and putting them in jail. So, when I first joined the Met I was happy to learn that my two-year probationary period included a compulsory six-week attachment to the Criminal Investigation Department – better known as CID.

The popular image of the detective branch of the Met in those days probably derives from TV programmes as much as anything else – for example, *The Sweeney*, a regular ITV series throughout the 1970s and early 80s. In it, detectives Jack Regan and George Carter, played by John Thaw and Dennis Waterman, wore loud kipper ties and jackets with wide collars, drank and smoked heavily, bent the rules and were politically incorrect even by the far less sensitive standards of those days. My experience of the real thing made Regan and Carter seem like models of enlightened policing.

'We got rid of one of your type before so it won't take us long to get rid of you,' was the welcome I received from one detective in the first days of my attachment. It's probably hard for anyone who hasn't experienced something like that to guess what it feels like. I wanted so badly to make a go of things in CID, and barriers were being put up before I had even started. I remember feeling a mixture of heightened nerves at the prospect of trying to be accepted, and resentment that it was obviously going to be so much harder than it needed to be.

This was, of course, in the days before ubiquitous mobile phones, and so if anyone at the Limehouse station wanted to locate an officer from CID after about 10 a.m., it would be necessary to phone the Oporto Tavern next door and ask for 'Sid Smith'. If it was just before or during lunch, chances were that a detective would be in the bar drinking with fellow officers, and sometimes with some of the more colourful local villains. If it was the afternoon, you might find them on the golf course.

The Police and Criminal Evidence Act gave some particular rights to suspects, but I recall these being routinely ignored. Sometimes a suspect would be arrested but no-one would be informed, so the clock didn't start ticking on the right to keep them in custody and no solicitor could be summoned. I was posted with two officers who detained a suspect in the street, then drove around with him in handcuffs in the back of the car. They interrupted their questioning to head off to buy fish and chips. On their return, one of the arresting officers pressed a handful of cold chips into the suspect's face. When I asked what was going on, the officer laughed and said, 'Who would ever believe I did that?' I considered whether to report this and other incidents, but all of us knew plenty of stories of what happened to anyone who grassed on fellow officers. In just one example, an Asian officer at Bow, who'd complained about fellow officers, was later attacked by criminals in the street. He called for emergency assistance, but none came, and he ended up in hospital with brain damage. Eventually, he left the force.

This was a period in which corruption among some detectives in adjacent areas of London was rife. Giving evidence to the Home Affairs Select Committee in 1997, Metropolitan Police Commissioner Sir Paul Condon said: 'I do have a minority of officers who are corrupt, dishonest and unethical. We believe, sadly, that they commit crimes, they neutralise evidence in important cases and they betray police operations to criminals . . . They are cunning, they are experienced, they are surveillance conscious.'

The same impression had been formed by Michael Fuller when he was a uniformed officer in Fulham. As he relates in his memoir *Kill the Black One First*, a temporary inspector was transferred in from a recent role in the Flying Squad:

> The new boss appeared and we got into line. Something about the stiff way he walked suggested it was many years since he'd been in uniform and right now he would prefer a suit. He made a few comments, and when he reached

the end of the line, he nodded at us. 'Right, you're all set. Go out there and get to work. Lots of stops. And make sure they're black.' Not long after, the same inspector was arrested and later found guilty and jailed for corruption going back to his days in 'The Sweeney'.

I have to say that I saw no direct evidence of any serious corruption during my short attachment to CID, but the careless racism and sexism, which I'd had to put up with throughout my training and probation so far, now became far more purposeful and serious. They would look down your dress, touch you up. One detective chief inspector literally chased me around a table in an interview room, until someone came in unexpectedly and I was able to slip out of the door and get away. Some of the officers had 'special relationships' with local prostitutes; the women would be allowed to ply their trade unhindered in return for sexual favours. One particular officer who drove the Area Van was the worst one to get sent out with. At the start of the night, he would pick up his favourite prostitute, called Bridget, and then have sex in the back of the police van before even starting the patrol. It was very difficult to ignore. In spite of this, an oft-repeated mantra among detectives was to 'avoid the 3Ps' – prisoners, prostitutes and plonks. ('Plonks' was the charming name given to probationary officers.)

At one point, I attended a leaving party for a retiring colleague, and in his speech the senior officer said, 'We were going to get you a Black and Decker, but. . .' now referring to me, 'we've already got the Black.'

When Deputy Assistant Chief Constable John Grieve eventually took over the inquiry into the investigation of the Stephen Lawrence murder, he accepted the charge of institutional racism, and went on to describe it in an interview as 'unwitting, thoughtless, stereotypical behaviour, showing ignorance and insensitivity in ways of talking to people'. However, I'd say that 'racist, sexist and nasty' would be a more accurate description of some of the CID officers I came across at that time, and once again I felt close to quitting. My attachment was supposed to be for six weeks, but after four I went off sick and told my boss I couldn't finish it. It was one of the most unpleasant times of my career.

In the light of such experiences, it's perhaps not surprising that the Metropolitan Police was having difficulties in recruiting and retaining officers from black and Asian communities. Relatively few applied, and there was an alarmingly high rate of resignations among those who did. As part of an effort to understand why so few people from ethnic backgrounds were joining the police, an exercise had been held in which every black and Asian officer in the Met was summoned to a series of meetings, at which they were encouraged to be open and frank about their experiences of racism and any other grievances.

The seminars, held over 100 miles away from London at Bristol University, were considered controversial at the time, given the compulsory attendance of officers based on their ethnic origin. Among those required to go was my friend Chris Donaldson. 'All sorts of jokes were going around at the time,' he remembers, 'like maybe they were going to gather us all together in one place and gas us when we got there.'

The Bristol Seminars, as they became known, revealed a depressing catalogue of experiences from the 350 officers who attended. The range of issues listed in the official report might well have been taken directly from my personal experience. They included: feelings of isolation and lack of support; the failure of supervisors to tackle inappropriate humour and behaviour; officers who complained were branded as troublemakers; the perception that career opportunities were restricted – particularly into CID.

The remarkable congruence between the findings of the seminars and my own experience was only surprising because I was one of the few, if not perhaps the only non-white officer in the Met, who was not present. I'd been prevented from going to Bristol by my sergeant, who reported upwards that I was on leave when they were due to be held. I wasn't, but, of course, he was my boss and there was nothing I could do about it.

The attachment to CID confirmed beyond any doubt that I was more suited to the kind of policing usually done in uniform. So I applied to become part of a community policing initiative called Home Beat, and was assigned to the Chrisp Street market area next to the Lansbury estate in Poplar. This was a perfect environment for community policing because the estate had been designed to include everything residents should need. Within a few streets, there were shops, pubs, churches, old folks' homes, open spaces and local schools.

This was a happy time for me; I was one of a team of four officers regularly patrolling the district, so I could get to know local residents, shopkeepers, market-traders and teachers. I attended community meetings to hear about the concerns of local people, and was called on to sort out things like disputes between neighbours and incidents of shoplifting. Occasionally, I would make up the numbers on night duties for other teams when required.

Even during this period, however, it wasn't all *Dixon of Dock Green*. One day, I received a call reporting 'shots fired' at an address on a council estate in Bow. The scene which greeted me when I arrived was more like something from a horror film. Lying in the street outside the house was the body of a young man with a mass of blood and gore where his face should have been.

The lad was only about 15 years old and he'd had a falling out with his girlfriend, who was the same age. He'd stood outside her house with a loaded shotgun and threatened to blow his own head off unless she came out. When she didn't, he fired the gun into his face and was instantly killed. I was assigned to clear the immediate area and keep people away from the body while other officers investigated the circumstances. I was just standing there for ages, with nothing to contemplate except the terrible tragedy which had befallen this boy's family, and the horror of what he'd done to himself. Images from the scene haunted my days and nights for a long while after.

Although I was generally happy at Chrisp Street, it was obvious that anyone who wanted to make progress would need to move around to get a range of experience. So I applied for a transfer and for a period I was based at Ilford, which was the police station closest to my own home, and where I'd gone to report the details of my burglary while training at Hendon. I managed to avoid the threatened 'bum stamping' initiation, but other female officers assigned to their first station in those days were less lucky. Just one example involved a WPC called Judy, who later wrote about the experience in *Voices from the Blue* (compiled by Jennifer Rees and Robert J. Strange): 'I was held down by three policemen while about forty watched as my breasts were station-stamped. It's something I never got over or forgot. Another colleague, fresh out of training, had the same thing done to her bottom but never got over it. She resigned the following day, too distressed to remain in the force.' Another called Mary recalled: 'I felt like a glove puppet because I had so many hands up my skirt. When making the tea, I kept a spoon in the boiling water to use when they came to show me their penises.'

I managed to avoid those particular problems inside the station at Ilford, but there were others in the community outside. As I lived in the area, I kept seeing people in the street that I'd arrested. One night, there was a fight outside a club called 5th Avenue and I apprehended one of the troublemakers. Next day, I was off duty and I saw him out and about, which felt a bit disconcerting. More troubling was when I was called to a domestic dispute and had to arrest a 6 foot 2 judo expert who was totally off his head on drugs. The day after, I was shopping in the local supermarket with my son who was staying with me, when I saw the same man. Fortunately, he'd been so 'out of it' the previous night that he didn't recognize me, and later when he went to court, he claimed that the arresting officer had beaten him up. When I came into court to give evidence – all 5 foot 3½ inches of me – the judge said, 'Really?' The man dropped his complaint.

Next, I asked for an attachment to the Hackney Community Safety Team under Sergeant Phil Gospage. The team consisted of a small group of officers trained to deal with racial and homophobic attacks, homelessness, crime prevention and, most important from my point of view, domestic violence. It was based in a small and friendly set of rooms at the back of the police station, discreetly tucked away so that victims of abuse could more easily report their concerns without being spotted by their neighbours. On the day in January 1996 when a reporter from *The Big Issue* came to research a feature on the initiative, I was just on my way out to visit an Asian family who had recently been the victims of a horrifying attack. A gang of youths had set upon the father with a cricket bat studded with nails, while the mother was dragged down the street by her hair when she tried to intervene. Their 9-year-old daughter had called the police, who'd taken an hour and a half to arrive, by which time the gang was of course long gone. Two youths were eventually arrested, but now my job was to try to rebuild the family's confidence in the forces of law and order. I visited them in the new council house we'd arranged and asked the mother about the panic button they'd been given. The woman answered in Urdu via an English-speaking neighbour that it wasn't working. When I asked to see it, the woman climbed on a bed and reached for a suitcase on top of a wardrobe. I told her that it wouldn't do much good up there, and had to arrange for a colleague to come round later that day to fix it.

I went on to tell the reporter of my anger at the English courts, which seemed powerless when dealing with racist attacks. I recalled a skinhead I'd arrested for giving Nazi salutes in the street and placing stickers on every door showing a black man in a noose with 'N———s Beware' printed underneath. He got a £50 fine for 'Behaviour likely to cause distress'. Does anyone think that bloke stopped doing what he was doing? I don't.

All the while I was keen to take whatever opportunities arose to advance my career, and so Shab and I went together back to Hendon for a course in Sexual Offences Investigation Training (SOIT). As its name suggests, the course teaches officers best practice in dealing with victims of sex attacks.

The police have, for many years, been criticized for what is often perceived as a lack of sensitivity when dealing with victims of sexual assault. Women have complained that they found it difficult to describe to men what had happened to them, and that when they did so, male officers were sometimes unsympathetic and discouraging. The introduction of SOIT officers was designed to encourage women to report such attacks in the first place, and to give them the best chance of being able to give their evidence effectively once they did.

As soon as a complaint was made by the victim of a sex crime, a SOIT officer would be assigned. In those days, the victim would be escorted to a so-called 'haven', which was a designated area, decorated and furnished to be comfortable and non-threatening. Sometimes these spaces were located inside a police station but sometimes not. The SOIT officer would take a full and careful statement about everything that had happened, and then ask the victim to stand on a big piece of paper while they removed their clothes so that any forensic samples could be collected. Nails would be clipped for traces of the attacker's DNA and swabs taken. Then later the SOIT would keep the victim informed of the progress of the investigation and, if and when the case went to court, would stay alongside them throughout the procedure.

Shab and I enjoyed the training, and especially the expertise it gave us in being able to offer genuine practical help to women in such circumstances. Although at the time of my own arranged marriage there had been no law forbidding a husband from forcing himself on his wife, what I experienced felt to me like rape. I was glad to be able to assist a number of victims of sex crimes to bring their cases to a successful prosecution. However, even with all the careful training and empathy, the reality on the streets sometimes threw up situations that could not have been anticipated.

One such incident took place in 1997 when a Turkish woman contacted the police to say that she'd been raped, and that her attacker was a respected figure from her local community. I was assigned as the SOIT officer, and was shocked to find that the woman had been appallingly injured by vaginal and anal penetration. The situation was immediately further complicated by the fact that she desperately did not want her husband to know what had happened, fearing that he might blame her for the incident, or regard her as in some way soiled as a result. The man was arrested and immediately admitted that intercourse had taken place but claimed it had been consensual. I believed the woman from the start, and the extent of her injuries bore eloquent testimony to the likely truth of her account. The accused man was charged and the case was awaiting trial, when suddenly he gave an interview to a local community radio station in which he complained that he was being victimized by the police. Against all laws forbidding the identification of rape victims, he named the woman concerned on air, and accused her of fabricating the case against him.

We went immediately to the radio station, but of course it was too late. We told them they'd broken the law, read them the riot act, and told them they may well be prosecuted for naming the victim. But the harm was done. Of course, the woman now withdrew her complaint and refused to testify against her attacker, so we had no choice but to drop the charges. It would not be the last injustice I'd have to find ways to come to terms with.

In another memorable case originating in the same period, I had to wait nearly two decades for the criminal justice system to get our man. I was on night duty when I was called to the scene of a reported burglary at a grocery store. The Asian couple who managed the business had two young children, who'd been asleep on the premises when the robbery took place. I was very used to finding the victims of crime upset and traumatized, but there was something about the scene which made me suspect that more was going on than was being reported. I did my best to persuade the couple to tell all, but they insisted it had been nothing more than a burglary. When checking the premises for potential evidence, however, I noticed that the woman's underwear had been discarded and so I collected it carefully and sent it to the forensic lab.

I had a sense that the woman didn't want to open up in front of her husband, so I took her to one side and asked if there was something else she wanted to tell me, but she insisted there was nothing. A report came back later stating that DNA from a male had been found on the woman's underwear, but there was no record of a match for the DNA in the criminal files.

It was one day nearly twenty years later that the phone rang and a detective told me they had a suspected rapist in custody and that his DNA matched the sample I'd collected all those years earlier from the burglary at the grocery store. Immediately, I went back to speak to the original victim and told her what had happened. Initially, she seemed pretty unhappy to see me, but we got chatting, and for a second time I urged her to let us know if something else had happened on that night. The woman was clearly reluctant to re-live the incident, but eventually she revealed that she had been raped, but she hadn't wanted her husband to know. As often happens, she was afraid he'd regard her as in some way soiled or to blame.

Of course, I completely understood why the woman should have felt that way at the time, but I asked whether she felt able to give a statement now. It was evident that the man was still attacking women, all these years later, and he had to be stopped. The woman said she'd think it over and undertook to discuss it with her children, who were now in their early twenties. The kids had been brought up in England and didn't have any of that sense that the victim is somehow to blame. They urged their mother to cooperate with us and she agreed to give the statement.

Her additional evidence was enough to force the man to confess, so he changed his plea to guilty and she didn't have to go to court. It had been a long time coming, but the rapist was eventually given a long prison sentence.

In yet another tragic incident from around the same time, I was called to assist when a mentally ill man had broken into his parents' home in Leyton, smashed up all the furniture and threatened to kill them. The first officers to be called to the scene had grappled with the man in the hallway, where he fell to the floor, hitting and smashing a glass table on the way down. He'd been hurt in the fall and so, still needing to restrain him, the officers turned him over to check for injuries. By the time I arrived on the scene, one of the officers was leaning over the prostrate man shouting, 'Please don't die, please don't die.' Despite their best efforts to revive him, the man died from what the coroner later concluded was positional asphyxiation. Outside in the street, the same officer wept on my shoulder, but I had to find a private place to go to cry myself, because, being a woman, I couldn't be seen to cry in front of the others.

All the night-duty officers on the scene were required to return to the police station, where we were confined to a room and questioned by members of the Independent Police Complaints Commission (IPCC). Anyone who'd had physical contact with the deceased had their clothes and property collected and were given tracksuits to wear instead. They were allowed to make only one phone call to their families, explaining that they'd be late but not the reason. They were eventually released at 7 p.m. that evening, twenty-one hours after the start of their shift, and several of them had no choice but to drive home. Then they were all suspended for three days while enquiries continued. We were all mortified when, later on, we attended the inquest at the coroner's court and the man's parents said, 'We wish we'd never called you.'

The question I'm left asking is, what else could our officers have done? He was threatening to kill his parents. If we hadn't been there, it might have been their funerals instead. All the officers involved were exonerated from any blame, but several still felt some guilt about what had happened. Later, as a result of this and similar incidents, we were given updated training in positional asphyxiation. Up until then, we'd been told to place suspects on the ground and handcuff them, leaving them there until we were ready to move them. What we all learned was that in that position it can be very difficult to breathe, especially for people who are seriously overweight. It's an issue that has hit the headlines in the United States in the most appalling way recently, with the death of George Floyd. These days, officers here are required to get those arrested standing as quickly as possible.

For anyone who works in the emergency services, there is

this huge feeling of failure when an individual dies on your watch, and it's something that never goes away. Increasingly, I was finding I needed to have strategies in place to help me come to terms with the everyday drama and trauma of life as a police officer, especially working in inner city or deprived communities. It's very hard not to start becoming cynical about the human condition, and to remember that, however many terrible things you might see in any given week, every single one is an appalling experience for the victims or those directly affected.

Equally, it can be difficult to find a balance between the natural human empathy that most of us feel when we come across distress and tragedy, and maintaining the protective shell that is necessary if we're to remain professional and objective. My own way of dealing with the dilemma has been deliberately to create silos in my mind, always trying my best to place the most traumatic incidents in one compartment, while keeping my personal and domestic life in another.

What that sometimes means is that people can be surprised that I'm able, when necessary, to speak about the most grim and ghastly events without displaying visible emotion. But that's because, when giving evidence in court, the judge and jury want to know the facts – they're not interested in how I felt about what happened. So, over many years, I have naturally become used to telling the facts as I witnessed them without adding my own take or enhancements. Does that mean I hardened myself to the underlying suffering of those involved? Not at all. It's just my own particular survival mechanism. Because

you can't go home every night and take the job with you; if
you do, you'll go crazy in no time at all.

CHAPTER NINE

'Never apply again'

One of the wide range of issues raised in the Bristol Seminars by black and Asian officers was that, while we might be tolerated, or sometimes even encouraged in the most junior roles in the service, the moment we begin to show ambition to rise through the ranks, attitudes towards us change.

When Michael Fuller decided to take that first step of promotion to sergeant, his immediate superior told him: 'I sincerely hope you're not going studying.' He later recounted the full story in his memoir *Kill the Black One First*: 'It was quite a while before I found out that this was no joke and that when I wasn't present he was openly talking to colleagues . . . about stopping me from taking any police exams which would further my career. In fact he was determined that I should not rise any further in the Met at all, because he was one of those men who thought that black people should always stay at the bottom of the pile.'

This was also to become a pattern for both myself and Shab, who recalls, 'I was a probationary WPC in uniform, but there was an "honour-based" rape case involving a young Bengali girl in Southend. I was asked by the local CID to assist, which I did, and they thought I'd done well. So then the local detective inspector told me they wanted me to join them permanently. Everything seemed to be going really well for me, but when I went back and told my inspector I wanted to join CID and to take the sergeant's exams, he went ballistic. Shortly after that he gave me a terrible PDR [Personal Development Report] and put on my record that I shouldn't be confirmed as a constable.'

Despite this discouragement, Shab went ahead and took the sergeant's exams and passed, scoring within the top 1 per cent of applicants in the Met. However, as soon as she applied for a posting as a sergeant, she was called in by her detective inspector, who told her, 'You don't want to be a DS.' When Shab said she was confused, he repeated, 'You don't want to be a detective sergeant.' Three days later, she was told that some performance issues had been raised against her, specifically that she had left property on her desk and failed to take a victim statement. After that, Shab felt her career was blighted. She didn't understand why her hitherto promising progress was suddenly floundering, but she submitted her application anyway. Later, she learned that her human resources manager had recorded that she was 'Only good for popular diversity in the borough'.

Meanwhile, I was having a remarkably similar experience in Hackney. In regular reports throughout my two-year probationary period, I was described as: 'A sensible, mature young woman who has a balanced outlook . . . she is polite and respectful to her supervisors and is popular with her fellow officers. She adopts a firm but polite line with members of the public and has no problem with the enforcement role.' All my grades on a wide range of criteria were As, B+s or Bs. I was praised for my ability to remain calm under stress and for my confident approach towards giving evidence. Indeed, the only negatives were that I had 'a problem keeping [my] hair tidy' and I tended not to enjoy being criticized. I had also passed my final exams with a mark of 81.2 per cent against a class average of 78.6 per cent.

Even before my probationary period had been successfully completed, I informed my senior officers that I wanted to take the sergeant's exams. I'd also heard that the Met was worried about the serious shortage of people from ethnic minority backgrounds among more senior ranks, and had consequently introduced the High Potential Development Scheme (HPDS), which was an accelerated promotion programme for young officers who showed promise. Naturally I applied, and from that moment, attitudes towards me changed.

I was called into a meeting with my chief inspector who said that he had no intention of putting me through to the scheme, and that I should 'never apply again'. Later, his report noted that my application for accelerated promotion would not be supported, 'and this arises from her poor interpersonal skills, as fully documented in her personal file'. He noted that he'd acquainted me with his view of my shortcomings, and that 'she is now under no illusion that she has much to do before she would be in a position to be a serious contender for the accelerated promotion scheme'. It was only ten years later that I saw my personal file, in which the same chief inspector had written 'this officer thinks she has the skills . . . [but] she hasn't got the credentials'. To this day, I have no real idea what this could possibly mean.

Despite all this discouragement, I decided to take the sergeant's exams and so I set about spending evenings and weekends studying for them. They involve a series of written tests. 'On the front of the exam paper were some notes in bold, and one of them was baffling,' recalled Michael Fuller, who had taken the same exams some years earlier. 'It said that anyone putting Masonic signs on their exam paper would be immediately disqualified,' he writes in *Kill the Black One First*. The significance of the instruction would only become apparent to Fuller, and to me, in years to follow.

After sitting the exam papers, candidates were confronted with five separate rooms, each presenting a different scenario. We were required to take charge of the scene and handle each situation with authority and confidence. Like my friend Shab, I also passed the exams with flying colours.

Promotion to sergeant is, of course, a big moment in the life of any career police officer, but for Shab and myself – each of us from minorities within minorities – the moment felt especially sweet. Both of us had grown up in a culture where little was expected of women other than unquestioning obedience, and both of us had needed to fight hard for every advance we'd made since early childhood. Steering a path through an organization as male dominated and white dominated as the Metropolitan Police involved us in new challenges every day. When to speak up and when to remain silent. When to stand firm and when to give way. Facing up to the need to do everything that bit better than the white man, around whom the whole structure had been designed to revolve. Now, though, both of us were sergeants, and suddenly we were in a position to give orders rather than always simply to receive them. For Shab and for me, managing down as well as managing up would create opportunities and problems in equal measure. First of all, there was nothing quite like a promotion to put a spring in our step. My first posting as a sergeant was to Waltham Forest.

This was a great time for me. I was one of three sergeants looking after twenty to thirty PCs. There were two other black constables in the station, which led to my first ever experience of going on patrol with another BAME police officer. It was terrific; such a novelty for people to see not one but two non-white police patrolling together. We experienced lots of goodwill from most people in the community.

Once again, however, the goodwill was less in evidence among some of our more Neanderthal colleagues. On one occasion, my friend Shab, another officer Gurdip Singh and I were talking together in one corner of a pub when a white officer approached and asked us 'Is this Paki corner?' Shab remembers being referred to as 'Bounty' by a female officer who constantly made racist comments about the Bengali community. 'Bounty', referring to the chocolate bar with a coconut filling, is a term of abuse well known to every black police officer in the country. Prejudice also came from a different angle when I accompanied a PC around a local estate and was told: 'All the people here are worthless, unmarried mothers, going round wearing leggings all day.' I had to point out that I was also a single parent, but that I didn't wear leggings and wasn't worthless. 'I didn't mean that,' said the PC. 'What did you mean?' I asked. He had no answer.

Later, the same young officer distinguished himself by sounding the alarm when what appeared to be an aborted foetus was found in the street. Traffic was halted and the area was cordoned off with red and white tape. Only at this point did someone examine the evidence more closely, to find that it was a gooey plastic toy in the shape of a baby dinosaur.

While a few streets around Wanstead are reasonably prosperous, Leyton more generally had lots of poverty and people living in divided houses and bedsits. As with many areas in big cities, the main problems came from gangs, which in this case were named after postcodes: E5, E9, E10 etc. Teenagers living in one district could find themselves being attacked simply for straying across a road into another postcode. Some complained of having to take huge detours to avoid a few streets where they felt in constant danger. Many of the gangs were made up of youths from the West Indian community, and most of the crime was drug related. Dealers in crack and cannabis were ubiquitous, but the Bengali and Somali community in particular used to chew 'khat', which was not illegal but sent them off their heads. Also known as 'African salad' or 'bushman's tea', fresh khat leaves are glossy and crimson-brown, resembling withered basil. Users claim the drug sharpens thinking, increases energy and cheers you up. Our experience, however, was that it also causes hyperactivity, manic behaviour, paranoia and hallucinations. The plant could be purchased at market stalls for around £3 a bunch. Tell-tale signs included red lips and red saliva, which would be spat onto pavements. (Hence the 'No spitting' signs put up by some councils.)

There was an established site for travellers in Clays Lane, Stratford, which my team regarded more or less as a no-go area. We would never get a call or a complaint because if someone down there had a grievance they would sort it out themselves. The travellers had constructed their own makeshift 'sleeping policemen' on the roads so they would have a warning of anyone approaching. The truth is that we were all a bit afraid of going down there, so we kept away if we could.

Now, aged 35 and with new responsibilities as one of the duty sergeants, I was still being called out to all manner of scenes of violent crime and human tragedy. One of them occurred in June 1998 and involved a call-out to a reported fire in a large 1930s terraced house in Dawlish Road, Leyton.

We arrived before the fire brigade and found the house burning fiercely. We'd been told there might be people inside, but could see flames and smoke behind the windows and it was impossible to get near. We started closing the road and keeping people back, and then the fire brigade arrived. We watched as fire fighters tried to smash the windows, but they were double-glazed and it was impossible to gain access. Then they tried to douse the flames, but by then the place was an inferno.

After several hours, the fire was brought under control and I was among those obliged to enter the house. It turned out that numerous backpackers had been living there. Four of them were dead and it was clear they'd been trying to get out but had been overcome. The interior staircase had been consumed in flames and it was difficult to get access to the entire house. One inside door was blocked because the charred body of a young woman was jammed up against it on the other side. I was terrified. I could see through the glass a body that had been burnt away and the teeth were bared in a sort of animalistic snarling expression. I can still see her now, slumped behind the door. The skin around her face had gone and I imagined the person dying in pain and absolute agony. You never forget that. Still reeling from the shock of what I'd witnessed, one of the fire fighters told me that it was my job to remove the bodies. I knew it wasn't, but the attempt at black humour failed me.

Everything in the house was burned to a cinder, and none of the neighbours could help with identifying the dead. We only knew that they were backpackers and someone thought they'd come from Australia. We had to contact the Australian embassy, then Interpol, eventually tracking down the families on the other side of the world and arranging for them to be informed by local police.

The cause of the fire turned out to be a candle which had been left alight when the occupants went to sleep. From that day to this, I never allow candles anywhere in my own house except in bathrooms. We keep a fire extinguisher in the hall and kitchen of our home, and always ensure there's an escape route through windows. People lock themselves in their houses at night, but for me the idea of being in a fire and not being able to get out is an unthinkable nightmare.

It was about this time that I received a call from my mother to tell me the lease had run out on their house in Handsworth and it would cost £20,000 to renew it, so they were obliged to move. My parents were still taking care of my son, but he was due to attend secondary school. I'd recently moved to a new house in Elm Park, Romford, but hadn't yet sold the house in Chadwell Heath. So I decided that my parents should come to live in my former home, which would mean that my son could attend the Academy just across the road. The arrangement also meant that he could stay within the stable family environment he'd grown up in, but I would see him so much more regularly. It was a significant step in being able to bring my family back together, after so many difficult years apart.

CHAPTER TEN

'Shi-ites and shitties'

My friend Shabnam Chaudhri and I kept in regular touch and did our best to cope with the slings and arrows of outrageous fortune. There had been many times when our mutual pledge not to 'let the bastards grind you down' had been reinforced by one of us on the other, seeking to impart the grit and determination necessary to turn the other cheek in the face of regular humiliation or provocation. Just one example Shab recalls: 'When I was in my first few weeks at Tower Hamlets, officers tried to make me go down to pick up all the condoms from the ground, saying I needed to find evidence for a sexual offence. I knew it was a piss-take and didn't go, because that sort of thing was pretty common with probationers.'

Shab took and passed the exams to become a detective, and was later assigned to Leyton as a detective constable, where she recalls, 'One day we had just returned from a raid where a handgun had been recovered. We were in the office about to debrief the job, when a fellow officer came in behind me, grabbed me around the throat and pointed the gun to my head, shouting "Get back or the Paki gets it".' There was general laughter and, although Shab didn't see the humour, she felt obliged to go along with the crowd. 'Not everyone laughed,' she recalls, 'a couple of colleagues came to me after and apologized. They said it was shocking and that I shouldn't have to take it, but you just can't make an issue about things like that.'

On another occasion, Shab was on night duty at Leyton police station and walked with a PC to the custody suite. 'I asked if there were any prisoners and he looked through the window, looked back at me and said, "No, only a sambo." I was totally shocked.'

Racial discrimination was an everyday experience for many BAME officers, and if at any particular moment we were not a victim ourselves, there was usually something going on close by to remind us of its presence. Every black or Asian officer serving in the Met during the late 1990s was aware of the situation facing Gurpal Virdi, who, having complained about racial discrimination in his job as a detective sergeant in West London, found himself accused of sending racist hate mail to himself and to other ethnic minority officers. He was arrested, suspended from duty and had his home searched. At a police disciplinary panel two years later, the Sikh officer was dismissed in disgrace, his claims of racism having been passed off as false allegations from a disgruntled opportunist. Virdi had to wait a further two years before an employment tribunal found that he couldn't have written and sent the letters, and that the force had racially discriminated against him. He eventually received £240,000 in compensation and returned to work.

But even in the face of humiliating defeat, the Met hadn't quite finished its persecution of an officer who'd had the temerity to complain. Another employment tribunal in 2007 found that the Met had victimized Virdi yet again by refusing him promotion because he'd previously won a race discrimination case against the force. Later, in 2015, Virdi told the *Guardian*: 'If you challenge the organisation you are a marked man.'

In Cleveland, 250 miles away in the north of England, 45-year-old Constable Nadeen Saddique had made no complaint, but still found himself on the wrong end of discrimination. Saddique was the only Asian officer among the highly trained firearms squad whose duties had involved guarding members of the royal family and Tony Blair. An eventual employment tribunal into his case heard that senior officers had wanted him thrown out of the unit from the outset, and that an inspector had been overheard telling another officer that 'I'll get that black cunt out of firearms, watch.' The officer had apparently agreed and was said to have replied: 'Who does he think he is? He's just a Paki.'

'I never wanted it to go as far as a tribunal,' Saddique told reporters, 'but after experiencing problems with discrimination for a number of years within the force and exhausting all avenues internally without success, I had to do something.' Saddique was happy to settle with his employer on the understanding that he would regain his previous status and resume his career, but that was to misunderstand the price that needed to be paid if any BAME officer made the mistake of failing to toe the line. He was later awarded £475,000 after another tribunal found that his career had been stalled and blighted as a direct result of having made the earlier complaint.

My friend Shab was also to learn this same important lesson the hard way. She'd been able to offer me support following the incident with the Area Driver during my probation, and again during my attachment to CID at Newham, and on various other occasions. Now, something happened which was to test her own patience and endurance and would put a blight on her career for many years to follow.

Shab's ordeal had begun years earlier when she attended the Community Race Relations training day, which had been introduced following the Macpherson report finding that the Met was institutionally racist. Among the others on the course were: Detective Constable Tom Hassell, who was 60; Detective Sergeant Colin Lockwood, 55; and 39-year-old Detective Inspector Paul Whatmore. Shab was the only non-white officer present when, according to her account, Hassell referred to Muslim headwear as 'tea cosies'. Then he went on to mispronounce 'Shi'ites' as 'shitties'. Warming to his theme, he added that he felt sorry for people who had to fast during Ramadan.

'When I corrected his pronunciation of Shi'ites he replied "Shi'ites, shitties, they're all the same".' Shab was astonished, not least because the entire purpose of the day was supposed to be about combating racism. She was also frustrated that Lockwood and Whatmore had failed to intervene, and felt she was owed an apology. But when she tried to raise her concerns with the borough commander, Shab's life changed beyond recognition.

'Everything and everybody around me instantly became obstructive and negative,' she recalls. 'My own team told me they couldn't speak to me because every time they did, the DI [detective inspector] would walk in and make them feel really uncomfortable. People I'd usually chat to started averting their eyes when I went by. A file containing intelligence material went missing from my desk, and I was told in confidence by another officer that a senior detective had taken it. At the same time, two DCs [detective constables] in the same office had been arrested for serious corruption and were treated better than I was.' Both of the other detectives were later convicted and sent to prison.

It took two years for the case to come to a disciplinary hearing, which found against all three men but recommended that no further action should be taken. After another appeal a year later, the finding was overturned and the men were cleared. Undeterred, Shab continued to pursue her case for racial discrimination. 'I was then approached by Leroy Logan [Chair of the Black Police Association], who said that the new head of diversity, Commander Steve Allen, wanted to resolve the top 20 high-profile race cases in the Met.' Shab agreed to meet Allen, and was subsequently awarded a five-figure sum in compensation, which she believes caused even more resentment in some quarters.

Although disappointing for Shab, this would have been the end of the matter had the issue not come to the attention of the, by then, Met commissioner Sir Ian Blair, who apparently saw an opportunity to demonstrate how seriously he was taking issues of racism. Blair declared that he found the decision to overturn the initial finding to be extraordinary and demanded it should be challenged. It took another three years for the tribunal to hear the entire story, at which Blair's intervention was seen as an attempt to 'hang [these officers] out to dry' in order to make a political point, and they were finally cleared. Having the matter looming over her neck for six years took a harsh toll on Shab's morale and prospects, and she felt herself to be in the wilderness for a very long time before her career would eventually be given a renewed boost.

The attempt by the Met to settle the most high-profile complaints followed in the wake of yet another example of the force's revenge against a black officer who didn't seem to know his place. Leroy Logan had been elected as the first chair of the Black Police Association, and quickly found himself confronting his bosses on behalf of a fellow black officer who'd been accused of dishonesty. Rather than engaging with him as an advocate on behalf of one of the Association's members, the Met began a thorough and forensic investigation into Leroy's own finances. Sure enough, Leroy soon found himself accused of having claimed £80 in expenses for a hotel bill which had already been paid directly. It was the clearest possible case of a simple administrative oversight, and Leroy was able to demonstrate that, far from embezzling money to which he was not entitled, he'd actually failed to claim some £600 in expenses which he was owed. Nonetheless, he had to endure an exhaustive investigation, including an interview under caution, before he was eventually found to have no case to answer. When he made a complaint to the employment tribunal, wiser counsels in the Met must have realized that it would be sensible to settle his complaint out of court, but Leroy would only agree to do so if all other outstanding grievances were treated in the same way. The result was that a number of disputes which would otherwise have gone to employment tribunals were dealt with far more quickly and efficiently.

Meanwhile, my relationship with Steve Reed had been going on for the best part of ten years, and on 12 January 2000, in the King George Hospital, Chadwell Heath, I gave birth to my second child, another boy, this time named Emil. I took three months of maternity leave and an extra month of accumulated time off, so that Emil was four months old when I needed to return to work. Luckily, my brother Satnam and his wife Lorna had a 6-month-old, so she was able to provide day-care for both children. I bought a twin pushchair and when the two boys, Emil and Talvin, were sitting alongside each other they looked like siblings, except that one had paler skin than the other. For the next eighteen months, Lorna had to endure a regular round of ignorant and offensive comments until Emil was eligible to go to nursery.

Notwithstanding the constant but generally low-level racism experienced by almost everyone with my background, this was a good time for us. My oldest son was still living with my parents but seemed happy and well adjusted, and my new family seemed settled and content. Steve and I both had busy work patterns, but we found time for a decent social life. Did I dare to allow myself to believe that things would go on more or less smoothly? If so, I was very much mistaken.

CHAPTER ELEVEN

A Death a Day

The next opportunity for promotion would be the highly significant leap from sergeant to inspector, and I was determined to take the first chance to move on and up. Always, however, there was the constant need to swim against the tide of a culture which was clearly and consistently stacked in favour of white males of a particular mindset. While belonging to the same golf-club or masonic lodge, or drinking in the right pub, undoubtedly oiled the wheels of progression for a certain kind of officer, none of these options were available to me, or for Shab Chaudhri, or for others who did not fit. My strategy, therefore, was to keep my head down, do the job to the best of my ability, and choose which battles to fight and which to leave for another day.

Once again, the prospect of more exams involved many hours of serious study in various aspects of the law. These tests required further attendance at an assessment centre where I was again confronted by a series of difficult scenarios designed to determine my knowledge and judgement, and then finally there was another challenging interview.

I passed every stage with flying colours, but there was another hurdle to negotiate before my promotion could formally proceed. Newly appointed inspectors have to be assigned to a particular section, where there is an appropriate vacancy. However, residual hostility in some sections against black or Asian officers meant that this was unlikely to be an easy matter. My problem was eventually solved by the intervention of a chief inspector called Steve Graysmark – who would later go on to marry my great friend Shabnam. Steve arranged for me to join him as an inspector at Newham – an act for which he later received considerable criticism and abuse from some colleagues, including senior officers.

Hard won as it was, this further promotion to inspector represented yet another highly significant milestone in my career progression and I was of course pleased and proud of the achievement. I settled into my new role with a determination to avoid being wrong-footed by the everyday prejudice I encountered.

My new rank and authority was quickly put to the test one evening when a police patrol chased a man in a stolen car which had crashed near a bridge between Barking and the Romford Road. The young driver escaped from the vehicle, jumped up on the bridge parapet, waved at police, and then leapt into the River Thames below. Local officers called me and also the fire brigade, whose expertise might assist in rescuing the young driver from the water.

The young man was swimming between boats and hiding underneath them, and we thought it most likely that he was carrying a stash of drugs and didn't want to be arrested. But if I was irritated by the antics of someone who was likely to turn out to be a petty villain, I was even more irritated by the senior officer from the fire brigade, who ignored me completely and reported on the latest situation to my sergeant. I had to tell him twice that I was the senior officer at the scene, but still the fireman seemed unable to comprehend that an Asian woman could be in charge.

I considered whether to ask my own officers to go into the water to arrest the young man, but since I couldn't know if he was likely to put up a fight or struggle, I felt strongly that it would be wrong to put them at risk by doing so. Eventually, my officers and the fire fighters managed to grab the car thief and drag him out of the water, but he later died in hospital from hypothermia. A plastic wad containing drugs was found in his mouth, which seemed to confirm our suspicion about the reason he was anxious not to be caught. At the coroner's inquest sometime later, the family accused us of allowing their son to die because he was 'known' to us. Of course, I regretted the tragedy, and I still feel sympathy for the family of the dead man to this day, but I remain convinced that my first duty had been to safeguard the lives of my own team.

After nearly twelve years together, and with our son now aged 2, Steve Reed and I were married at Redbridge Registry Office with just a few family members at lunch, and then a party for 200 that evening at the Met's Chigwell Sports Club.

Most of our guests were police officers. It was a lovely day, which felt so different in every way from the first time I'd been married more than twenty years earlier. This time I'd chosen my own husband and, like every willing bride, I hoped and expected it to be a long and happy marriage.

Meanwhile, the area of Newham that I was policing was among the most deprived in the country, scoring in the bottom quarter in the most significant indices of employment, poverty, crime, domestic incidents and infant mortality. So many of the everyday crimes were in some way related to hardship and deprivation, and perhaps most depressing of all was the high number of unexplained or sudden deaths in the borough. The situation became of such concern that a new regulation was introduced that would have serious consequences for my working life. Whereas before, any sudden or unexplained death would be attended by whomever was the officer on duty of relevant rank, this new rule required that all such deaths should be attended by a police inspector. This meant that I was being called out to attend every single unexplained death, and that was at least once a day. Quite often it was more frequent than that.

Most of these call-outs involved older people who had died in accidents or from sudden illness, but many were murders, manslaughter or suicide. There were also frequent cases involving younger people who had died in any manner of dreadful circumstances. One that sticks in my memory was when I was required to attend a house where a teenager had hanged himself. The boy was not that far removed in age from my own eldest son, and I found it difficult to get past the thought of the agony parents and other family experience after a suicide.

The infant mortality rate in Newham was among the highest in London, and very often it was far from clear whether the death of a baby had been accidental or otherwise. I attended scenes of infant deaths that seemed to be simple tragedies, but also others where they had been thrown off tables, or cut, or sometimes raped. On one occasion, doctors at the local hospital removed the nappy from a dead baby, to find that it had been chopped with a knife across the buttocks and a chunk of muscle removed. The effort involved in continuing to behave professionally when faced with those responsible took its own toll.

It seemed that every day brought a new and sometimes bizarre tragedy for families who were often entirely innocent of any blame. Police at Newham believed they might be dealing with a serious crime when we were alerted early one Sunday morning to the discovery of a foetus buried in a shallow grave in Woodgrange Park Cemetery next to Manor Park. A patch of disturbed ground was enough to indicate something amiss, and the removal of a few shovelfuls of soil revealed a white plastic bucket with an NHS label on the side. Inside was a tiny but fully formed foetus. As the duty inspector, I was in charge of the scene and immediately I ordered that the area should be secured. However, just as my operation was getting under way, a Muslim family appeared alongside to attend the burial of their 1-year-old child. Since some adherents of the Islamic faith forbid the presence of women at the funeral service, I ordered all the female officers at the scene to remove themselves, and then I also moved a discreet distance from the ceremony. I was among those who were surprised to learn that some Muslims bury their dead without coffins, and we watched from afar as the baby was interred with her tiny body aligned towards Mecca.

Once back in charge of the scene, we discovered that another label on the white bucket indicated a patient's name and NHS number. Officers were dispatched to the address, where the woman and her husband immediately broke down and told their story. The mother had miscarried her baby at Newham Hospital, and staff had given the foetus to the parents for them to arrange a burial. Unable to afford the cost of a funeral, and not knowing what else to do, the husband had come to the cemetery by night, dug a hole, deposited the foetus and bucket, and covered it with soil. I found their story heartbreaking. Can you imagine being in such a situation? Nevertheless, we had no choice but to return the child's remains to the parents so that an official burial could be arranged.

On another occasion, I was among the officers called to the crematorium when workers sifting through the charred but not completely consumed remains from a recent funeral discovered that there were two skulls instead of one. The area was sealed off as a crime scene and the forensic team was called. Later, it transpired that there is an African culture which favours burying a coconut to sustain a dead body through its journey to the afterlife, and the shell of the coconut had survived the flames. It was a rare lighter moment in an otherwise unremittingly grim time.

Day in day out, night in night out, the other inspectors and myself would be witnessing tragedy in every shift. Afterwards I would return home, often in the small hours of the morning and go to see my own tiny son Emil, asleep in his cot. On those nights I would pick him up and cuddle him, and think about how it could so easily be him that was hurt. It was as close as I have come to serious depression in all my years of service, and I knew that I would soon be in need of a change of duties.

CHAPTER TWELVE

'Police officer or single parent'

Notwithstanding the appalling crimes and situations I faced in my daily duties as an inspector, my life was settling into a pattern where I felt content in my marriage, I had satisfactory childcare arrangements, and I was doing a rewarding job alongside people I enjoyed working with. One of them was a young officer (we'll call him Robert), whose last job had been in the Directorate of Professional Standards, and who was therefore receiving no cooperation from fellow officers. I felt sorry for him and gave him whatever help I could.

One day, Robert and I were among a group of officers who'd been at Chigwell for a training course, and afterwards everyone went to the pub for a drink and a chat before going home. The conversation turned to gossip, and in particular we spoke about various people within the force who were having affairs with colleagues. I tend to be a bit naïve in such matters, and I said something like, 'I just don't understand how people can do that, to betray their partners in that way.' Eventually everyone else left, leaving only Robert and I in the pub, and I could tell that he had something on his mind.

'I feel very bad to be the one to say this to you,' he said eventually, 'but you've been a good friend to me, and so I need to tell you something that everyone knows about, except you.'

Robert went on to tell me that my husband Steve was having an affair. The woman involved was someone I'd already met – her name was Shen Mertkol. She was Turkish, and was my husband's civilian admin assistant at Edmonton. Robert thought that the affair had been going on for some time.

I felt as though I'd been kicked in the stomach. I'd been married for only a relatively short time and we had a young son. It seemed possible from what Robert told me that my husband's affair had even pre-dated our marriage. My instinct was to confront Steve straight away, but I managed to remain sufficiently calm to give myself time to think carefully about what I wanted to do.

I went home and managed to conceal the turmoil going on inside my head for a few days until the following weekend, when Steve told me he was due to be working the early shift. I said goodbye to him on Saturday morning, but a little later I telephoned the station and asked to speak to my husband. The operator checked and replied that Steve wasn't due to be working that weekend. I then asked if I could speak to Shen Mertkol and was told that the civilian assistant didn't work on Saturdays. At this point I took two suitcases and filled them with my husband's clothes and belongings. I then called him on his mobile and asked where he was.

'At work,' he replied.

'You aren't because I just telephoned them,' I said.

There was a pause and then Steve said, 'They must have made a mistake.'

I'd heard enough and told my husband that his belongings were in two suitcases on the front lawn of our house. 'I suggest you might want to collect them within an hour,' I said, 'because I think there's a danger they might catch fire.' With that I ended the call, closed the curtains, turned out the lights and put the bolts across all the doors. After an hour, there was a loud banging outside, but I ignored it and eventually the noise stopped. I felt wounded and betrayed, and was clear in my own mind that our marriage was over.

Now, though, I was in a terrible dilemma as I needed to work out how I'd be able to continue with my chosen career at the same time as being a single mother. The hours were long and demanding, childcare was expensive, and I knew I would struggle financially. I wanted nothing further to do with my husband but realized that if I was going to manage on my own, I'd need to rely on him continuing to provide some financial support for our young son.

Meanwhile, I had some very immediate issues to deal with. Suddenly, I was all alone with no arrangements in place for my son's care for the coming weeks. I had no choice but to call my chief superintendent to explain the situation and ask for a week off to sort out some childcare. He instantly refused my request and told me, 'You can either be a police officer or a single parent.' Now desperate, I called on my younger brother

Satnam and his wife to move into my house for a week to take care of Emil, while I worked out a longer-term solution.

Steve went into rented accommodation, and after several weeks he began to ask if I could forgive him. Among the excuses he used to justify his behaviour was that he'd become fed up with having to defend me as an Asian woman in the force. That really hurt. The idea that he was somehow having to apologize to colleagues for me not being white-skinned. Steve begged me to let him return to the house so we could start again. At first I refused, but there was no escaping the fact that I would need his financial support to bring up our son. Eventually, I told him I was prepared to give our marriage another chance, on the condition that he gave up seeing the other woman and transferred to another police station.

Steve agreed to my conditions and moved back home, and I felt determined to make a go of our marriage. I hoped we'd be able to make a fresh start but when, after a few weeks, I learned that my husband had started seeing his mistress again, I felt hurt and doubly betrayed. As far as I was concerned, it was all over, but there remained a whole chapter of pain and trouble ahead, before the marriage was finally at an end.

CHAPTER THIRTEEN

The Diversity Directorate

S teve stayed in his rented accommodation and I became subject to a campaign of hatred. One morning, I came out of my house to find that all the tyres on my car had been slashed. There was no evidence beyond my own suspicions that Steve had been involved, and nor could I prove that he was responsible for a number of late-night anonymous phone calls. A series of abusive emails, on the other hand, were undoubtedly from him. My friends encouraged me to complain about his behaviour to his senior officer, but I knew that to do so might mean he'd lose his job, and therefore be unable to pay maintenance for Emil. Since my main priority now was to look after the best interests of my son, I felt I had no choice but to find a way to cope with it all.

I managed to employ an au pair to come to live in with Emil and I, but I still found it difficult to maintain the routine shift pattern of earlies, lates and nights. And, of course, life as an operational police officer was continuing to throw up its share of unexpected and often traumatic incidents.

One afternoon in August 2003, I'd just held the parade meeting as the duty inspector in Forest Gate when a call came in to say that a row had broken out over a parked car, and there had been a shooting. Two men had been executed in the street.

I know it sounds odd, but for an instant I didn't take it seriously. You're always getting hoaxes or garbled messages or people misunderstanding what they've seen. Nonetheless, I was only a few streets away and so I instantly set off with my driver to the reported address at the Forest View Hotel on the Romford Road.

When I arrived, I could see a small crowd, and among them a man was kneeling on the pavement. People parted as I approached, and I wondered whether he'd been hurt and was crouching down. Only when I got up close could I see that he'd been shot in the head. It was instantly clear that he was dead, and had just slumped down and ended up in a kneeling position, but it was so bizarre to see him like that. For a moment it seemed unreal.

My attention was then drawn to another small group standing nearby. I walked across to discover another man lying in a spreading pool of blood. He had also been shot.

As a police officer, you get all too used to scenes of violence, but even today it's unusual to see people killed by gunfire on the streets. It's a shock.

My immediate action was to report what I'd seen and summon further help. Then, to cordon off the area as far as

I could, to prevent the scene from being viewed by passers-by. I felt traumatized myself and was acutely aware that there were children in the vicinity. Reinforcements arrived within minutes and as soon as the crime scene was completely under control, we set about finding witnesses and taking statements.

It had all started, we were told, with a dispute over a parked car. The 52-year-old Amarjit Singh Tiwana and his 25-year-old nephew, Rajinder Singh Tiwana, had parked their van outside the hotel, which belonged to their family. At around 2 p.m., the drivers of two cars in the road found they were blocked in and began sounding their horns. Amarjit came out and moved the van, and the first motorist drove off without incident. But, unfortunately for Amarjit and Rajinder, the driver of the other car was a convicted robber and drug dealer called Ayub Khan. Witnesses reported that Khan had become increasingly angry and started shouting at Amarjit and Rajinder, pointing to his car as if it had been damaged. One witness saw Khan push Rajinder in the chest as if he wanted to start a fight. When Amarjit tried to explain, Khan replied, 'I don't give a fuck,' and repeatedly shouted, 'Shut up.'

Ayub Khan was still angry as he drove away, and about ten minutes later he came back with two other Asian men and started to damage the van which had blocked the road. Then one of the men pulled a gun out of a bag – later identified as a MAC-10 pistol capable of firing 1,000 rounds a minute. He opened fire, killing both Amarjit and Rajinder. Amarjit's 26-year-old daughter, Harjinder Tiwana, was standing nearby and watched in horror as her father and cousin were executed

in cold blood beside her. But her horror must have turned to
terror as the gunman aimed the weapon at her. She said later
that she thought she was about to die, but that perhaps the
gun had jammed. The three men fled.

TV and newspaper reporters were quickly on the scene,
and we were left with the task of trying to calm the family and
witnesses, and to preserve the forensics. Khan left the country
after the attack but was extradited from Bangladesh in 2010
and eventually found guilty of double murder at Woolwich
Crown Court. He was jailed for a minimum of twenty-six years.

Incidents of this kind were, of course, unusual, but they took
their toll as I was juggling the difficulties of an anti-social shift
pattern and my commitment to my son. I managed it for two
years until, finally, I could do it no longer and I began to look
around for a new role in which I could maintain something
resembling family life, while still making a contribution to an
area I felt passionate about. My thoughts turned to the issue
that, in some way, visited every day of my professional life.

The perennial problem of institutional racism, which had
been described in the Macpherson report, was confirmed yet
again in February 2003, when Her Majesty's Inspectorate of
Constabulary (HMIC) issued its fifth major report on the same
theme over the previous ten years. The report was entitled
Diversity Matters, and once again commented on the lamentable
gap between intentions and outcomes in trying to address
deeply ingrained problems:

> Training alone can never achieve necessary organisational
> change . . . Too often, evidence was found of systematic
> failure amongst line managers to address inappropriate
> behaviour or attitudes on the part of their staff. In some
> instances, the manager was the source of the problem.

The problem described in the report – and the urgent need for
radical change – could scarcely have been more vividly illustrated
than by an episode of the BBC *Panorama* series broadcast a few
months later in July 2003. Entitled 'The Secret Policeman',
the programme reported that an undercover journalist named
Mark Daly had applied to join Greater Manchester Police, but
had secretly been filming throughout his training. It revealed
what may be the most stunning catalogue of racism ever seen
on British TV.

The episode opened with some headline vox pops spoken
by fellow young officers, and secretly recorded by Daly. They
included, 'A dog that's born in a barn is still a dog; a Paki that's
born in Britain is still a fucking Paki.' And, on the subject of
stopping drivers, 'I'd stop him cos he's a Paki. Sad, innit? But
I would. He's a Paki and I'm stopping him, cos I'm fucking
English.' Later in the episode, one young policeman boasts
how he imposed an on-the-spot fine of £260 on a driver
without insurance 'because he was a fucking Paki', and then
forced him, his wife and three children to walk half a mile
back to their holiday camp. At the same time, he stopped a
white woman who was similarly driving without insurance,
but let her off with a warning.

The programme went on to describe how there was only one Asian cadet in the group, and how he had been called 'fat' and 'smelly' and 'the fucking curse of the class'. The recruits resented what they saw as the preferential treatment afforded to him because he was from a minority.

Perhaps most nauseating of all were the remarks of one young cadet on the subject of the recent murder of Stephen Lawrence: 'He fucking deserved it and his mum and dad are a fucking pair of spongers.' His comment on the people who killed Stephen? 'They fucking need fucking diplomatic immunity, mate . . . they've done for this country what others fucking should do.'

One officer had recently joined Greater Manchester Police from the Met and was in a good position to make a comparison. 'The Metropolitan Police is the worst for racism. That force, man. Jesus.' Now concerned that the scandal might be about to visit at its door, the Met immediately ordered an internal inquiry into the young officer's record from his time in London – who he'd worked with, and whether there'd been complaints about him in the past. Nothing of note was revealed.

The then Home Secretary, David Blunkett, made the elementary mistake of reacting publicly to a programme he hadn't actually watched, instantly dismissing it as 'a stunt' and accusing the BBC of 'trying to create news'. However, a short while later he managed to view the episode and quickly apologized, declaring that its revelations justified the way they'd come to light. Blunkett said the task now was 'to root out racism in the force', and that meant implementing new assessments and training of recruits to weed out those who should not be in the police service. Senior police chiefs from all around Britain described themselves as feeling 'physically sick' by what they'd seen and heard. Measures would be taken to educate recruits and junior officers in what many would regard as simple civilized behaviour.

I was among the many officers who were sickened and disgusted by the *Panorama* programme. Apart from the utterly vile views expressed in it, lots of us just felt embarrassed to be part of an organization where there was an undercurrent of such ugliness and ignorance. The programme renewed my determination to be an active part of the solution, and I successfully applied for a job in the Diversity Directorate based at New Scotland Yard. The role would involve some travelling, but at least it was mostly done in daylight hours so I could take good care of my youngest son.

The Directorate concerned itself with a wide agenda of policies designed to address the yawning chasm between the current state of the service, and the fair and integrated modern police force that many of us wanted it to become. Among the highest priorities was the matter of recruitment: finding ways to encourage members of ethnic or other minority groups to join the force, to redress the catastrophic imbalance between the racial and ethnic mix of the police and the community we seek to serve. The Directorate also seemed to me to be a genuine attempt by the Met to take account of the different ways that policing was perceived by members of minority communities. It concerned itself with the continuing controversy about the widely differing rates of stop and search for black and Asian people, on the one hand, and white people on the other. Also on its radar were concerns over domestic violence, especially towards Asian women – a subject that was particularly close to my heart.

And so began two years in which I was largely away from shift work and dealing directly with street crime. The job involved evaluating the impact that new laws and policies might have on ethnic and other minorities, inside and outside of the force itself. Some basics of daily life, which anyone might expect to take for granted, such as providing tampons for female prisoners, had been overlooked in official legislation or regulation; the Diversity Directorate made it part of its business to identify and resolve such anachronisms and anomalies. As well as attempting to address all the different kinds of discrimination experienced every day by ethnic minorities, inside and outside of the force, the Directorate was tasked with taking the sting out of some of the many employment tribunals involving members of the force. Officers from our Directorate would meet with complainants to try to understand their grievance, and to find informal resolutions which would remove the need to go through the whole business of a tribunal.

This was the first time I was based at New Scotland Yard in Victoria, and I recall feeling proud and impressed to be working in the building. The legendary headquarters of the Met is probably the most famous police building anywhere in the world, and this was well before the cutbacks which later made it feel shabby and neglected.

All the most important people in all the squads – the top detectives and the commanders – were based there, and it felt like quite an achievement just to be among it. My office was on the ninth floor, five floors above a canteen where you could rub shoulders with the top brass. To one side was an area known as 'Peelers', where senior officers would hold social gatherings and leaving dos. One floor up, there was a rather smarter dining area where half a dozen tables with white linen and decent cutlery were waited on by uniformed staff. This was where the most senior officers and their guests would dine, but more junior ranks could book a table in exceptional circumstances.

It was during my time in the Diversity Directorate that I first met Rod Jarman, who was a detective chief superintendent in charge of some 200 officers in the Racial and Violent Crime Task Force. His division had been set up directly in response to the murder of Stephen Lawrence and had at its disposal nearly 50 per cent of the entire resources devoted to murder in the capital city. Rod remembers taking a call from his senior officer, Cressida Dick, who told him about this female inspector 'who badly needed a break from a punishing shift pattern'. Could he find a role for her? He did, but it was not until eighteen months later that Rod and I would become romantically involved and eventually marry.

Notwithstanding the well-meaning efforts of officers like Rod, it's fair to say that the work of the Diversity Directorate, and other initiatives put in place to combat inherent racism, had only marginal and at best mixed success. Two years later in 2005,

'The Secret Policeman' programme and its aftermath were the subject of a further report published by the Commission for Racial Equality (CRE), which included warnings that police training on race issues had now become so heavily politicized that it risked making officers cynical and defensive rather than more tolerant and understanding.

The report had been written for the CRE by a former Director of Public Prosecutions, Sir David Calvert-Smith, QC. It said that training was now often focused on lists of politically correct and incorrect words, which officers should or should not use, and failed to instil a 'core ethic of respect' for all racial groups. Sir David cited Home Office research suggesting that community and race relations training 'had not made a major impact on forces'. It lacked clear organization and provoked cynicism on the part of some officers. There was even a danger, the report said, of a backlash from some white officers who felt the message coming out of the police hierarchy was inconsistent and incoherent.

The CRE report went on to recommend, yet again, that more effective training was needed, because the police service still attracted some recruits who were racist, and because some middle ranks in the police still did not take racism seriously. 'Unfortunately,' Sir David said on the BBC *Today* programme, 'you will never get rid of recruits who want to join the service in order to bully people and a number of those will want to bully black people.' The CRE report added that, on race, the police service 'is like a permafrost – thawing on the top, but still frozen solid at the core'.

Despite the very best and most determined efforts to effect radical change in the culture and outlook of the Met, it seemed that little was being achieved. The nasty underlying layer of xenophobia and misogyny remained intact and apparently unreachable.

CHAPTER FOURTEEN

Making History

Towards the end of 2005, my thoughts were turning again to the possibility of promotion, and my attention was drawn for the second time to the High Potential Development Scheme (HPDS). This was the programme I'd expressed interest in as a probationer, but at that time had been told 'never apply again'. However, since the scheme was not run by the Met itself, but was a nationwide initiative, I hoped I might not face the usual barriers. If that kind of discouragement was going to put me off, I'd have quit the force on scores of occasions over the previous ten years. So I applied again, and was invited for three days of testing and vetting to see if I would qualify.

It was scheduled over the weekend of Mother's Day and I suspected it would be a waste of time so I almost didn't go. There were ten candidates and each of us was closely monitored by one of the assessors for the entire duration of the course. There were psychometric tests, then an interview, followed by a series of meetings in which we each had to take the chair and orchestrate the discussion. There was an exercise in report writing and some aptitude tests, and at the end of Sunday I returned home exhausted and fairly sure my application would fail. In fact, I got a call just two days later – I'd been accepted. I was absolutely over the moon.

The HPDS is designed to identify officers who show sufficient promise that they might make it to the very top ranks of the police force. The idea was that our careers could be analysed to identify significant gaps in our service thus far, so that attachments could be arranged to round out our experience. Acceptance on the scheme was another highly significant milestone for me and seemed likely to be a turning point in my career. My success was reported in *The Big Issue*, which quoted me: 'It's been really good. The HPDS has changed my career, it's opened several doors for me.' I was keen not to miss an opportunity to raise a flag for diversity and added that I'd like to see the scheme targeted at under-represented groups. 'So perhaps we are losing a bit of potential there. This could help target individuals and improve the demographic profile in the senior ranks.' The appended photograph of me looking authoritative, alongside two old white judges dressed in red robes and long wigs, seemed like a sign of the changing times.

An immediate consequence of my acceptance onto the HPDS was that I was invited to attend a course run by the National Policing Improvement Agency at Bramshill, known then as Centrex. The college was based in a Jacobean mansion in Hampshire, set in 25 acres with a deer park. It provided training for senior police officers from every British force, as well as from other countries. The three-week course was attended by some thirty high-fliers from forces up and down the country and involved a range of management skills, including budgeting, personnel management and other capabilities necessary for senior officers of the future.

I was one of just a handful of women and the only non-white face among the group. I was well used to being in a minority of a minority, so that wasn't an unusual experience for me, but as I looked ahead one morning at the programme for the day to come, I was in for a surprise. In and among the guest lecturers on matters of law, finance, dealing with outside organizations, and so on, was a speaker from the Order of Freemasons. I was dumbfounded, and immediately approached the organizer of the course seeking an explanation.

'He's just here to talk about the organization,' I was told, 'its history, charity work, how subscriptions are paid, stuff like that.'

'But aside from anything else,' I said, 'the Freemasons are all about recruiting men. They don't want people like me.'

The course organizer was not fazed. 'Well, you might not want to hear about it,' he said, 'but others do.' He went on to indicate that there was nothing secret, and suggested I should sit quietly through the talk.

I was astonished. Not only did I know that the Freemasons didn't want any women in their organization, I also had a very strong feeling they didn't especially welcome people of my skin colour or religious background. I refused to stay there and 'sit quietly', so I walked out of the room, preferring to wait alone outside.

When I look back on that now, I think it was the first really big mistake I made in my career in the Met. The incident marked me out as a troublemaker who wasn't prepared to sit silently and smile while the old boy network of middle-aged white men continued to dominate the police force for ever. No matter how hard I worked, or how much I might achieve, it always felt like swimming against the tide. Whereas white men had the constant momentum and flow of a supportive culture, people like me were always trying to walk up the down escalator.

Much has been written and reported about the role of the Masons in the police, but to be fair, there is evidence that – whatever else it may be – Freemasonry may not be quite as 'institutionally racist' as I had suspected. In his memoir *Kill the Black One First*, Michael Fuller (Britain's first black chief constable) recalls an attempt to recruit him after he had also been successfully admitted to the Met's high-flier scheme. When he replied that he didn't often join clubs, he was told that the Masons were much more than a club and that they did lots of good work for charities.

'But who else is in your lodge?' asked Fuller.

'Some are only for police. Others take all sorts. That's what makes it so interesting.' Fuller asked for more details of the membership. 'Police, judges, a few criminals,' he was told.

'You mean police and judges and criminals all sit and eat together?'

'It's not like that,' was the reply. 'Some people have done time, that's all.'

Fuller decided not to join.

My friend Chris Donaldson, the young black officer who'd originally persuaded me to apply to join the police, is disarmingly candid about the Freemasons: 'I joined because I thought it would help my career in the Met,' he says, and then smiles, 'but, unfortunately, it never did.'

Meanwhile, the ambition which had propelled me onward since schooldays and my decision to take ten O levels when everyone else was taking five, had not deserted me, and the next step on my ascent of the mountain would be promotion from inspector to chief inspector. It was a leap I'd attempted twice before, but now having gained a place on the HPDS, perhaps it was finally within my grasp.

The first time, my friend Shab and I had applied at the same moment, and both of us were rooting for the other as the results were due to be known. I always made sure I was away from the office when these outcomes were expected, because I know I'm likely to have a little cry, and I never want to do that when I'm at work if I can help it. So Shab and I were together when we received the disappointing news, and I admit that we shed some tears. The second time I was on my own, but the result was the same. This time – my third attempt – my success in getting onto the HPDS and my work in the Diversity Directorate had allowed me to broaden my experience, and had also placed me in a series of high-profile events where I'd been required to interact with the public and with elected officials.

I arranged to be working out at my local gym when the call was expected. When it came, and I learned I'd been promoted to chief inspector, I confess to shedding tears of a different sort. This promotion made me the most senior female police officer of Asian background in the Met – and it felt huge.

What a distance from the two-up two-down terrace in Tiverton Road in Smethwick, with the tin bath hanging on the wall in the backyard. And what a very long journey for the 5-year-old girl who began primary school speaking little English, with parents who spoke no English, and whose main ambition for their daughter was that she should become an obedient wife. Whereas, at one time, my life seemed destined to be that of a subservient spouse of a man I had not chosen, having to account for my every move, now I felt I'd managed to become very much my own person, with a pride in my independence. The road to this point in my career had involved overcoming a lot of hurdles and obstacles, and there'd been many times when my pact with Shabnam involving 'the bastards' had been sorely tested. Now, though, with this recognition and promotion, I'd made history, and could feel that my achievement might serve as an inspiration and encouragement for other young women, and especially those from ethnic minorities. My new position thrust me into the public eye at a level I'd scarcely been prepared for, but I was determined to embrace the opportunities and challenges it presented.

My promotion re-motivated me in my long-term ambition to persuade more people from the black and Asian communities to come forward to join the police. Notwithstanding that my own experience of racism within the Met had been patchy at best, I remained convinced that the only long-term solution was to achieve a significant increase in the proportion of people from minorities, and especially at its most senior levels. I took part in a whole range of recruitment drives in many areas, but was most keen when they were situated in Southall or other places where a high proportion of the catchment and possible audience was from the minority communities. I knew enough, however, to realize that no-one would be taken in by any attempt to airbrush away the difficulties. In an article for a weekly free newspaper designed to promote employment opportunities called *Works for Me*, I wrote: 'As an Asian woman there have been difficult times at different points in my career, but over such a long period of time it would be unbelievable if it had been plain sailing. There are plenty of raised eyebrows when I attend meetings as the senior police representative ... I am not always what people expect of a police officer. I'm not trying to conform to an image of a police officer, and challenging stereotypes is what drives me on.'

At the same time, I was also trying to rebuild my personal life after my separation from my husband. My new relationship with Rod Jarman was going well, but my ability to build a normal life was circumscribed by what was turning into a long-running and highly acrimonious dispute with my ex. We couldn't agree financial terms for the divorce, and there was disagreement too over Steve's access to our son. I accepted that Emil should see his father from time to time, but discovered that he was sometimes merely taken back to Steve's house to watch TV.

More than anything, I now just wanted to get him out of my life, so I offered to buy him out of any financial interest in our assets, including his share of a house we had recently moved to in Abridge. I also said I'd settle for a reasonable figure as his contribution to bringing up our son. He wouldn't agree to either and so the matter was inevitably going to court.

As happens so often when couples split, everyone outside the marriage felt entitled to have their opinion, and I found myself in an awkward position among our neighbours. Everyone took sides, and I was told I couldn't go the village ball to be with our 'friends' on our normal table because they felt awkward. I was hurt and upset, but saw no reason why I should be ostracized, especially as I'd been the injured party in our marriage. So I booked a separate table and took a group of my loudest and most fun-loving friends. We were the first ones on the dance floor when the band began to play, and the last ones off. The group then went back to my house for a noisy after-ball party. Later I was told off by the ball committee, who said my friends were not considered the 'right type' for the village.

Feeling ostracized was not the only cause for discomfort in the local community. My son Emil, now 6 years old, was doing well at school; he was bright and worked hard, and was good at sport. He was also the only non-white child in the school. So if you happened to be a mindless moron with no experience of people from a different background, anyone with a non-white face might seem to be a potential target. And so it was that two idiots from Emil's school put on balaclavas and attacked him, calling him a terrorist and bruising and grazing his face. Of course, I went to the school to complain, but was greeted with a response of the 'boys will be boys' variety, and left with very little reason to think the incident would not be repeated. I made up my mind there and then that it was unfair on my son to make him grow up in a place where there were no other non-white children, and so I decided to move again, this time to Sevenoaks.

When the divorce settlement eventually came to court, my husband argued I should support him financially because my career and earning prospects were better than his. He also claimed a share of the house in Chadwell Heath, even though I'd bought it before I met him. Although she spoke no English and the whole matter was strange and traumatic for her, my mother was compelled to come to court to give evidence that the Chadwell Heath house was her only permanent home. Fortunately, the judge could hardly take seriously the idea that a single mother would have better promotion prospects in the Met than Steve as a single man, and he was forced to accept quite a lot less than I'd offered him for his share of our assets, and to pay more in maintenance for Emil than I'd asked for. I might have hoped that most of the inevitable pain and distress surrounding the end of our marriage was behind me, but unfortunately it was not to be.

CHAPTER FIFTEEN

'It's you!'

The re-election of Tony Blair in May 2005 for his third term of office came as a surprise and disappointment to many who had opposed his determination to go to war in Iraq. Aside from the controversy about so-called weapons of mass destruction and the countless deaths of innocent people on all sides, some blamed the UK's involvement in the war for the subsequent murder of fifty-two people in the London tube and bus bombings in July 2005. One of the bombers had left a video which sent out a chilling message:

> Your democratically elected governments continuously perpetuate atrocities against my people all over the world . . . Until we feel security you will be our targets and until you stop the bombing, gassing, imprisonment and torture of my people we will not stop this fight. We are at war and I am a soldier. Now you too will taste the reality of this situation.

Tensions were consequently running high in all areas of the country, and especially in London, where a further tremor came with the news that the police had killed an unarmed civilian – Brazilian Jean Charles de Menezes – as he boarded an underground train at Stockwell station. In what was later revealed to have been a tragedy of errors, police had mistaken de Menezes for a bomber, and ended up shooting him to death as he sat among bewildered and horrified commuters. Suddenly, it felt as though the war that had been conducted in far-off lands was being fought in the streets of Britain.

Not only had the enemy brought the war to a place where it couldn't be ignored, but the attackers were not frenzied jihadis wearing funny clothes and communicating via grainy videos. The four men who blew up themselves – and scores of innocent members of the public – on tubes and buses had been fermenting their hatred in the quiet suburbs of Leeds and Aylesbury. If they could have planned the murder and mayhem while hiding in plain sight, who else was plotting against us and how could we stop them before it was too late?

The National Community Tension Team was organized by the Association of Chief Police Officers and involved the Home Office, the Muslim Council of Britain, local authorities, youth organizations and other groups concerned with harmony in the community. I joined as deputy commander in January 2006.

The job was based in Birmingham, but I was tasked to tour the country with the intention of persuading members of the Muslim community to join local liaison committees. The stated motivation for the exercise was to find ways to combat

Islamophobia, and this was indeed an important aspect of the objective. Equally crucial, though, was the need to find ways to gather intelligence for Counter Terrorism Command about young radicals who might be planning violent crimes such as the London bus and tube bombings. Naturally, there was initial suspicion, especially among some of the young men, and it required tactful negotiation to win their confidence. Coming originally from a minority community myself, I found it easier to empathize with the concerns of the Muslim groups. On the other hand, in the Muslim community, just as in the police, my gender sometimes proved to be an obstacle to being taken seriously.

When I tried to organize a community meeting among Muslims in Leicester, the men at first insisted that separate gatherings be held for themselves and for the women. When I resisted, the leaders agreed to a single meeting, but then demanded that women should sit separately and must not be allowed to speak. Although it was irritating always to be slighted by the men, I was able to turn it to my advantage because, of course, it's always the women in such communities who really know what's going on. I was able to extract useful information from groups of Muslim women in Coventry and Redbridge, as well as Leicester and a number of other towns throughout the Midlands.

There seemed to be a sort of unofficial hierarchy among the radicalized Muslims. The highest status was enjoyed by the Saudis, next were the Pakistanis, and finally there were the Somalis. It tended to mean that the Somalis were prepared to go further – be more reckless and daring – just to prove themselves worthy of the others.

Several months into my attachment to the National Community Tension Team, a rumour was picked up that radical Muslims were planning a spectacular outrage which would involve kidnapping someone in uniform, who would then be beheaded on video for circulation on the internet. The intended victim might be a soldier or a police officer, and would probably be from an ethnic minority. This, of course, put me centrally in the threatened group. News of the rumour caused a speedy review of priorities, and Operation Gamble was put in place to track down and arrest the plotters. I was required to return to London to brief relevant teams in the Met, and orders were issued that police officers should not go on patrol alone. There was even talk of not allowing BAME officers out at all while wearing our uniform.

The investigation went on for six months and after identifying a group of suspects, our team and intelligence officers intended to investigate for a further two months before making any arrests. However, when one of those under suspicion was seen purchasing a video camera, it was feared that the crime might be imminent and so plans were brought forward. Just before 4 a.m. on 31 January 2007, some 700 of our officers raided eight homes and four businesses in Birmingham, including a corner store, two Islamic bookstores and an internet cafe. Eight men were arrested, and then a ninth later the same day. The man later identified as the ringleader, Parviz Khan, admitted to the plot and was sentenced to life imprisonment, to serve a minimum of fourteen years. Another of the accused was found guilty of failing to report the plot and four others were sentenced to up to seven years for supplying equipment to Pakistan-based militants fighting coalition forces in Afghanistan.

It was eighteen months before the wider concern dissipated sufficiently for the exercise to be discontinued, and I found myself unassigned and on gardening leave until a new job could be found for me. I had no way to know that I would be so close to events when, six years later, the nightmare threat was eventually carried out on the streets of Greenwich.

My increasing experience of dealing with elected officials and outside institutions had been put to good use following the London bombings of 7 July. The heightened feelings of insecurity among Londoners in particular, alongside the destabilization of ethnic communities, led the Met to stage a programme of meetings designed to inform and reassure the public. I helped to set up a facility at the Queen Elizabeth Hall for people who'd lost loved ones or had other enquiries, and I was called upon to attend a series of public meetings, several of which were characterized by fear and bad temper. At one meeting in particular, things threatened to get out of hand when the senior police officer chairing it was shouted down. He was trying hard but with the best will in the world the people didn't believe he really understood what they were going through. I discreetly took over running the meeting and managed to restore calm.

The Met's commissioner Ian Blair had also set up a series of focus groups to discuss issues arising for sections of the community with so-called 'protected characteristics', and among them were

groups representing gays and lesbians, and ethnic minorities. It
was my role in these focus groups, as well as my work following
the London bombings, that led to a new and entirely unexpected
highlight in my career.

I had been happy but very surprised when I heard that I'd
been nominated in the prestigious annual Asian Women of
Achievement Awards. Previous winners of the awards included
the then director of Liberty Shami Chakrabarti and the successful
actress Nina Wadia. However, when I was informed that the final
decisions were voted on by the public, and that no serving police
officer had ever actually won anything, I was content to settle
for an enjoyable and stress-free evening at the formal ceremony
at the London Hilton on Park Lane.

I put on my best uniform and invited my eldest son and my
friend Daisy Reid as my guests. My (by now) husband Rod was also
attending because of his role in the Met's Diversity Directorate.
When our party was shown to a table right at the very back of
the auditorium, it confirmed for me that I'd be able to enjoy a
few drinks and a thoroughly pleasant but uneventful evening. So
much so that, when the time eventually came for BBC newsreader
Sophie Raworth to announce the award in my category, I was
hardly listening. It was left to my friend Daisy, who was paying
rather closer attention, to nudge me and whisper, 'It's you!' I
was genuinely stunned, and only had the few moments it took
to weave my way between what seemed like a maze of tables to
collect myself. Having shaken hands and had my picture taken
with Sophie, I was obliged to say a few words. Even now I can't
remember what came out, but I believe I managed to tell the

assembled crowd that I was overwhelmed, humbled and extremely grateful to the public who had voted for me.

No sooner had the reality of the honour begun to sink in, than I was informed that I was wanted as a guest on the BBC's Breakfast TV show the following morning. This left me only a few short hours to get home, grab whatever sleep I could, before getting up at 5 a.m. to be back at White City. I remember the hour sitting in the studio giving intermittent live interviews to the morning audience as a happy blur.

CHAPTER SIXTEEN

Croydon

Even though I had overcome all the technical hurdles to reaching the rank of chief inspector, I once again faced the need to find an operational posting where there was a vacancy at that level. This was seldom easy for BAME officers, and so when I discovered that a position existed in Croydon for which there were no other applicants, I applied. The local chief superintendent was not encouraging, but in the absence of other candidates he had no choice but to accept me. This was in an area which presents a wide range of challenges for many of the public services, including the police. All my operational policing roles had been in areas with problems of deprivation, but nothing had quite prepared me for what I would be faced with here.

One of the troubled and troublesome areas under my command was the New Addington estate, which has long been a centre for crime and anti-social behaviour, and scores low on every measure of social deprivation. In a 2013 survey by the *Croydon Advertiser*, it was said to be the worst place to live in Croydon, based on life expectancy, numbers of incapacity benefit claimants, people on income support, local schools and health services, unemployment, teenage pregnancy, crime, school exam pass rate, public transport accessibility, and access to open space.

The adjacent Fieldway estate, in particular, found itself in the unwelcome glow of the public spotlight in 2011, when a local resident was recorded on video as she subjected surrounding passengers on the Croydon Tramlink to the most vile racial abuse imaginable. When the footage was uploaded onto YouTube and started to go viral, complaints were made to the police and the woman concerned was arrested and charged with a racially aggravated public order offence. The upload was viewed 11 million times in a few months, and she was sentenced to twenty-four months' community service (and also to receive treatment for her mental health).

This was a very dangerous area for street crime in general, with patrolling officers not exempt from becoming victims. Any individual police officer on the beat alone would be liable to be attacked by gangs of youths, sometimes just for the fun of it. The situation was so bad that I insisted officers should only patrol the streets in pairs, and even then they were often vulnerable and prey to ambush. It wasn't just on the estates or in hidden areas. This could happen in broad daylight in Croydon town centre.

Violence against the police would most often occur when they were engaged in a stop and search of a young person.

Before they knew it, two of my officers interviewing a suspect together would find themselves surrounded by the suspect's friends, then jostled, then shoved to the ground, then punched and kicked before reinforcements could be summoned. Mostly the incidents involved young men, but occasionally they involved young women too.

I remember one occasion when we arrested a young woman for taking part in an assault on a patrolling officer. Her parents were summoned but they refused to believe their daughter could conceivably have been involved in such an incident. I had to show them the CCTV footage, and they stood there watching the girl kicking the officer while he was on the ground. That's what it took to make them believe us.

On another occasion, one of the officers beaten up was of West Indian origin, so that at least we were able to add that it was a racially motivated attack to the eventual charge sheet.

One particular challenge was the presence in the town centre of Lunar House, which was the headquarters of the Border and Immigration Agency of the time and its main screening unit. Lunar House is a huge, ugly and forbidding twenty-storey building, which wouldn't look out of place in the post-war Soviet bloc. It opened in 1970 and, along with its neighbour, Apollo House, is said to have been inspired by the moon landings. Many people have had plenty of time to consider the irony of an inspiration from the space age, because at 5 a.m. each day, queues of aliens in various states of desperation would start lining up around the block for what could easily be a four- to ten-hour wait to be seen. Some were merely students seeking to renew their visas, others were asylum seekers in flight from wars in far-off countries, while some were illegal immigrants seeking to cheat the system in order to remain in Britain.

I got to spend time with some of the Home Office staff who had to decide if someone had a justifiable fear of returning to their homelands. One young man complained to me that every single person he interviewed – including men, women and children – claimed to have been raped. You could easily see how someone hearing that day in day out could get jaded and cynical, but I had to point out to him that they probably had been. We have no idea of the trauma that most of these people have been through.

The presence of such a mêlée of disparate and desperate humanity frequently caused frustration and tension among those queuing, and among the local community. The situation gave rise to difficulties for us in trying to maintain order, and we often found ourselves in the middle and being blamed by both sides.

Many of the people queuing at Lunar House were vulnerable in some way and were therefore prey to all kinds of criminal activity. Sometimes, young foreign women in the queue would be lured away to a nearby house and subsequently pressured into prostitution. But, as well as trying to protect the vulnerable, we were frequently called to sort out the conflicts which arose when frustrated people met what often seemed to be inflexible bureaucracy. On such occasions, we could very easily become hate figures for the mob, with consequent fall-out upon ourselves.

One example hit the headlines in September 2007, when more than 200 people from the Gatwick No Border Camp gathered to protest what they believed was the mistreatment of refugees and asylum seekers at the hands of the UK immigration authorities. Just an hour into the demonstration, a man was seen leaving Lunar House, crying, shouting and clearly distraught. Three police officers grappled the man to the ground and continued to restrain him as he lay face down. His face was cut in the fracas, and he was shouting: 'Help me, help me! They are against poor people. This is what happens to poor people. These people are not human.' The man was arrested and taken away in a waiting police van.

Some of the demonstrators protested to other officers at the scene about the level of force used and were invited to go to the police station to make a formal complaint. The group proceeded en masse to Croydon police station, where officers invoked Section 14 of the Public Order Act 1986 (imposing conditions on public assemblies) and penned the protesters in. Two of the protesters refused to comply and were then arrested, handcuffed and put in the cells. 'I went to complain about police heavy-handedness,' one of them said later, 'and immediately got assaulted by a policeman myself.' It had been a not untypical day in the life of the Croydon constabulary.

As I had managed to rise through the ranks, I was of course less liable to be subjected to direct or overt racism, but one way and another the Met never let me forget for very long that I wasn't quite 'one of them'. An example from this period occurred when my boss, Superintendent

Adrian Roberts, was applying for promotion to the rank of chief superintendent. In the course of an interview to test his aptitudes and management skills, he was asked: 'If you had a female Asian officer under your command who was disgruntled because she hadn't been promoted, how would you handle it?' The question was hardly hypothetical because Roberts was indeed my next in command and I, in common with just about every other senior officer in the Met, had been disappointed when I'd been turned down for promotion. I was outraged when Roberts told me what had happened. Now I was being used as a bloody exam question.

Throughout my time in the Met, I'd gained plenty of direct experience of policing public events. Now, though, for the first time, my more senior role required me to take overall responsibility for planning and directing police strategy in dealing with large crowds, so I attended a public order course at the Met's specialist training centre in Gravesend. The facility consists of a series of roads bounded by fake street-frontages, in which the trainers simulate aspects of crowd control, including demonstrations, rioting and football crowds. With bricks and petrol bombs falling all around, it can feel very real and very terrifying.

Ever since the disaster at Hillsborough, crowd control has been taken extremely seriously by all police forces up and down the country, and any senior officer put into a position where they're in charge of a huge crowd knows that the stakes can be very high indeed. Even after the training, I was required to shadow the officer in charge at matches involving Crystal Palace, Charlton and Millwall, and all of them passed without major incident. Years later, I found myself among the senior team controlling a football crowd when I realized I'd forgotten to bring any gloves. One of the specialist officers dealing with football hooligans offered to lend me his spare pair, with the warning, 'But be careful because they're my DNA gloves.' I was confused, until he explained. These were the gloves he wore when he was likely to get into a ruck with unruly football fans, and so they could well be covered with DNA from the spilled blood of those he'd arrested. He carried another pair, quite clean, which he'd hand over to investigating officers if there was a complaint of police brutality. Looking back on it now, I probably should have taken the officer to task, but my priority was to coordinate a complex strategy for the day and it slipped through the net.

Eventually, I was ready to plan and take full responsibility for my first match at Charlton, when the opposing team was Sheffield Wednesday. I'd made all my preparations carefully and felt ready to take charge on the day. What I'd failed to realize, however, was that among Sheffield Wednesday's more prominent fans was the Met's commissioner, Bernard Hogan-Howe; and what I'd also failed to anticipate was that, just as I was about to start my briefing, the commissioner himself would arrive in person – on horseback! Happily, I managed to keep my nerve and deliver the briefing, and subsequently enjoyed an uneventful day, despite being under the scrutiny of the most senior police officer in the land.

For the moment at least, my professional life seemed to be going relatively smoothly. Coming just around the corner, though, were a series of incidents that would bring my private life into the public gaze in ways I could scarcely have imagined.

CHAPTER SEVENTEEN

The Cannabis Farm

My husband Rod and I were now living in Kent, but my former husband Steve had a home in Hertfordshire, so access visits for Emil were problematic. The difficulties got worse when our son was picked for the school football team which often had fixtures on Saturdays. One weekend in September 2008, when Emil was due to be with Steve, he phoned his father to tell him he had an important football match which he did not want to miss. Steve was unhappy, and the call did not go well.

On the Saturday morning, I was standing on the touchline with Rod, cheering on Emil, when I saw Steve arriving. He was accompanied by the woman with whom he'd originally had the affair, Shen Mertkol. Cross words were exchanged, and then Shen approached my son directly, apparently trying to hand him a note. I was angry and told her to leave him alone, and I'm not proud to admit that I swore at her.

Keen to prevent an already heated situation from boiling over, Rod began to steer me away from the confrontation but as he did so, Steve fell in behind us, shouting abuse. Again, Rod tried to defuse the situation, telling Steve that if he was dissatisfied with the custody arrangements, the way to deal with it was through the courts rather than by making a scene on the touchline of his son's football game. Nevertheless, the pursuit continued, until eventually I broke free and turned to push Steve away. With my 5 foot 3 inches versus his 6 foot 2, this was an uneven clash and I slipped and fell onto the muddy ground. Steve seemed to have achieved what he wanted.

'I've got you now, you stupid bitch,' he shouted, and then proceeded to call the local police to report me for alleged assault.

Now anxious that this unpleasant saga shouldn't continue in front of our son, I took Emil and left. Steve's girlfriend Shen was wearing heels that were unsuitable for a football pitch, and had been a long way away from the confrontation, so when the local bobby eventually turned up to investigate, Rod was the only witness. He had already made up his mind to tell the whole unvarnished truth of what had occurred, not least because at that time he was a commander in the Met and was also applying for the post of assistant chief constable of the Kent force. When the hapless young constable realized that the dramatis personae of this mini-drama were an inspector, a chief inspector and a commander of the Met, he quickly retreated back to the local station to allow more senior heads to take a view.

There the story might well have rested in peace, but for the fact that some helpful person called the newspapers, and the prospect of a 'senior cop strikes former husband' headline obviously caused great excitement in the world of the tabloid press. In fact, by the time Chinese whispers had enhanced the story, the printed version was a far more compelling account of how a 'senior cop strikes former husband's *mistress*'. Shen, who had been hundreds of yards distant at the time of the row, was reported to have been the victim of the 'crime'.

The consequence of fresh interest from the media was that I was asked to attend the local police station at Tunbridge. There I might have been arrested, except that when word of all this reached my boss at Croydon, Adrian Roberts, a call was made to Kent police to find out what on earth was going on. Subsequently, the assistant commissioner of the Met, Tim Godwin, telephoned the chief constable of Kent to make a specific request that his chief inspector should not be arrested. So instead, when I arrived at Tunbridge police station, I was escorted to the office of the detective chief inspector, where I was interviewed about the incident under caution. I was not, I'm keen to emphasize, taken to the cells. It was perfectly clear to the investigating officers that there had been no incident which needed to involve the law; nonetheless, to avoid any suspicion of being seen to be partial towards 'one of their own', they were obliged to make a report for the Crown Prosecution Service – it would be for them to decide what should happen next. As a result of this, Rod and I had our first direct experience of receiving the kind of press attention most people would wish to avoid.

There followed a series of unannounced visits to our home by journalists and photographers, and over subsequent days and weeks the story was reported in the local paper, as well as the *Daily Mirror*, *Daily Telegraph* and on the BBC. The news even spread as far as the *Ahmedabad Mirror* published in Gujarat, which featured a photograph of me with the headline: 'UK's top cop of Indian origin bashes up ex-husband's lover'. Most of the reports mentioned my inclusion in the High Potential Development Scheme, which led one online reader of the *Evening Standard* to comment, 'It ought to be called "the Home Office's fast track Higher Potential Scheme which aims to take any old rubbish as long as they're asian [sic] and prepare them for senior ranks, ignoring whatever trouble their greed or stupidity gets them into along the way" scheme.' Another online reader remarked, 'If you fast track them because of their colour or creed and for no other reason, what do you expect. Sod the hard working white women and men in the force.'

The press coverage just made Rod and me angry and irritated, but the effect on our 8-year-old son was more traumatic. One day, Emil returned home from school accompanied by our au pair, to find the house surrounded by a phalanx of reporters. They had to take refuge in a neighbour's house for several hours, only later sneaking indoors via the garden. It was many weeks before Emil could be persuaded to return to school, and only then after the head teacher personally took him on a tour of the perimeter fences to demonstrate that the premises were secure.

As if the whole thing had not already been blown completely out of proportion, the Met convened what's known as a 'Gold Group', at which representatives of various departments gather to anticipate and discuss the damage that might be sustained by an individual and the force as a result of a particular incident. I was represented by a member of the Police Federation, and the Met was represented by Deputy Assistant Commissioner Maxine de Brunner, whose suggestions included that I should ensure my living room curtains were closed after dark.

The Crown Prosecution Service decided to take no further action against me, but that wasn't quite the end of it. Next, the matter was investigated by the Met's Directorate of Professional Standards, which found that the inevitable publicity created by the incident had caused a stain, and I was deemed to have brought the force into disrepute. The entire episode gave me a valuable insight into what can happen to an innocent individual when she unwittingly finds herself in the crosshairs of the British press and media. It's like suddenly you lose control of your life, and you're waiting to be knocked about by whatever or whomever chooses to turn your private business into public property. Later, I put the citation for my bad behaviour on the wall-facing side of a framed certificate for outstanding service to the public.

After the incident, which had traumatized our son and damaged my career, I sought and was granted a legal injunction requiring Steve Reed to keep away from Emil, at least until he reached the age of 16. His father was allowed to write a letter, which would remain sealed until that time. I eventually waited until after my son had taken his GCSEs before giving the letter to Emil to read.

Life had scarcely had a chance to return to normal when another missile appeared out of the clear blue sky. It all started when I put the Abridge house up for sale after I moved to Kent, but the housing market was in the doldrums. Eventually, following a period of several months with no prospect of a sale, I was advised to let the house to tenants until the market picked up. I therefore changed the mortgage to a buy-to-let, altered the insurance, and advertised it on HouseWeb. Before long, a very charming young Vietnamese couple came along, looked around, and said they wanted to take the tenancy. They provided references which checked out, had the utility bills transferred into their names, and began paying their rent regularly and on time.

Weeks passed and from time to time Rod and I would go out of our way to drive past the Abridge house, just to ensure that everything seemed in order and that the gardens were being kept tidy. There was never much sign of life, but if it was after dark, there was usually a lamp on behind curtains in the living room, indicating that the house was occupied. Following the move to Sevenoaks, however, there was less opportunity to keep an eye on the Abridge property, but the rent continued to be paid and there were no reports of anything untoward from neighbours. Until one day there was.

On the morning of 13 March 2010, I took a call from the family next door to our former home. They didn't want to worry me, they said, but at about 1 a.m. they'd heard sounds of what seemed like fighting at the back of the house. Some glass had been broken and people had been shouting and running into the garden. I thanked them and then called the tenants, but could get no response. That morning I was due to take Emil to his football game, and so Rod volunteered to drive back to the house to see what the fuss was about.

When he arrived there was no sign of any problem at the front of the house, so he went around to the back, where it was immediately clear that there'd been a break-in. There was broken glass on the back patio and the doors were open to the elements. Rod took a few steps inside and what he saw stunned him. Every part of the floor was covered with several inches of soil, and there were hundreds of plants growing under sunlamps and a makeshift irrigation system. He has been around long enough to know that he was looking at a cannabis farm.

He immediately stepped back to call the local police, and when they arrived and he re-entered the house, what they discovered was a disaster zone. All the carpeted floors, upstairs and downstairs, were now buried under a thick layer of soil. A large round hole had been cut in the ceiling between the ground and first floors, apparently to allow plumbing and electricity to circulate more easily. Water had been diverted from the bathroom taps to provide an irrigation system. Even the loft was full to capacity with cannabis plants.

There was, of course, no sign of the Vietnamese couple but there were signs that a fight had been followed by a quick getaway – among the personal belongings left at the house was medicine for treating epilepsy.

The first reaction of the local police was that Rod and I must have known what was going on, but they were soon reassured. Rod had by then served thirty-one years in the force and reached the exalted position of deputy assistant commissioner. The embarrassment of having been taken in was sufficient punishment, not to mention the bill for some £43,000 to make the property habitable.

We claimed on our insurance, but sure enough we were to be disappointed. The small print had required us to check the premises personally every six months, and it had been seven since we'd last visited. Even though the use of hydroponics speeds up the growth of new cannabis plants, the insurance company insisted that those in the house were at such an advanced stage of growth that they must have been more than six months old. And, after all, we were both senior police officers and ought to have known better. It all added up to a refusal to pay out.

We were at a loss about what to do next. The house would need a massive amount of work, but we couldn't go on paying the mortgage and funding the repairs at the same time without a tenant. The loft was still full of cannabis plants which local police seemed to be showing no inclination to take away. Eventually, we discovered Mario, a Romanian builder, who offered to repair and renovate the house in exchange for being allowed to live in it for a discounted rent. The arrangement suited all sides, and eventually the house was serviceable, but not before Rod and I had once again found ourselves in the national newspaper headlines in a way we didn't relish or welcome.

Some helpful person tipped off the press that a house belonging to a senior police officer was being used as a cannabis farm. There followed a flood of enquiries from the media, and in what may have been a sincere effort at damage limitation, the Scotland Yard press office advised us not to contradict the journalists' assumption that the house belonged to Rod. After all, it had been he who'd dealt with everything, and anyway he was about to retire so the story could do him no harm.

However, the incident was to have a further sting in its tail when the press then received another tip-off that the house actually belonged to me, rather than to Rod. The implication was that I'd been happy to shift any criticism to my husband, and several newspapers had a field day at the further expense of my reputation. In fact, the question of whether it was Rod or me whose name was on the title deeds hadn't seemed to either of us to be relevant. Why should it? We're married. What possible difference could it make? Of course, it made no difference, but it did provide a further opportunity for those who later wished to place hurdles on the progress of my career.

CHAPTER EIGHTEEN

The Pope and I

It wouldn't take a psychiatrist to work out that my particular interest in so-called 'honour-based' crimes is rooted in my personal experience of an enforced first marriage and the domestic abuse that followed. The consequences for individual young girls and women of being forced to marry someone they've never met, of female genital mutilation and other abuse, have never been taken sufficiently seriously in this country, and from my earliest days in the police I wanted to do my bit to put that right. So when I was asked to give some support to the Women's Interfaith Network, founded by Lady Gilda Levy, I jumped at the chance. Gilda set up the network to bring together people from all religions and ethnic groups, to show that the subjugation of women isn't a genuine part of any of the actual religions themselves – mostly it's a construction by the groups of men who've run them for their own benefit for centuries.

Talking to representatives from the most orthodox branches of the Muslim, Sikh, Jewish and Christian religions made me realize that, whatever the differences between them, they have one thing in common – they all treat women as second-class citizens. Even at the most basic level of regular worship, orthodox Muslims and Jews both keep women in separate spaces, while my own experience of marrying into an extreme Sikh family left me in no doubt about their views on gender equality. In most of the various Christian churches too, you'll usually find the men wearing the fine robes and dispensing the sermons while the women are sweeping the vestry and dispensing the tea.

I hoped that my experience in reaching out to people from different minorities would make at least some contribution to the important work of the Women's Interfaith Network. What I absolutely did not expect was that my contribution would eventually be recognized, and so what followed came as a bolt from the blue. I was asked if I wanted to meet the Pope.

At first I thought it must be someone's idea of a joke. I'd read that Pope Benedict XVI was due to come to Britain. He'd been invited by David Cameron, and the visit was already attracting criticism and controversy. Some of the voices raised against it were concerned about the cost of his security, while the majority were protesting against the Pope's views on a range of issues, from abortion to the role of women in the priesthood. I'm not a religious person myself and have to admit that I hadn't made a personal study of the views of this particular Pope. But before I got to thinking about any of that, I needed to ascertain that this wasn't all some kind of a wind-up.

It wasn't. As part of his itinerary, the Pope was coming to St Mary's University in Twickenham, where he'd be meeting people representing different religions, denominations and inter-faith groups. In recognition of the work I'd done for women within the police, and in the Women's Interfaith Network, I was to be presented to His Holiness, and to receive a gold medal. I can honestly say that I have never been more amazed by anything in my life.

Naturally, I expected that the Met would be happy that one of their senior officers should be recognized in this way, but when I applied for permission to attend the ceremony wearing my uniform, I was in for another surprise. The answer came back: no, I was not allowed to wear my police uniform; in fact, I was not allowed to go at all. The reason was apparently that part of the controversy surrounding the Papal visit was that he'd been insufficiently firm on the subject of child abuse among the priesthood. Any association, therefore, between the Pope and the Met might reflect badly on the police.

So, in the course of his visit to Britain, Pope Benedict XVI would be meeting the Queen, the Prime Minister, the Archbishop of Canterbury and the First Minister of Scotland, among many others – but he wasn't going to be meeting Chief Inspector Parm Sandhu, in case his views on paedophile priests should rub off on my uniform.

I decided to take the matter to a higher authority and secured a personal interview with Deputy Chief Constable Rose Fitzpatrick, who took no time at all in telling me she couldn't help. So now I had a decision to make. Would I obey an edict handed down by people whom I suspected might be motivated by jealousy – because they hadn't received a similar invitation? Or would I follow my conscience and attend the ceremony anyway, in spite of the order not to do so? I informed the organizers that I'd be there.

So what does one wear when you're meeting the Pope? Something demure obviously. Certainly nothing in any way revealing. I tried on several of my best outfits, but couldn't work out why I wasn't finding anything that felt quite right. Then I realized; obviously, I should be wearing my police uniform. I'd already decided to disobey a clear instruction not to attend the ceremony, and so I thought 'What the hell?' On the morning of 20 September 2010, I put on my smartest chief inspector's uniform and set off for Twickenham.

What can I say about meeting the Pope? In the course of my work, I've met the Queen and the Duke of Edinburgh several times, I've met Prince William, prime ministers and individual senior politicians. In no case could I say that I was unduly nervous at the prospect. However, the thought of meeting this man, who had risen to the top of a church representing hundreds of millions of the faithful; whose every utterance was noted and taken to heart by the devout across the entire world? Yes, I felt nervous.

The event was ticketed, but nonetheless there were huge crowds. These, of course, included scores of uniformed police officers, so I didn't feel in any way out of place. I wondered what my seniors would think or do when they saw the photographs, but I decided I'd worry about that later.

I was still feeling a sense of eager anticipation during the opening prayers and speeches, but as the moment approached when I would be introduced, I gradually felt completely calm. The Pope seemed to exude a quiet charisma which put everyone close to him at their ease.

When eventually my turn came around to meet him, I was first of all surprised at how small he is. I'm just 5 foot 3 and a bit, and he is shorter – a little old man with white hair, wearing a white cloak and dress. When I glanced down and saw that he had on the most impressive pair of bright red shoes, for a moment I had the irreverent thought that if he clicked them together he'd be back in Kansas. But now the Pope, the actual Pope, the head of an estimated 1.3 billion Catholics in 232 countries, was reaching out with his right hand, and something possessed me to grasp his hand in both of mine.

The Pope smiled and gave me his blessing, and then asked a question: 'Do you have children?'

'Yes,' I said, 'I have two boys,' and so he blessed them too, then handed me a gold medal, and two smaller medallions to give to my sons.

In my everyday life I try to keep words like 'awe' out of my vocabulary, but I'm not ashamed to say that I was awestruck by my meeting with the Pope. Of course, by then I had read up on his views about women in the priesthood, and abortion, and a range of other matters, and naturally I profoundly disagree with many of them. But when I met him I felt myself to be in the presence of a good man, someone who wanted to bring people together rather than push them apart. Maybe I'm wrong, but that's the way I felt and feel.

And I never heard a word about it from New Scotland Yard.

CHAPTER NINETEEN

The London Olympics

Most of London had celebrated when it was announced that the capital city was to host the Olympic Games in 2012. For the Met, however, the prospect gave rise to a whole world of problems and responsibilities. Less than twenty-four hours after the original announcement on 6 July 2005, the London bombings had killed 52 people and injured 700, and from the very first moment, the scale of the security risk was not lost on any of us. The world would be watching, and London would be a target for every radical group which wanted to put their grievance on a global stage.

By 2011, plans were of course highly advanced, but when a vacancy arose for a chief inspector to coordinate and oversee arrangements for the deployment of officers and resources to cover the Games, I decided to apply.

Whenever you go for advancement in the Met, any important gaps in your CV will hold you back, and so I was always looking for opportunities to get into and learn about things I hadn't been involved with before. A massive logistical operation of this kind was outside my immediate experience, which was precisely the reason the task appealed.

I got the job and, under the supervision of a commander and as part of a team of senior colleagues, I embarked on a year of detailed and meticulous planning, including how to deploy thousands of officers along with horses, dogs and other support, to ensure the safety of athletes, dignitaries, tourists and members of the public. And all the while, the many other priorities of policing London would need to be covered as well.

The priority that quickly barged its way to the top of the list was, of course, the outbreak of rioting which followed the shooting by police of Mark Duggan in early August 2011. Duggan had been targeted as part of Operation Trident, which was an intelligence-led investigation into gang warfare in the capital. Officers had reliable information that he was carrying a firearm, and believed he was on his way to shoot a member of a rival gang. When they stopped a minicab he was travelling in, he tried to make a run for it. Shots were fired, and Duggan was later pronounced dead at the scene.

Word leaked out from the Met after the shooting that there'd been an exchange of gunshots, but it was established later that a gun recovered at the scene hadn't been fired. At the time, no-one was aware of the precise circumstances; all we knew was that the already strained relationship between parts of the community and the police in the area was at boiling point, and the shooting of Duggan was likely to push it over the top. Two days later, on Saturday 6 August, what started out as a peaceful protest march from the Broadwater Farm estate to Tottenham police station began to get ugly. Apparently, the officer sent out to speak to them was a chief inspector, while demonstrators were demanding to meet someone more senior. That night and during those that followed, rioting broke out in Tottenham, and spread to Brixton, Enfield, Islington, Wood Green and then all over much of the capital and further afield, eventually causing at least five deaths and many more injuries, as well as an estimated £100 million worth of damage in London alone.

The unusually rapid spread and apparent organization of the rioting was attributed to the use of social media. Rioters were able to share information about intended targets and move hundreds of people around very quickly. But the very thing that started out as a useful tool for the criminals turned against them, as we began receiving hundreds of photos and videos recorded by ordinary local people. Detectives set about analysing the images, along with CCTV from our own cameras and those of local authorities, and were quickly able to identify and arrest hundreds of those responsible.

Three years later, an inquest jury found that Mark Duggan hadn't fired a weapon, but that he had been lawfully killed. However, the circumstances surrounding the shooting remain in dispute to this day. It's natural that people will ask how it can be justice that a man was shot and killed when he hadn't actually fired his weapon, or maybe wasn't even holding it at the time. But I'd ask people to put themselves in the position of the officers at the scene. They know this man is carrying a gun. Good intelligence tells them he's on his way to commit a serious crime or maybe a murder. They are highly trained, but of course they are on edge. They stop the car he's travelling in, he makes a run for it, and for a split second it may seem as though he's reaching for a gun. Do they wait until they or one of their friends is shot and maybe killed before taking action? Surely not. No-one wants to see anyone gunned down by police on the streets of London or anywhere else, but my own feeling is that if you carry an illegal and loaded gun, it's very hard to blame the forces of law and order if you come to harm. No doubt some people will disagree with me, but that's my opinion.

Within a few days of the shooting, the riots had led to well over three thousand recorded crimes in London alone, and police had made hundreds of arrests. The whole thing was a tragedy for the Duggan family, and then for many other families who had loved ones killed or injured, as well as literally hundreds more who lost their homes or businesses in the mayhem.

News of the riots obviously resonated around the world, and can't have improved the image of London as the home of the forthcoming Olympics, so we redoubled our efforts to ensure the safety of everyone planning to come. A major obstacle in the way of deploying the maximum number of police onto the streets during the Games themselves was the obligation for all officers involved in any particular prosecution to give evidence when the case came to court. The obvious need to deal speedily with prosecutions involving tourists or visitors would mean that an inordinate number of officers would be taken off patrol, often on the day following the arrest. If any of them failed to turn up, defence lawyers were quick to claim that the narrative of evidence was incomplete and so the prosecution would fail. In the search for a solution, it was even suggested that anyone and everyone arrested in the course of the Games should be made to languish in jail until after the closing ceremony, when all the cases could be heard at once. The immediate prospect of prisons bursting at the seams with a multinational cohort of well-meaning drunks seemed too ghastly to contemplate, so for the moment the problem remained unresolved.

It was clear that, unless a solution could be found to the problem, scores or hundreds of officers, who were needed for all-important and sometimes urgent operational duties, would otherwise be waiting in the anterooms of courts all over London. I therefore devised a scheme in which a sworn statement could be read into evidence, without the need for the officer to appear in person. Once the detail was formulated, I coordinated and then chaired a meeting involving the Lord Chief Justice, the Chair of the Olympics Working Group on Crown Courts, and the Chief Prosecutor, all of whom readily accepted and declared themselves willing to adopt the new procedure. These novel arrangements did indeed free up hundreds of officers to be on the streets where they could be more effective, and brought about a radical change in courtroom procedure, which remains in effect to this day.

Even with the new resources now freed up, we were going to be up against it in providing secure cover twenty-four hours a day for the duration of the Games. One piece of luck was that the Olympics were taking place during Ramadan. This meant that our Muslim officers would be fasting during the hours of daylight, and so would likely welcome the prospect of working the night shift when they were allowed to eat and drink. This coincidence of timing made it considerably easier to deploy resources across twenty-four hours. However, our efforts to keep the peace got off to an unfortunate start when hundreds of cyclists took part in the Critical Mass London ride on Friday 27 July, to coincide with the opening ceremony, and clashed with officers trying to restrict traffic near to the Olympic site. While Danny Boyle's spectacular show was taking place inside, ugly scenes erupted outside and were caught on camera, leading to 182 arrests.

Just about every officer in London and the home counties was stretched to the limit in ensuring the safety and security of the hundreds of thousands of people who had crowded into the capital city for the Olympic Games. All seemed to be going more or less according to plan, but that was before we first heard about a girl by the name of Tia Sharp.

It was on the first Friday after the opening of the Games that Christine Bicknell and her daughter Natalie Sharp walked into a Croydon police station at 10 p.m. to report that Natalie's little girl, Tia, was missing. The two women were accompanied by Christine's partner, Stuart Hazell.

The family told police that 12-year-old Tia had been staying for a few days at her grandmother Christine's house on the New Addington estate. Christine had been away at the time, but the child was happy to be looked after by her long-term partner, Stuart Hazell. Hazell said Tia had set off on her own to Croydon around lunchtime, but had not been seen or heard of since. Officers carried out a quick search of the house and then sent out cars to tour the local streets overnight. Next morning, they launched a public appeal. Word of the missing child spread quickly among local residents, many of whom were instantly keen to join in the search. We started house-to-house enquiries while neighbours began to circulate hastily prepared flyers.

I had organized a detailed roster for every available officer on essential security duties, but suddenly this incident was increasing in priority. Hazell's account was corroborated by a neighbour, who told police he'd seen Tia leaving the house and heading down the path at around noon on that day. Notwithstanding the word of the witness, however, suspicion naturally fell upon Stuart Hazell as the last person known to have seen Tia alive. Officers quickly learned that Hazell's mother had been a prostitute and his father had been in jail, and so he'd been brought up in care. More significantly, he had a history of thirty separate convictions for offences, ranging from dealing in cocaine to grievous bodily harm and racial abuse, and had served three prison sentences.

Needless to say, the decision was quickly made to carry out a second search of the house in which Tia had reportedly stayed alone with Stuart Hazell. Once again, though, no trace of the child was found.

By the start of the week following her disappearance, concern for Tia's safety was reaching fever pitch, and police found themselves facing criticism for the level of resources we were devoting to the search. Local people were saying that the incident was being treated as low priority because the family involved were 'white trash'. They believed that if they'd been more middle class or from a more privileged area, we'd have deployed more officers and the child would have been found.

The criticism stung, and by mid-week we had authorized more officers to come off duty at the Olympics to help find the missing child. The deployment made it necessary to revise the carefully made plans for security at the Games. The world might be watching the stadium and its surrounds, but the community was much more concerned about young Tia Sharp – and the local people would still be here long after the tourists and athletes had gone home.

Detectives looking for proof of where Tia went after leaving the house viewed some 800 hours of CCTV and followed up 55 reported sightings, but all proved fruitless. A third search was carried out at Tia's grandmother's house, this time using specially trained dogs, but again it drew a blank.

Eventually, on the following Friday morning, and with no progress in the search for missing Tia, Stuart Hazell left the house early. When Christine woke she became aware of a dreadful smell which seemed to be strongest on the upstairs landing of the house. The police were called again and carried out a fourth search, and this time found Tia's decomposing body wrapped in black plastic and shoved into a corner of the loft. Items of clothing she'd been wearing when she went missing were also found in various carrier bags.

Now Stuart Hazell was on the run, and police issued an appeal to the public to avoid approaching him, but to call 999 immediately. That same evening, he was seen on CCTV buying a bottle of vodka from a shop in Cannon Hill Lane, Merton. News footage of the arrest shows a helicopter flying above, while some twenty or more officers hold back the crowds. Various shouts from those assembled onlookers include 'Let us have him for five minutes' and 'I'll stab him myself.'

Despite being guilty of the most disgusting perversions that many hardened officers had ever seen, Hazell wrote to his father from prison denying that he was a 'nonce'. He pleaded not guilty and put Tia's family through four days of agony in court as they had to hear everything that had happened to the child. Then he changed his plea to guilty and was sentenced to a minimum of thirty-eight years in prison.

Naturally there was a barrage of criticism of the detectives for failing to find Tia's body, and it was later acknowledged that the child had been in the loft since the moment she'd disappeared and had been overlooked in three searches. An internal inquiry put this down to human error. Two constables were given guidance, and another was banned from carrying out any searches in the future.

The tragic murder of Tia Sharp was an appalling ordeal for the family, which was prolonged and exacerbated by errors made by the investigating officers. It was also a dreadful embarrassment for the Met, and the only cold comfort for me was that our failings were not attributable to any lack of officers or resources.

Nonetheless, when something like that happens, there isn't a single officer in the force who doesn't feel regret that we've let down the community we're here to serve.

CHAPTER TWENTY

Own Goals

Policing the international and multicultural visitors attending the London Olympics obviously provided the Met with a golden opportunity to present itself as an enlightened and modern force, so there's little doubt that whoever was responsible for public relations will have been delighted with the poster of a glamorous female of non-specific BAME appearance carrying a Heckler & Koch semi-automatic rifle. What they might not have known was that Carol Howard was already well on her way to being totally disenchanted with her treatment, in what might be one of the most macho police departments. Carol was the only woman in a team of seventy officers at the time, and one of only twelve in the 700-strong Diplomatic Protection Group, just two of whom were black.

Growing up in Peckham in the 1980s and 90s, Carol remembers her uncles complaining about constantly being stopped and searched on the streets. Nonetheless, she'd been attracted to the police from a very young age and took an early opportunity to sign up for work experience at her local station. She had a baby at 18, but then joined the Met as a station receptionist aged 21 and began her officer training three years later. The graduation photo from Hendon shows her with a big smile. 'I was so proud of myself,' she later told the *Guardian*, 'especially because I was the only one [of the recruits] that had a child.'

After an attachment investigating child abuse, Carol Howard applied to join the Diplomatic Protection Group, defending embassies around London. Very quickly, though, her new boss, Inspector David Kelly, seems to have decided she was not up to the job and appears to have embarked on a course of action that a later employment tribunal found was designed to 'undermine, discredit and belittle' her. Howard later told an employment tribunal she thought Kelly's behaviour might be partly explained by the fact that he was attracted to her but she did not reciprocate. He allegedly ordered some other officers to ask her if she was sleeping with another PC in the unit, but they refused. He booked her in for extra training, and told colleagues to investigate if she was absent through illness, on one occasion sending a marked police car to watch her home.

All this was bad enough, but when Carol reached a point where she could stand it no longer and made a complaint, what had been a perpetual irritation turned into a nightmare. She had been instructed not to discuss her complaint with her inspector, but nonetheless Kelly confronted her. 'He was jabbing his hands in the direction of my face, shouting, "Who's telling you not to speak to your chain of command?" He was so loud and so aggressive, and I felt so intimidated by his stance, by his demeanour, the way he was shouting, and the fact he still had his Glock [pistol] on him.' Carol later complained that two sergeants had witnessed the verbal assault, saying, 'You could see that they felt uncomfortable. They knew [it] was inappropriate, yet neither of them intervened.'

Carol sought advice from the Met's Black Police Association, and spoke to the Chair, Janet Hills. Janet immediately spotted the potentially seismic own goal for the force of a public airing of allegations of racism and sexism from the Met's poster girl for the Olympics. 'I went to see a very senior officer and said, "You really don't want to be reading in the newspaper what this officer is saying."' Her warning had no effect and the matter was escalated to be heard by an employment tribunal.

The tribunal found that Carol Howard had been discriminated against because she was a black woman, but also that she had then been victimized for having made the complaint in the first place. The Met was found to have launched an 'insulting, malicious and oppressive' smear campaign against her, in which it was leaked to the press that she had previously been accused of assault and of possessing an indecent image of a child. The tactic of using unofficial leaks to the press was one that had already been used against me, and would be again. In Carol's case, the assault allegation had involved her former husband who had quickly withdrawn the complaint, while the 'child porn' turned out to be a photograph of her own 6-year-old daughter taken while sleeping.

It seemed to be a story that could scarcely get any worse until it became apparent that, in cases where an officer had made a complaint, the Met had a deliberate policy of deleting any evidence of racial and sexual discrimination from the files. The tribunal went on to criticize Met commissioner Sir Bernard Hogan-Howe, who considered Howard's ordeal an isolated incident, accusing him of attempting to 'brush it off as insignificant'.

The tribunal found in favour of PC Howard and awarded her compensation of £37,000. Even as she emerged from the tribunal victorious, but not triumphant, Carol was feeling the bruises. 'Today is not a day for celebration,' she told journalists, 'I have been put through a two-year ordeal in which I have been bullied, harassed and victimized simply because of my gender and race.' Subsequently, she brought a further action for discrimination against the Independent Police Complaints Commission (IPCC). This time she lost, but her defeat at the second tribunal wasn't quite enough for the Met. Later, she was accused and charged with downloading emails containing personal information in breach of data protection laws. The case went to court, where Carol argued that she'd been collecting evidence in support of her whistleblowing complaint about discrimination. The jury took just half an hour to acquit her, but of course she understandably described the ordeal of the trial as 'a nightmare'.

The treatment of Carol Howard led to yet another full-scale investigation, this time by the Equal Opportunities Commission, which found a reluctance among black officers to make a complaint because of the likely reprisals. One officer told the investigators that 'individuals are living, if you like, in a culture of fear of raising their head above the parapet because if they do then they might as well consider leaving their career behind or not going to get promoted or they will be disciplined through no fault of their own'. The 2016 report, called the *Section 20 Investigation into the Metropolitan Police Service*, found a series of weaknesses and made recommendations for improvement.

What happened to Carol Howard was just one of a number of examples illustrating the lengths the Met seemed willing to go to when defending themselves against any officer with the temerity to complain about racial discrimination. However, even this very public own goal was soon to be echoed in another incident involving the now retired sergeant, Gurpal Virdi. Having humiliated the force by winning an employment tribunal and damages of well over £200,000, Virdi controversially elected to return to his former job, and work towards his thirty years of service. When he eventually retired in May 2012, however, there were no speeches or thanks or formalities – instead Virdi was unceremoniously escorted from the building.

Once again, though, the Met hadn't quite finished with him. Following his retirement, Virdi set about involving himself in local politics, and in particular the rehabilitation of youth offenders. His activities in the community occasionally put him into contact with the local police, but otherwise he tried his best to forget the many negative aspects of his experience of the Met. Then one day, he received an unexpected visit from the police, and was stunned to hear that he'd been accused of a serious sexual assault on a 15-year-old boy whom he had arrested – twenty-eight years earlier. Perhaps not surprisingly, Virdi had no memory whatsoever of any incident, but was entirely certain he had never assaulted anyone. Nonetheless, the Met helpfully issued a press release detailing the charge, which ensured that Virdi was dropped by the Labour Party on whose behalf he was standing as a candidate in the local elections.

Since the allegation was that he had beaten and abused a minor, including inserting an extending baton into the boy's anus, Virdi was also suspended from his work with young people, and made effectively unemployable while he waited for the charge to work its way through the justice system. When eventually it came to court, the jury took less than an hour to acquit him of all charges – not least because the particular baton allegedly used in the assault had not been introduced into the Met until ten years later, and also that the police's own records proved that he had not even been the arresting officer on the occasion of the alleged assault. The then Deputy Assistant Commissioner Fiona Taylor defended the Met's actions, telling the *Guardian* that, 'Once allegations such as these were raised by the victim it was only right that we investigated them thoroughly and impartially. We presented the evidence to the CPS [Crown Prosecution Service] who decided the allegations and evidence should be heard by a jury.' In his subsequent book, *Behind the Blue Line*, Virdi makes a persuasive claim that the charge would never have been pursued by the Met but for his refusal to toe the line and remain silent about discrimination in the force.

Since the very beginning of my long career in the Met, incidents such as these involving Carol Howard and Gurpal Virdi were a constant background to my working life. On a day-to-day basis I went about my business managing very significant resources and responsibilities; I got the job done, and I went home to my family. However, there was always some controversy going on involving myself, or Shab, or one of the few BAME officers of either gender. When I look back on it now, I was always aware that we had to try harder than everyone else, had to be better prepared than those around us, because we were never going to be part of the club. There was never going to be anyone looking out for me, watching my back, in a way that sustains the majority of white, mostly middle-aged men who reach senior positions in the Met. It was a lesson I was about to learn the hard way.

CHAPTER TWENTY-ONE

'Help for Heroes'

It was a few weeks after the Olympics that I received a call from Deputy Assistant Commissioner (DAC) Mark Simmons to give me the good news that I was to be appointed as one of two superintendents at Greenwich. I would be reporting to Detective Chief Superintendent (DCS) Richard Wood and would start work there 'on Monday week'. I was delighted at the prospect of a return to front-line policing and began to look forward to a fresh start in a new place. However, when a week went by and I'd heard nothing further, I called DCS Wood to enquire about my responsibilities. I was surprised by his response.

'You're not coming here,' he told me. 'There's been a mistake.' When I enquired about the nature of the mistake, Wood replied: 'I've re-organized and I don't need you.' Later, he would claim that this re-organization was nothing to do with me, and that he'd voluntarily reduced his own establishment by one superintendent to streamline management. Not only was this not within his authority to do, but it fails to explain why my appointment replaced a previous incumbent, and the role was re-filled after I'd left.

Naturally, I reverted to DAC Mark Simmons, who said I should ignore what Wood had told me. He confirmed my appointment at Greenwich and told me to turn up there on the following Monday as arranged. When I arrived, armed with my pot plants to cheer up my new office, Richard Wood repeated that he neither needed nor wanted me on his staff, and that I hadn't been allocated an office.

I was now faced with a dilemma. I'd been instructed by the DAC to report to Greenwich as one of Richard Wood's two superintendents, but the man I was supposed to be reporting to was saying he had no role for me. Immediately, I realized that if I turned and went away or found it necessary to call on Simmons to back me up, I would forfeit any chance I might ever have of establishing my own authority in the borough. Looking around the management floor, I saw straight away that there were four offices next to each other which were intended for the senior leadership team, two of which were clearly designated for the two superintendents. On this Monday morning, however, one of them was still occupied by the chief inspector, Mike Balcombe, and he was showing no sign of moving. There were some moments of embarrassment, and then someone suggested that I should find a space on a lower floor which was allocated to more junior ranks.

I knew this was a moment of truth. If I collected up my belongings and headed to the floor below, I would never be taken seriously in the future. I took a deep breath and issued a direct order to Balcombe to vacate his office immediately. Then, leaving my pot plants on the window ledge, I went for a walk.

Out in the street, stressed and destabilized, I was physically shaking as I called my husband Rod. What should I do if I returned to find that no-one had moved? 'Stay calm and keep your nerve,' he advised. 'If you have to revert to Mark Simmons now, you'll never live it down.' I agreed and waited an hour before returning to the fifth floor where I found that Mike Balcombe had vacated the middle office. Mike would later turn out to be a great friend and supporter to me, but for the moment I'd won a small victory and my pot plants had a new home.

So now I was nominally one of two superintendents in the borough of Greenwich, but had to find a way to fit into a structure created by a boss who had openly made me unwelcome and declared that he had no use for me. It was clear that Richard Wood had been ordered to take me into his establishment against his wishes, and appeared to show no motivation to make my appointment a success. In the following days and weeks, it seemed to me that most of the appropriate tasks were being allocated to the other superintendent, Chris Hafford. Thickset, of stocky build, with thinning but close-cropped hair, Wood and Hafford even appeared to have been cast from the same mould. Meanwhile, I was asked to take on what I regarded as a hotchpotch of miscellaneous tasks, many of them relatively menial, and which scarcely seemed to add together to form an

identifiable job. There had been a spate of thefts of mobile
phones, for example, and I was put in charge of coordinating
efforts to combat the crime. The borough had relationships
with a number of outside groups, which made contributions
to police resources for specific tasks; I was asked to ensure
that all these complied with regulations, while Superintendent
Hafford remained in charge of both Operations and CID.

The closest I got to operational policing was when I was
duty superintendent overnight, and one particularly harrowing
incident began with the report of a young man collapsed at
a bus stop near Shooters Hill. When I arrived at the scene,
I learned that the boy had been lying on the pavement for
perhaps an hour while pedestrians had walked by and cars
had driven beside him. It was later discovered that four buses
had come and gone while he'd been prostrate on the ground.
I arrived with my driver at the same time as an ambulance,
and we blocked the road while four medics tried to revive
the young man. Eventually, though, he was taken to hospital
where he was pronounced dead, with the likely cause being
simple heart failure.

It fell to me to identify the young man and to track down his
family. The only clue was a name tag in his rucksack labelled
McDonalds, so I went to the local branch at Greenwich where
they recognized his photograph and were able to provide the
young man's address. He lived, it turned out, in a block of flats
just a few yards from where he had lain dying and unattended
for an hour earlier that same evening. All I could think of was
that his parents were probably at home, watching the TV

or having their dinner, entirely unaware that their son was laying outside in the street just a short distance away. It was yet another of the tragedies which were becoming increasingly commonplace. I remember that he had these round lenses in his glasses. We were told that he'd been working evenings to save up money to put himself through college. Even today, many years later, I still well up in tears if I have to relate this story. I guess I'm thinking of my own son and how he's out and about in the same sort of way.

Among the more important duties assigned to me in the course of my day job was to review the role of part-time staff in the department. It was something I felt keen to support, not least because a liberal policy on flexible working tended to remove some of the barriers standing in the way of women and ethnic minorities. I was dismayed when the responsible officer from Human Resources told me that Richard Wood was opposed to part-time workers and wanted to reduce or abolish their presence on his team. When it started to become clear that my report was going to recommend an increased role for part-timers, I began to receive increasingly panicky phone calls at home from this officer, warning that Wood was likely to be furious. Undeterred, and knowing I'd likely have to face the consequences, I stuck to my guns.

While I was determined to make the best of my situation, I struggled to understand why I found myself in such a disadvantageous position compared with Chris Hafford, who was my colleague of equivalent rank, but remained in charge of the key crime-related departments. There was no reason to suspect that what I was experiencing was due to racism; more likely it was that officers like me simply didn't fit in with the male-dominated culture and infrastructure which had run the Met for such a long time.

This homogeneous culture was recognized and well understood by my husband Rod, who'd risen through the entire career structure of the Met, retiring – after thirty years' service – as a deputy assistant commissioner. He had seen it all, and was a constant and good sounding board, always able to remind me of who I am and what I was trying to achieve.

Following the end of his long and distinguished career in the Met, Rod had set up a new company specializing in training individuals in leadership skills, and targeted at police forces at home and internationally. When the new company was established in 2010, he needed to appoint directors, so, in common with thousands of people who invite their partners to join the board of a new company, he invited me to join as a non-executive. After all, my experience was entirely relevant and complementary, and I would be a useful source of advice.

Naturally, a police officer is obliged to register and obtain approval for any such outside appointment, simply to ensure that no conflict of interest arises. In this case, the aims of the new company were entirely compatible with those of the Met, and so official approval for me to join the board was freely given. All went well, and Rod's business began to prosper.

However, officers are obliged to renew such approvals regularly, and I was surprised when my new boss at Greenwich,

Richard Wood, decided to raise a question about my role in my husband's company. The matter was accordingly referred to a higher authority, and again my appointment as a non-executive director was approved. That might have been the end of it; however, sometime shortly afterwards, I received a call from the New Scotland Yard press office to tell me about an enquiry from a journalist about my role in my husband's company and asking whether it was compatible with my duties as a senior officer. I have no reason to suspect that Richard Wood was responsible for the leak, and he vehemently denies it.

Notwithstanding the source, there followed what turned into a regular series of reports in various newspapers, in which my directorship was questioned. The latest selection appeared as recently as February 2017 and included the *Daily Mail* online, where the reporter claimed something resembling a scoop.

A senior officer in the Metropolitan Police has been unveiled as the co-director of a private police training company, despite strict guidelines concerning outside business interests.

Parm Sandhu, borough commander of Richmond Upon Thames and the highest ranking Asian woman in the Met, is co-director of Rod Jarman Associates (RJA), which 'provides advice, training and development to all aspects of policing and community safety' . . .

When asked about Parm Sandhu's role with RJA, the Met said her interests had been 'registered'.

The *Mail* went on to elaborate with a quote from a peer who clearly knew nothing about my particular situation:

Baroness Jones of Moulsecoomb, a former member of the Metropolitan Police Authority, said: 'It is appalling that a senior officer has outside interests that appear to breach the Met's own rules. The Yard needs to conduct an urgent review to see how this was allowed to happen.'

What the report failed to mention was that the position had been registered in line with regulations the moment it had first arisen, and had been approved a number of times since. It had scarcely been 'unveiled' because it had never been secret. Once again, though, I found myself on the receiving end of adverse publicity, and the inevitable resulting rumour and whispering campaign, for an allegation which had no merit whatsoever.

Day in day out, throughout my time at Greenwich, I felt ignored, devalued and excluded from most of the important decision-making in the running of the borough. But it wasn't just me. Several of the other women in the team also experienced a constant pressure to be seen to perform in a world where the rules were made up and enforced by men. All this meant that, when my younger sister was diagnosed with a serious medical condition and needed some support, my heart sank at the prospect of having to seek some flexibility in my pattern of work. I should add that my sister lived with me during this period, was single, and was also a Metropolitan Police Service employee. Nonetheless, I was refused permission to accompany her for her treatment and on one occasion I was even made

Receiving the Asian Woman of Achievement award from Sophie Raworth.

(Left) Remembering Shafilea Ahmed.

Happy Birthday Shafilea

14 July 1986 - 11 Sept 2003

(Below) Meeting his Holiness at St Mary's in Richmond.

(Left) Carol Howard, the ideal BAME poster girl for the Olympics.

(Below) With Anthony Joshua at the 2012 London Olympics. I met him through my role as Olympic planning manager.

Policing a demo by cyclists outside the 2012 London Olympics; maybe not the best use of the thin blue line.

Richard Wood.

Chris Hafford.

Commissioner Bernard Hogan-Howe liked to be in amongst the action.

Being interviewed by local TV after taking over at Twickenham.

Meeting Prince William at Hendon.

With Superintendents Shabnam Chaudhri and Nusritt Mehtab.
By 2019 all three of us had been under investigation.

Left to right: former Commander John Grieve, who founded the Diversity Directorate and investigated police corruption in the murder of Stephen Lawrence and in Northern Ireland; Stephen Lawrence's father Neville; me; John Azah from the Kingston Racial equality Council, who gave powerful evidence to the Home Affairs Select Committee about discrimination against BAME officers in disciplinary proceedings.

Me, Doreen Lawrence and Cressida Dick, the first female commissioner, who says the Met is no longer institutionally racist.

With my friend Daisy Reid, Cressida Dick and Rod
at my retirement from the Met.

With Rod and Emil on my last day in the Met.

to attend a meeting to which other boroughs had sent more junior members of staff, meaning I was unable to be there to support my sister as a result.

In that part of my time at Greenwich, when I was allowed to get on with matters to do with solving crimes, I turned my attention to a new phenomenon that police forces began referring to as 'county lines'. The idea had been dreamed up by drug gangs with a view to extending their territory for dealing, while eluding the police and without necessarily clashing with rival gangs.

We first learned about it because bright young kids from good families and prosperous backgrounds were being reported missing. They'd turn up after a few days, sometimes with an unexplained sum of money in their pockets, and often too terrified to say where they'd been or what had happened to them.

It turned out that local drug gangs had been selecting young teenagers who looked like anything but a drug dealer. Sometimes they would be promised an adventure and some easy money, and other times they'd be promised a beating. In either case, the victim would be taken and driven to another town many miles away and introduced to a hard-up local person who was in some way vulnerable or with special needs. The local person would usually have no idea what was happening but would be told they could earn some money for keeping quiet while their house was used for a few days. Their newly arrived young guest would be given a 'burner' phone – one not traceable to a particular owner – and told to field calls from local drug users. Callers would collect their purchases at this new address, and by the time the neighbours complained, or the local police were alerted, the scam had moved on to somewhere else.

The result was that we had all these parents who were worried sick, having no idea where their children had gone for days on end. The problem was that, when the kids turned up apparently unharmed after a few days, there was often no direct evidence that a crime had been committed at all.

We had to wait for another five years, until October 2018, to get our first conviction for a county lines offence. Zakaria Mohammed, 21, from Birmingham was convicted under the Modern Slavery Act after he was found to have exploited two 15-year-old boys the previous January. They had gone missing but were eventually found shivering in a squalid flat in Lincoln. Mohammed was given a prison sentence of fourteen years.

Meanwhile, it was six years since I'd been part of Operation Gamble, the investigation set up in response to a rumour that radical Islamists were planning to capture and behead a member of the police or another uniformed service. At that time, the nightmare had been averted, but on Wednesday 22 May 2013, at 2.20 in the afternoon, it became a reality.

I was the superintendent on duty in the police control room at Charlton in southeast London when a flurry of 999 emergency calls came in at the same time. Some reported that there'd been a serious incident at John Wilson Street in Greenwich, and others spoke of a man having been beheaded and lying on the road.

When something like that happens, you don't really believe what you're hearing. Despite the warnings we'd been getting on and off for several years, the idea of someone having their head cut off on the streets of London was way outside anything we could ever have expected. And yet here we were. Two officers wearing civilian clothes were close by the area, so they were quickly sent directly to the scene. I asked for pictures from local CCTV, and after a short while a screen showing the feed from a camera in Artillery Place flickered into life.

The monitor showed blurred images of two black men walking around in the road, apparently carrying large knives or machetes, and talking to passers-by. Instantly, a call was sent out to Specialist Firearms Command for an armed response unit – Trojan – to attend. Within three minutes of the first call, the two plain-clothes officers were on the scene and reporting in on their mobile phones. They described a man lying in the road in a pool of blood, and said that the two attackers were still walking around holding huge knives. No-one was tackling them, but nor did they appear to be threatening anyone else.

At that moment, we had a vital decision to make. Whether to send in these two unarmed officers to tackle the two men and try to carry out an arrest, or wait for the arrival of the specialist armed unit which was on its way. As there seemed to be no immediate danger to anyone else at the scene, it was decided to wait. The tension was dreadful as minutes ticked by.

Unknown to us at the time, the two attackers were explaining to passers-by their reasons for deliberately driving their car into an unarmed man, and running him down in the street. Witnesses said later that they'd assumed the collision had been accidental, and that the driver and passenger had left the vehicle to help the injured man. They were, of course, then horrified to see them set about hacking him to death with knives and a machete.

When the immediate butchery had stopped, three brave women went to the bleeding man to see whether they could assist, but it was instantly obvious that he was way beyond help. A former schoolteacher, Ingrid Loyau-Kennett, spoke to one of the attackers and asked the reason for the assault. One of them, later named as Michael Adebolajo, seemed to be more concerned about offending the sensibilities of onlookers than for his victim. He told a passer-by, 'I apologize that women had to witness this today, but in our land women have to witness the same.'

In our control room, the seconds were ticking down towards the arrival of the Trojan unit, but to me the whole thing seemed to be going on endlessly. We could see that various members of the public were gathering to look, while amazingly others seemed to be walking by as though nothing had happened. At one point, an ambulance drove towards the injured man and swerved round him when the two armed suspects were seen standing nearby. It was clear that the two attackers might have had the opportunity to attempt an escape, but showed no intention of doing so.

Just minutes after the initial 999 call, the first Trojan unit carrying three officers arrived at the scene. Videos shot by various witnesses show the two attackers appearing to split up, and Adebolajo is seen to run directly at their BMW car, wielding a large knife. The car draws to a halt, but Adebolajo is within a few feet of it before the marksmen are able to get out. An officer in the back of the car fires two shots from a machine gun and the attacker collapses in the road. Moments later, the other attacker – Michael Adebowale – also runs along the pavement, apparently aiming a handgun at police. Four more shots ring out and he too collapses to the floor. However, both men are still moving, and two more shots are fired in quick succession as they lay on the ground. I was among a group of officers witnessing this in fragments as it unfolded at the scene, and it was of course one of the most dramatic and traumatic moments of my professional life.

With the imminent danger apparently over, the immediate task was to attend to the victim, but again, it was instantly clear that nothing could be done. The next challenge was to identify him, but officers were instructed not to search his pockets for fear of disturbing any forensics. The only clue was that the victim was wearing a 'Help for Heroes' T-shirt and a backpack, and so we sent officers to the local barracks to ask if anyone was unaccounted for. The question was asked, 'What colour is he?', but his injuries were so appalling that it wasn't possible to give a positive answer. In the end it was a distinctive watch on the man's wrist that confirmed his identity.

Lee Rigby had been a drummer in the Royal Artillery based at Woolwich, a former machine-gunner in Afghanistan, whose fate had been sealed because he was walking close to the barracks and was wearing the distinctive T-shirt.

The natural thing for the chief superintendent to do in the immediate aftermath of the incident might have been to call me – the duty superintendent with a relevant background in both riot control and the National Community Tension Team – to manage the scene. Instead, Richard Wood ordered me to remain where I was in the control room while he attended the scene with his preferred deputy, Chris Hafford. Junior colleagues around me in the control room registered surprise that our senior officer had gone to the scene at all, and suggested that – if he'd been determined to do so – he should have been accompanied by me as the duty superintendent. I was embarrassed and felt it was another example of gender discrimination against me, but this was hardly a moment to be making a fuss about status.

The incident caused an instant and understandable swell of horror and outrage among the local community, and we were put on alert for vigilante actions or reprisals. These fears were justified. Very quickly, the English Defence League (EDL) swamped the area, trying to take advantage of the situation, and organized marches and demonstrations against Muslims. The next day, in Woolwich market, some thugs ripped a burka from a woman out shopping and slapped her face. I was among senior officers called upon to organize and chair community meetings to try to calm the local Muslim population and others who were feeling vulnerable. Rumours began to spread that another uniformed person might be targeted, and police, army and cadets were all told not to wear their uniform off duty or to and from their stations.

Lee Rigby came from Rochdale, where his family was understandably devastated by his violent death. Unfortunately, an already appalling situation was made even more difficult for the police by what turned into a confusion over his next of kin. It transpired that one year before his murder, Lee had separated from his wife Rebecca, leaving her with their 2-year-old son Jack. He was now engaged to another woman, Aimee West, who was also in the army and currently serving in Afghanistan. However, Lee had not changed his will, and so the army and police had no choice but to deal only with his wife, who thus received all the public sympathy and all the compensation.

When something like this happens, you inevitably get caught up in dealing with the unfolding events. It's too late to prevent the initial tragedy, and you are focused on minimizing any further risk to the public or your own officers. It's only afterwards that your mind goes over the real horror of what's occurred, and then all of us have to learn to deal with it in our own way. For me, I try to work as hard as I can to keep whatever happens in my professional life completely separate from my private and family life. Whenever I've failed to do that – and find myself reflecting that what I've seen happen to someone else's family could just as easily happen to mine – well, that way madness lies. If I allowed those thoughts to spread and fester, I wouldn't be able to do my job. So I take on board the dreadful things that regularly happen, I do whatever I can to learn from them, and then they find their place in accumulated experience and I try to move forward. I won't say I always succeed, but it's the only way I know how to do it.

CHAPTER TWENTY-TWO

'He went berserk!'

Although I felt very strongly that the responsibilities I'd been allocated at Greenwich were not always commensurate with the seniority of my superintendent rank, I was determined to ensure that I discharged my duties with diligence and professionalism. One of these duties was to check over and sign off what was known as a 'directed surveillance authority', which required particularly careful judgement and handling. These are highly sensitive and secret operations in which detectives are authorized to carry out invasive electronic and other surveillance on a suspect. Requests for such authority need to fulfil a wide range of criteria, and regulations require that they should be approved individually by an officer of superintendent rank or above who has also received specific training.

On 11 September 2013, such a request came in from Sergeant Sohrab Peerbaccus, who was leading an investigation into a series of hi-jackings that had been carried out by members of the travelling community on lorries delivering to wholesale warehouses in the Charlton area. In one incident, a driver had attempted to tackle the raiders and had been run over in the getaway and killed. Two individuals were suspected of the crime, and authorization was needed to install surveillance and listening equipment to monitor their conversations.

I went through all the details with Sergeant Peerbaccus, assuring myself that the request fitted all the necessary criteria, and then I approved and signed it off.

Next day, I was out of the office at a Crime Fighters meeting when I received a message to call Sergeant Peerbaccus. When I did, he said he needed approval for an amendment to the authority that had been agreed the day before. I offered to go through it with him, but he replied that there was no need, as the matter was being dealt with. When I enquired how this could be so, Peerbaccus explained that, in my absence, he had contacted Mark Gilchrist, who was Richard Wood's staff officer. Gilchrist had undertaken to arrange for an approval of the amendment.

I knew that DCS Wood was away on a specialist training course in Scotland, designed to get him through his third attempt at further promotion to the most senior ranks in the Met. I was therefore alarmed at the possibility that Gilchrist might be planning to issue the authority himself. In addition, I also understood that – even had he been present – my senior officer had not received training in some important recent amendments to the approvals procedure. I immediately called Gilchrist's office and left an instruction that he must not give the approval, and went in search of a computer with compatible software to enable me to go through the request myself. I was then able to review the proposed amendment and sign it off.

There the matter might have ended, except that I was concerned about what might have been a serious breach of the law. Directed surveillance authorities were comparatively rare and always sensitive, and there could have been trouble for all of us if procedures were not followed to the letter. The email from Peerbaccus to Gilchrist seeking authorization was headed 'for you', with the possible inference that Wood had delegated this particular authority to Gilchrist – which would have put them both in breach of the rules. Nevertheless, I was well aware that anyone who complained to or about a senior officer could quickly be regarded as a troublemaker or someone with 'attitude', so I decided to seek advice from my personal mentor, who was at that time the chief constable of Derbyshire, Mick Creedon. Mick told me that the incident could well have involved a breach of the law of the land, and that to remain silent about it might make me complicit. I had no choice, he said, but to follow up the matter.

Even at this point, rather than follow the letter of the rulebook and refer the matter directly to Professional Standards for formal investigation, I preferred to try a more collegiate approach. The following Monday was DCS Wood's first day back in the office, so I deliberately arrived at work early so few other colleagues would be around. When I went in to see him and reported my concerns, I entirely expected him to share my worry and simply clarify the situation with Gilchrist, or indeed anyone else involved in the approvals process. Instead, his reaction was rather different. He went berserk.

I was utterly taken aback when he started shouting at me. He asked me, who did I think I was. Was I accusing him of delegating authority improperly? Detective Chief Superintendent Wood found it totally unacceptable that I would challenge the conduct of a senior officer. He was shouting and pointing his finger at me, and at one point I believed he had lost control completely. I genuinely believed I might be violently assaulted. I asked him if I could leave the room and he specifically forbade it, telling me I could leave when he said I could. The door was closed, preventing me from going, and I felt bullied and harassed and terrified.

In and among what felt like uncontrolled ranting, Wood managed to say that he was allowed to delegate authority if he wanted to. Although I felt intimidated and overwhelmed by his overbearing manner, I did manage to summon up the courage to tell him that he wasn't. At this point, Wood called Gilchrist into the office and asked him about the authorization request. Gilchrist denied that he'd intended to authorize the application himself, and said he'd planned to find me or, failing that, would have tried to contact Wood by telephone.

Wood was still incandescent and told me I was going to be investigated. When he finally allowed me to go, I returned to my office and, against all my usual determination and practice, I burst into tears. What had just happened? What on earth had I done to provoke such a reaction? While my relationship with Richard Wood had been strained from the beginning, I instantly knew that it had entered a whole new phase, and there could be no going back. After a few minutes, and as soon as I could calm down enough to trust myself, I called my husband Rod. He had never heard me this distressed at work and was concerned. When I managed to talk him through the headlines, he cautioned me that Wood would be likely to deny my account of the meeting, and that I should immediately make a careful and detailed note of events. I hung up the phone and did exactly that, and, indeed, Wood has consistently maintained that the meeting was calm and businesslike.

Instead of referring the matter to the Directorate of Professional Standards which would be likely to carry out an objective inquiry, Wood and his boss, Deputy Assistant Commissioner Simon Letchford, asked Chief Superintendent Stephanie Roberts from the nearby borough of Bromley to investigate. At the time, I had no reason to believe the inquiry would be anything other than fair, and so it was with an open mind that I agreed to go to an interview with Roberts. The facts were straightforward; I had taken the only action available to me if the force was to live by the letter of the law. Several weeks later, Richard Wood called me into his office.

'The inquiry has reported, and its findings don't reflect very well on you,' he told me.

Naturally, I wondered how this could be. I asked to see Roberts' report, but Wood refused to show it to me. Instead, he repeated that it did not reflect well on me and told me I needed to apologize to Mark Gilchrist, who was 'very upset that his integrity had been called into question'.

Some years later, I managed to obtain a copy of Stephanie Roberts' report, which states her intention to interview everyone involved in the incident, but includes no record of any interview she might have conducted with Richard Wood. Nonetheless, it states, 'I have spoken to all identified parties in this report and I cannot find any evidence to support wrongdoing'.

It was impossible not to feel that I'd been undermined and any authority which might have accrued to me as superintendent in the borough had evaporated. Even worse than that, I'd been perceived to have made a complaint about a senior officer, an action that had proven to be an unforgiveable sin in so many other instances. I had crossed a line and, although of course I didn't realize it at the time, my professional life would never be quite the same again.

Now desperate to remove myself from a situation in which I felt bullied and under-valued, I decided to apply for further promotion, so I compiled a detailed record of my work during my time at Greenwich. Notwithstanding the fact that I'd had to cobble together a coherent role out of the various tasks assigned to me, the account reads as a substantial compendium of tasks and achievements. However, when it comes to the end section in which my line manager is required to comment on my account, Richard Wood takes the opportunity to make further criticisms: 'She was given opportunities to deputise for me although she did not maximise these which could have been influenced by some personal difficulties she experienced at the time.' I can only imagine that the 'personal difficulties' referred to were that I had asked for six days off in order to accompany my sister for her medical treatment. Wood later denied that he had ever refused permission for me to take the time off.

As if all that wasn't sufficiently helpful to anyone considering whether to employ me in a new role, Wood hadn't quite finished. 'In terms of the evidence she provides on this form much of this was not activity driven by her but by other SLT members. She would benefit from ensuring she takes personal responsibility for issues by providing guidance and leadership as opposed to merely delegating issues to junior officers.'

Now I felt that my career was at a crossroads. While my progress up to the rank of chief inspector had not been without hurdles and the occasional tripwire, I now began to feel the force of a more systematic determination to undermine me. The obstacles put in my way were no longer merely matters of ignorance or casual spite; it seemed as though there was something in the fabric of the force that was out to thwart any further progress.

I genuinely had not the slightest idea why Richard Wood took against me from the very beginning. I specifically do not accuse him of being racist. I can only imagine that I had not been his choice at the outset, and therefore he felt little if any obligation to make a success of my appointment. With the bad feeling that followed my complaint and the inquiry now poisoning the atmosphere, I felt I had no choice but to ask DAC Mark Simmons to lift me out of my role in Greenwich.

To his credit, Mark Simmons understood my predicament, and could probably guess at the reason it had come about. He had overruled Wood from the very moment of my appointment as a superintendent at Greenwich. His authority had been enough to enforce the placing; what he could not do was to ensure I received a welcome or a chance to prove myself.

CHAPTER TWENTY-THREE

'Belittle, intimidate and bully'

I considered myself especially fortunate to have as my mentor the chief constable of Derbyshire, Mick Creedon. Mick was among those senior officers who recognized the serious problem caused by under-representation of black and Asian officers in the police, and he often said he regarded me as an important role model. He was therefore dismayed when he learned what had happened at Greenwich, and he quickly undertook to find some way to keep me in the force.

With his help, I was eventually reassigned to Her Majesty's Inspectorate of Constabulary (HMIC) as a staff officer working for Zoë Billingham, at the time HM Inspector of Constabulary and latterly also of Fire & Rescue Services. The Inspectorate describes its role as making independent assessments of police forces and policing; according to its website, the Inspectorate asks 'the questions that citizens would ask' and publishes 'authoritative information to allow the public to compare the performance of their police force . . . against others'.

The first day in my new job felt like arriving at a place of safety, after all my recent tribulations. I had been made to feel like a lame duck, and had lost so much confidence. Zoë Billingham spent the first hour with me, outlining the way the department worked and my duties within it. Suddenly I remembered what working in a well-run and professional outfit should be like. We were to have regular one-to-ones, which were not rescheduled or cancelled at the last minute. The senior team was collaborative and shared a sense of purpose, just as you'd hope any serious place of work would. It was refreshing and restorative.

The day-to-day work of HMIC involved carrying out regular inspections of all forty-three forces against a range of criteria, and then producing an order of ranking in each category. I occasionally travelled with my new boss to assist. Zoë's watchwords were always 'no surprises'. She would be upfront about any problems, stating them clearly there and then, so that her opinions could be questioned at the time if necessary. She didn't want to carry out the inspections and write up a report, which the force in question would then read, question and resent long after she'd gone home.

Zoë Billingham may have inherited her good sense and forcefulness from her mother, Labour MEP (later Baroness) Angela Billingham, and indeed may have been influenced in her frankness by her father-in-law, that veteran scourge of government of every hue, Dennis Skinner. In either case, I remember Zoë as one of the most impressive people I ever worked for.

I had been assisting Zoë in HMIC for only a few months when, in August 2014, Mark Simmons telephoned my home at 10 p.m. one night and asked if I would like to be deputy area commander at Bromley. Simmons said that if I took the role, he'd recommend that I be promoted to chief superintendent.

I was naturally excited, and I only had one misgiving – but it was a big one. I would be reporting to Chief Superintendent Chris Hafford, who'd previously been deputy to my old *bête noire* Richard Wood. I knew that the two men were close and I was concerned that Hafford might bring with him some of the hostility I'd felt from Wood. I also had to take into consideration that Zoë Billingham was keen for me to remain at HMIC, where I was developing a range of strategic skills. She kindly asked me to stay, and also asked if I really thought it was wise to go back into the fray of daily policing so soon. But I knew that staying away from an operational role for too long would damage my chances of further promotion, so in the end I accepted the job in Bromley.

My misgiving proved to be justified, even before I took up my new posting. In the days before I was due to start work, Hafford sent me a copy of an advertisement for the role of staff officer to the Commissioner with an accompanying note stating, 'Do you fancy this?' I declined to apply for the alternative job. Then, I received a second message from Hafford telling me that he would be on holiday when I arrived, but that I should report to Chief Inspector Pete Turner, who was acting up during his absence. I felt that requiring me to report to an officer two ranks below me was a deliberate attempt to humiliate. The Met would later insist that Turner's local knowledge and previous experience acting up in the borough made him a natural choice to deputize while Hafford was away.

It was an inauspicious beginning but, despite my initial concerns, I was determined to throw myself into the senior management of the borough. My new job involved leading a team of three chief inspectors and 600 staff, chairing committees involving outside institutions and managing huge resources. My list of activities reads like a blizzard of acronyms, targets and policies, but one that did make a genuine impact in the real world of crime detection and conviction was a pilot project with officers adopting body-worn video cameras.

The use of these personalized cameras has been surrounded by controversy since they were first introduced, raising as it does questions of practicality, and concerns over privacy and ethics, among others. However, supporters of their use point to the reduction in complaints against the police, as well as the many occasions when having the camera as an objective witness has served the interests of justice more easily than more compromised witnesses were able to.

One case involved in the pilot project was that of a woman who'd been given shelter in a safe house because her violent husband was due to be released from prison. At midnight on the day of release, a 999 call was received from the woman but, due to some confusion about the address, police eventually arrived at the house some hours later. Officers equipped with personal body cameras were horrified to find the woman bleeding from the mouth and with several missing teeth; her leg appeared to have been broken and – unbelievably – an attempt had been made to scalp her. The man was, of course, arrested, but later the woman declined to give evidence against her husband.

It sounds amazing when you hear that. People often wonder how a woman can refuse to give evidence after such an appalling attack, but the answer is depressingly simple. She will have been terrified that if she helped us to put him in jail, he'd eventually get out, and when that happened, he would come round again and kill her.

In most circumstances, the police would have had no choice but to withdraw the prosecution, but in this case the evidence was there for all to see on the recordings from the body cameras. Indeed, my boss Chris Hafford later took the opportunity to boast of the success of the body-worn camera pilot in the Bromley Borough Commander's Newsletter from April 2015:

This month saw Bromley officers secure the first body-worn video (only) successful trial in London. The officers from my Community Safety Unit worked tirelessly to secure the first conviction based only on the evidence of body-worn video. The suspect had a long domestic abuse history and his various victims, including our one, were unwilling to support a prosecution. Working closely with the CPS prosecutions, Met Prosecutions, staff at Bromley Mags and the BWV [body-worn video] programme team, the contested trial went ahead, and the defendant was found guilty and sentenced to six months imprisonment.

The feedback regarding the initial investigation, victim care and trial preparation was excellent and I'm confident we will learn valuable lessons from this investigation to help future victims.

I was proud of my role in the project – and probably wrong to have hoped to receive any of the credit.

Alongside the comprehensive programme of administration and management which always goes with these senior roles, I also remained determined to use my personal knowledge and experience to advance some of the causes I continued to support and believe in. While there were always limits on what I could achieve for the Women's Interfaith Network as a lowly PC, sergeant or even inspector, this was exactly the kind of 'above and beyond the call of duty' activity that my new more senior rank made possible.

I also gave support, in my own time, to the Sharan Project, founded by Polly Harrar, a charity which supports women at risk, especially from honour-based abuse. I got further stuck into my work as the Met's lead officer in coordinating policy on honour-based crime, chairing a bi-monthly meeting involving the Home Office, the Foreign and Commonwealth Office, the NHS, Ofsted and the Royal College of Midwives, where policy on everything from enforced marriages to female genital mutilation (FGM) is coordinated. I was the London lead on FGM, undertaking a range of activities designed to educate and eventually to reduce the incidence of this terrible crime. Over the following years, there would be many attempts to bring a successful prosecution against one of the parents or medical staff involved in carrying out these procedures, but at that time the first successful guilty verdict was still several years away.

However, while my voluntary activities were going well, the opposite was the case in my full-time job at Bromley. Exactly as I had feared, and exactly as had been the case in Greenwich, I felt from day one that I was unable to do a thing right in the eyes of my boss. It seemed to me that every possible opportunity was taken to belittle, intimidate and bully me.

A typical example occurred when a young officer whom we'll call Barbara Brown had been working for a year in an acting role. She had been doing very good work and, as her line manager, I had assured her that when the vacancy eventually came up, she would be given the job. However, when I returned to work after a weekend off, I was told that Chris Hafford had reversed my decision and given the job to someone else. 'Well, you weren't here,' I was told. The Met would later argue that Hafford was my line manager and that it was by no means unusual for a senior officer to countermand decisions made by their juniors.

What I was now experiencing as a hostile work environment obliged me to think about every decision I made in the context of how it would be viewed by the male officers I believed were seeking to undermine me. So, when I was approached by Barbara Brown and a colleague we'll call Jennifer Scott to support their complaints about bullying and gender discrimination, I knew my response would provide another defining moment in my career. Jennifer's allegation of bullying by a particular officer ended in a heartfelt cry for help, which felt all too familiar:

> [The named officer] . . . has ruined my life for almost two years. I am aware that I was coming home from work and shouting at my children. I had resorted to drinking alcohol every night in order to cope. I was also struggling to sleep every night through worry. This has had a devastating effect on me but the tablets are assisting with getting me back to a happy place.

Once again, I had a difficult decision to make: I could stand by what I had seen and experienced and give truthful evidence, which would no doubt lead to my further isolation from the male-dominated team running the borough, or I could take the easier route and decline to support the female officers and hope for a quieter life. On 20 August 2015, I was interviewed by the 'fairness at work' officer, who minuted my answers as follows:

> I spoke the truth about how negatively the female officers were being treated. I stated that as a woman and even as a female superintendent I could not pull rank to make decisions. I said that Bromley was an awful environment for a woman to work. I also stated that this discrimination extended past Bromley. The blame for the issue at Bromley affecting those female officers was a sexist clique.

Subsequently, I was summoned by DAC Simon Letchford and admonished for my action in supporting the two women. I could not have demonstrated any more clearly that I was not 'one of them', and the battle lines were being drawn.

Eventually, just six months after my move to Bromley, on 5 February 2015, Hafford sent a densely typed three-and-a-half-page memo, which included what I felt was a highly critical assessment of my performance. It begins:

> I'm aware that I have a very full day tomorrow including a trip to NSY [New Scotland Yard], so thought I would spend some time this evening setting out my thoughts on your development plan. Clearly these are my thoughts only, and although we have had two discussions this week, we haven't had the opportunity to finalise and are [sic] your development plan.

The report was rambling and in places scarcely comprehensible, but the Met would later deny that it was in any way hostile or intended as anything other than constructive.

But I had had enough. I felt I'd been undermined by senior officers at Greenwich, and then had to endure the same thing after my transfer to Bromley. As far as I could tell, it was yet another case of the old-boy network closing ranks against someone who didn't fit their stereotype copper. For more than twenty-five years, I had been determined to overcome whatever obstacles the force could throw at me. Time and again, I had needed to call upon the resolve I'd shared with

Shab when we were both probationers all those years ago at
Hendon – don't let the bastards grind you down. But now, after
a harsh and concentrated two years of feeling systematically
under-valued, slighted, humiliated and ground down, my
determination was slipping. I went on sick leave, and such
was my desperation that I also took the unprecedented step
of emailing the commissioner, Bernard Hogan-Howe. The
subject of my email was 'Staff in confidence'.

Dear Commissioner
I am taking the unusual action of writing directly to you
as I believe no one in the organisation is listening to me.
As you may know I am currently sick with stress, this
is my first period of sickness absence in over 20 years.

I feel it is important that you are aware that this is the
end result of nearly two years of bullying which has
occurred after I raised an incident of wrongdoing with
my then line manager. I have worked to manage this and
to carry on with my role but this is no longer possible as
I have been subject to a series of undermining briefings
and actions. The final straw being my recent referral to
Occupational Health which is inaccurate, suggests I am
only sick due to not getting through promotion processes
and indicates a lack of care.

I believe my position in TP [Territorial Policing] is now
untenable and have requested a managed move which

has not happened. I therefore feel there is no place for me in the organisation and, with great regret, I am taking advice on what action I can take to protect myself.

Parm Sandhu

I did not receive a reply.

As it happened, this crisis in my career coincided with my father becoming seriously ill, and I was glad to be able to have some time to nurse him in what would turn out to be the final months of his life. He'd been in and out of various institutions for treatment of his depression, and for many years I'd been missing the man I'd known when I was growing up. In the hours between taking care of my father and mother when they most needed me, I reflected on my current situation and my own future. For much of my career, I'd found the work tough but satisfying. My varied postings in operational and administrative roles had given me a wide breadth of knowledge, which could of course be useful to me in the private sector. A future outside the force for someone of my background and experience could be an attractive one, not least because my husband Rod was still building his new business. On the other hand, I still felt strongly that my role in providing a model for younger women, especially from minority backgrounds, was an important one. There were few enough Asian women in the higher ranks of the Met as it was: if I also threw in the towel it would represent a significant step in the wrong direction.

Meanwhile, my boss Mark Simmons remained supportive

and continued to urge me to return to work as quickly as I could. I told him I would as soon as he could find me a suitable job, but privately I thought I might sit out the next six months, for which I was entitled to full pay, and then put in my papers. Throughout my career, I had been resolute that I would reach my thirty years of uninterrupted service, but for the moment I just couldn't see a way to continue, unless there was some radical change.

When my father eventually died in July 2015, I knew his passing was a relief for him and for my mother. Nonetheless, it was still a shock when it came, and I spent many hours remembering the days of my early childhood, recalling the much younger man who'd walked with me to the library every week, who taught me to love reading even though he hardly read at all himself, and who never quite managed to feel welcome or at ease in the country he'd made his home years before I was born.

Shortly after my dad's funeral, Mark Simmons called with the offer of a job which would enable me to 'get back on the horse' if I chose to do so. The role was to throw me right into the aftermath of what arguably have been the two most traumatic and disgraceful episodes in the history of the Met.

CHAPTER TWENTY-FOUR

'Your Indian heritage'

It has become more or less accepted that the murder of Stephen Lawrence had a deeper and more enduring impact on the Metropolitan Police than any other single crime in its history. The debate throughout the force over the finding of institutional racism by the Macpherson report has remained live and vivid at all levels, and continues to cause shame in some sections, and indignation in others. The original finding arose largely as a result of the actions of officers at the scene of the crime, and then the conduct of the murder investigation that followed. The report dragged into the spotlight an ugly culture, which had been lying not far beneath the surface for several decades.

As the Met prepared its response to the publication of the Macpherson report, Michael Fuller, a senior officer of Jamaican background, was asked to explain to his white colleagues how the circumstances around the murder of Stephen Lawrence illustrated the existence of institutional racism in the force: 'It proves there's a link between prejudice in the criminal justice system and what happens to black people,' he told them. He details what he said in his memoir *Kill the Black One First:* 'They're more likely to be stopped and searched, more likely to be arrested, more likely to be convicted and their sentences tend to be harsher. Black police officers have to wait longer to be promoted, are more likely to be disciplined and their punishments are likely to be stiffer. And, of course, they're much more likely to leave the force. As for crimes with black victims, they're less likely to be solved. The statistics are all there if you want to look at them.'

Perhaps even more shocking than the situation described by Macpherson was what emerged later about the means by which the Met had sought to protect itself from criticisms arising from the investigation. Revelations that undercover officers had been tasked to infiltrate the Lawrence family in order to discredit their legitimate complaints about the lamentable police performance shocked even hardened cynics.

The Ellison Review was set up in an attempt to get to the bottom of a viper's nest of inter-tangling suspicions and rumours about corruption and establishment cover-ups of inefficiencies and worse. Among its serious criticisms of the Met was the apparent inability of the force to produce documents and files relating to complaints against individual officers.

The same complaint had also been made following the various inquiries into the brutal killing of Daniel Morgan in the car park of the Golden Lion pub in Sydenham in March 1987. Morgan was a private investigator whose business, Southern

Investigations, seems to have been a barely disguised conduit for channelling illegal payments from newspapers to corrupt police officers. It's believed that the 38-year-old was planning to blow the whistle on what he knew about corruption in the force, but – before he could – he was hit on the head several times with an axe, and found lying next to his car with the weapon buried in his face.

When set against the allegations that serving police officers were involved in this crime, had then engaged in covering it up, and before that had profited for many years from robbery and corruption on a grand scale, the sin of bad record-keeping seems to pale somewhat. However, the crime has been the subject of five large-scale inquiries and has thrown up some 750,000 individual documents, few of them computerized or searchable. The Met's apparent inability to locate files relevant to this case constituted yet another important concern for Scotland Yard's Directorate of Professional Standards.

Following the publication of the Ellison Review's report in March 2014, and judicial criticisms of record-keeping in the Morgan case, the Directorate was tasked to pull together and impose some system on the many thousands of files which had been piling up in dusty store-rooms in individual police stations all over the metropolitan area. Under the management of Deputy Assistant Commissioner Fiona Taylor, the unit set about retrieving, collating and digitizing some 150 files a week, crucially making them searchable. Where once there might have been three complaints filed in one station against an officer, and four more at their next posting, and three more at the next one after that, it would now be possible to search an officer by name and come up with all ten, with the possibility that a pattern of behaviour might be recognized and acted upon.

The Directorate of Professional Standards was spread over four floors of what was then New Scotland Yard, and had its own budget in the region of £24 million. While the days of Frank Serpico (the New York cop played by Al Pacino in the film based on his life), where officers in such a unit were openly despised, may have been no more, the unit was so secretive that its one-time boss, Neil Basu, used to refer to it as the 'ghost squad'. 'We felt kind of excommunicated from the Met,' he told BBC News. 'I sort of joke about it now, but I can't remember being invited to a leaving do for the three years I was on Professional Standards.' Basu, who was then a relatively inexperienced detective inspector, said he was 'wide-eyed' at the extent of the corruption he came across. 'My God, none of us realised it was at this level. What we were looking at here were people who were drug-dealers, conspiracy to commit kidnap, conspiracy to commit violence, serious assaults, perhaps even attempted murder.'

It was to this unit that I was now seconded, with the task of helping to administer its important work. Almost immediately, the collation began to throw up patterns of misconduct that might previously have gone unnoticed but were now visible. Whereas a single allegation by a drug dealer that a detective had seized drugs for his own profit might be dismissed as the predictable lashing out of a felon, half a dozen allegations made by different people in different areas were now catching the eye.

We sent officers to all thirty-two boroughs, quite literally asking them to search cupboards, basements and disused garages for lost files. On one occasion, an officer found an old hard drive which was obsolete and damaged, and I had to authorize the cost of £150,000 for an expert and his assistant to unlock and rebuild it, so the contents could be examined. It turned out to contain important information, including about former Detective Sergeant John Davidson, who had been accused of corruption in the investigation into the murder of Stephen Lawrence. Davidson was later cleared.

I was frequently shocked by what the exercise revealed, and scores of officers were called in for questioning as a result of files being brought together. Many who had long since retired came along with their lawyers – in some cases to help them explain how they'd found the money to buy their second homes or wine bars in Spain.

The job was challenging and rewarding, and after my experiences in Greenwich and Bromley I was happy to spend a period out of the day-to-day front line. Still, I retained my passion for operational policing and an ambition for further promotion. I'd been assured that my most recent application to ascend to the rank of chief superintendent had been rejected only because there were a limited number of jobs and too many qualified candidates. I was also told that I would have been the next in line. 'Dust yourself off,' was the advice from Commander Nick Downing, 'and we'll look for a next opportunity for you.'

As it turned out, I didn't have long to wait. As good as his word, Nick Downing called me again just two weeks later to say that a temporary vacancy had arisen as borough commander at Richmond and Twickenham. The incumbent chief superintendent, Colin Kennedy, had been the subject of an allegation of misconduct and was suspended pending enquiries and a hearing. The acting position would last at least six months but was open-ended, and would involve promotion to chief superintendent, at least for the duration. The only problem, Nick Downing told me, was that whoever took the job would have to be in place within twenty-eight days.

An abrupt end to my current role did not suit DAC Fiona Taylor, but she generously undertook to find a way to cope so that I could take up the opportunity. I was delighted. Aside from housing the legendary rugby ground, Twickenham was a relatively quiet borough as far as law and order was concerned, certainly in comparison with my previous beats in east and southeast London. However, it was a chance for me to get back into uniform and to show what I could do if given a chance to run something of my own.

It was therefore with a significant bounce in my step that I started my new role in west London in July 2016. The announcement was welcomed by local newspapers, several of which ran photographs and features about the appointment of the Met's most senior Asian woman officer to the borough. I was made less welcome, however, by the chief executive of Richmond council, Gillian Norton, who told me that she didn't want me in the post because 'I want Colin Kennedy back.' I received a similar sisterly welcome from the local Conservative Member of Parliament, Tania Mathias, who said very much the same thing. (Later, Mathias was much more supportive of me, but subsequently was ousted in the 2017 general election by Vince Cable.) When I attended my first Safer Neighbourhood Board, I was curtly informed that its members would be complaining about my importation in place of Colin Kennedy who, unlike me, was a local person with roots in the local community. (I assumed this was a reference to me hailing from Sevenoaks, rather than from the sub-continent.)

All this was fairly hard to take, but I knew I had nothing to do with the cause of the vacancy, and equally that I could do nothing about the unhappiness caused by the suspension of Kennedy. However, when I found the representative of the local Police Federation sitting opposite me and complaining about my arrival with the words, 'We know all about your background,' I was not similarly powerless. I threw him out of my office.

If all this was not bad enough, I was then informed by the other superintendent on the borough, Rob Applegarth, that he felt he should have been given the job of filling in while Kennedy was away. Applegarth was a direct entrant into the police, having been in the armed forces and, as far as I was aware, had only worn the dark blue uniform for around eighteen months.

'So, you've been in the police for a year and a half and I've been in for twenty-eight years,' I asked him, 'but you think it should have been you rather than me who took this job?' I remain unconvinced that Applegarth ever conceded the point.

Day-to-day policing was, for the most part, a less fraught affair than I'd previously experienced. Much of the crime involved online fraud, and a significant population of elderly residents were prone to the evils of door-to-door conmen.

I attended regular reviews of events in the borough, and one day was surprised to hear about an incident in which police had been called when a man was accused of groping a woman on a bus. Officers had questioned the man on the roadside, but eventually decided to let him go free with a warning. Passengers on the bus were astonished that no further action was being taken – and when I heard about it, so was I. I issued an order that officers should go to the man's house to arrest him, but I later learned that the instruction had not been carried out.

One of the passengers on the bus had been made so angry that he put an account of the incident on Facebook, along with the man's name and address, which he'd overheard during the police interview. As a result, the alleged groper had received threats and now apparently felt in danger in his own home. We found ourselves in the extraordinary position of providing extra security for the man who'd been accused of inappropriate behaviour. Needless to say, questions were asked about whether this was a good use of police resources.

The relative prosperity of the borough didn't make it completely immune from the types of crime more associated with deprivation, and one day I went on a routine patrol with Home Beat police responsible for a troubled estate in

Twickenham. My officers suggested that we might pay a visit to someone they knew well – a very talented artist, but also a habitual cocaine user. We knocked on the door of a flat in a high-rise, which was opened by a man with a fresh and alarming gash, which started above his eye and extended halfway down his cheek. It was clear that he wasn't happy to see us, but nevertheless he was persuaded to invite us in.

The flat was full of beautiful works of art, which the man used to sell in an area close to the market square in Kingston. The only trouble with this arrangement was that he used the money he made to buy drugs, which then brought him onto the radar of local dealers, as a result of which he'd been 'cuckooed'. What that meant was that criminals would knock on his door and demand entry with threats of violence, then use his flat for several hours or days to sell illegal drugs. Callers to burner phones would be told to come to this particular address, the deal would be done, and eventually the dealers would be on their way. This had been happening regularly, but on this day the artist had tried to resist, and so they'd made an example of him to deter others.

The artist had no hesitation in relating the story because he knew we couldn't arrest or prosecute anyone without him as a witness, and it was more than his life was worth to give evidence to us. So often the frustration of our job is that we know who the guilty people are but are unable to gather the evidence necessary to bring them to justice.

We got slightly more satisfaction when investigating a spate of burglaries, including at a house in Castlegate, Richmond, where items stolen included a box containing the ashes of a pair of twins who had died at birth. Naturally, the parents were heartbroken. Eventually, we received information about a suspicious VW Passat which, when it was stopped, was found to contain crowbars, hammers and rubber gloves. Three men from Poland were arrested and eventually convicted, and investigating officers were able to invite the bereaved parents into the local station to return the precious remains of their children.

In Richmond, just as in most big cities, one of our jobs as police officers is to try to fill in the gaps left by inadequate social service provision, especially in the area of mental health. A relevant case from the time began when we took a call from a mother who was distraught that her 37-year-old son had lost control of himself and had left the house in a state of agitation. The man had mental health issues and she was concerned for his safety.

Ben Rich was eventually tracked down and taken to Kingston Hospital, where it was said he should be transferred to the more specialist Springfield University Hospital in Tooting. Officers remained with the man for many hours while he waited to be transferred, but when he was eventually admitted to the facility, he absconded again. The next thing we heard was another call from Mum saying he'd returned to her house and that she was afraid. When our patrol car arrived a few minutes later, officers saw Mr Rich driving out of his mother's road in a sports car. They followed, and there was a chase, which ended when Mr Rich drove his car underneath a lorry, injuring the lorry driver and the driver of another vehicle, and killing himself.

A two-year-long inquiry eventually absolved the police from responsibility but was highly critical of the health and social services. It was just another of the hundreds of tragedies caused every year by inadequate and uncoordinated provision of welfare support.

By no means all my experiences with colleagues were negative, and my stay in Richmond brought me into contact with one particular officer whose approach reminded me of one of the reasons I'd wanted to join the force in the first place. I already knew PC Paul Dowsett as someone who'd been giving up his spare time to work with local police cadets for more than eighteen years. Over that time, he'd given a helping hand to hundreds of young people, often steering them away from a life of crime and towards a career in the police. One day, Paul asked me if I'd meet a young man he'd been looking after but who, at just 10 years old, was too young to join the police cadets. The boy, who I'll call Jamie, had an absent father, and a mum suffering from serious depression. Jamie was very close to his mum and used to stay off school to take care of her when she was especially unwell. One day, though, Jamie's mum insisted that he should go to school, but by lunchtime he was so worried about her that he returned home to see how she was. When he let himself in, he found his mother hanging above the staircase with a rope around her neck. The 999 operator told him how to cut her down, and Jamie was still trying to perform CPR on her when the ambulance arrived and she was pronounced dead.

Jamie went to live with his grandfather, and Paul had taken the boy under his wing, helping to keep him safe and out of trouble until he could join the cadets. I was glad to agree to have Jamie with me for a day of work experience, and at lunchtime I took him out to a nearby café. He was a truly lovely kid, and I watched as he wolfed down a huge plate of sausages and chips and then went onto pudding, declaring how great it was that his grandad wouldn't have to cook for him that evening. Then he took out an old mobile phone, carefully prized off the back panel, and produced a £20 note that his grandad had given him to pay for his lunch. Of course I refused, but he insisted. The boy's grandad wanted him to pay his way. I could have wept.

As well as the operational role, my new job involved a wide range of civic and ceremonial responsibilities. Among the VIPs I had to meet and greet were Zac Goldsmith and latterly Vince Cable, who came across as a very nice man. I frequently found myself obliged to attend evening events and then face the prospect of a long and late-night commute back to my home in Sevenoaks. Eventually, the frequency of long days and nights obliged me to bring a few changes of clothes into the office and install a camp bed in the corner. Overall, I was enjoying the change of pace, even if my new base was a four-hour round-trip from my home, and I felt equal to the responsibilities of borough commander.

I also enjoyed and appreciated the opportunity to attend an 'insight day' for people who might be in line to attend the Strategic Command Course at the College of Policing. However, even a routine day mingling with the most senior officers in the land could not pass without a reminder that I was not 'one of us'. On my way into a meeting on the first morning, I fell in behind a senior officer who was speaking on his mobile phone. He knew I was there and within earshot of his conversation, but was complaining to someone that he was having to look after 'some black guy from London'. Then he said, 'It is like being at school and having to look after the younger kids.' Another day, another incident of gratuitous racism; however, before long, even though I was out of the way in the sticks, I was soon made aware that someone somewhere had it in for me.

In July 2017, I was asked to see my boss, Julian Bennett, who told me that information had been received from an anonymous source that I was not putting in the hours and was 'not visible' in the borough. I was amazed. I was, in fact, regularly working fourteen to sixteen hours a day as the borough commander, including weekends. Initially, I thought he had confused me with someone else. I was disgusted that yet again I was being subjected to allegations with absolutely no truth to them.

It all came to an end in February 2018, when several boroughs in west London were amalgamated as part of force-wide cuts in manpower and resources, effectively making my role redundant. My predecessor Chief Superintendent Colin Kennedy was exonerated, found to have had no case to answer, and subsequently retired.

Once again, I found myself as a highly qualified and reasonably well-paid police officer, but with no assigned role. I took the next opportunity to apply for promotion to the rank of chief superintendent, and passed all the tests except one, and so would not be given the job. When I discovered later that the particular psychometric test that I'd failed had been found to be potentially biased against people from ethnic minorities, I had a tough decision to make.

Ever since the Bristol Seminars nearly thirty years ago, people from ethnic minorities have remarked that if we complain or make a fuss, we're instantly marked down as troublemakers. By that point in my career, there'd been a series of incidents where I'd had the choice of sitting back and taking it, or standing my ground. I have no doubt that my decisions to stand my ground have had the effect of labelling me a troublemaker, and here I was again – feeling on the wrong end of an injustice, but unsure whether it was in my best interests to make a complaint or to keep quiet.

I decided to appeal against the decision not to appoint me as a chief superintendent on the grounds that one of the psychometric tests was racially biased. However, keen as always not to let the grass grow under my feet, at the same time I applied to head up the anti-terrorism project known in the Met as 'Prevent'.

I didn't get the job, and the (white, male) officer who did was the same rank as me and arguably less well qualified. Nonetheless, I welcomed my consolation prize of being appointed second in command. The appointment was, of course, conditional on a security clearance by New Scotland Yard, but I felt confident that there would be no obstacles; after all, my existing clearance by MI5 was at the level of developed vetting (DV), which is the highest that can be obtained. But I was in for yet another surprise. While the security services seemed to be completely satisfied that, after twenty-nine years of exemplary service with no trace of any suspicion, I was no kind of a security risk, the Metropolitan Police was not. In fact, nothing could have prepared me for the email from Vetting Compliance summoning me to an interview:

> Please can you attend Empress State Building 6th floor lift lobby where a member of the team will collect you, to conduct an interview *to discuss your Indian heritage* [my emphasis]. Please bring with you Passports covering the past 10 years including Passports or Identification documents [sic].

I was born in Britain and have lived in Britain all my life. I have never been accused of anything which would call my loyalty into question. I have worked in many roles opposing radicalism in a whole range of ethnic groups, have been positively vetted by MI5 to the highest level, and I have only been to India three times in my entire 54 years to date – yet now the security people at Scotland Yard wanted to meet me to discuss my Indian heritage. I duly turned up for the interview, and while one of my interrogators flicked through the pages of my passport, another embarked on the questioning.

'How often do you go back?'

'Back where?' I asked. 'To Handsworth?'

'No, to the Punjab.'

'I've never been to the Punjab,' I said. 'That's where my

parents come from. Not me.' I did not want to make a mistake, so I offered more detail. 'I've taken three holidays to India over the years, but have never been to the place my family came from.'

'What about your parents?'

'My father is dead. My mother is housebound. And even when they were able to, they hardly ever went back to India. I think my mum has been back twice in my lifetime. They made this their home.'

By now, the other officer had finished thumbing through the pages of my passport.

'I see you've been to Russia?'

I confirmed that Rod and I had indeed been to Moscow for a holiday. We had visited Red Square, photographed the Kremlin, that sort of thing.

'Did anybody speak to you?'

I confirmed that lots of people had spoken to me. I was on holiday.

'But they will have known you were a police officer?'

I was left to wonder about the significance of this while the other officer continued.

'And I see you've also been to China?'

'Yes, that's right. Great Wall. Forbidden City. All the tourist stuff.' Now I felt the need to be more helpful. 'We like going to places we've seen in the movies,' I explained. 'It's a hobby. We've also been to Transylvania and to the Vatican.'

This seemed to satisfy my interrogators. 'Well next time you go to China, let us know, will you?' I confirmed that I would and, seven minutes after the interview began, it was over.

A week later, I was at a leaving party when I ran into my boss, Mark Simmons. By now I had chosen to see the funny side of the incident, and so I related the story to a gathering of officers. Simmons was horrified. 'What are we going to do about it?' he asked. I said I was perfectly happy that nothing should be done about it. I was entirely willing to pick up the cudgels on behalf of principles that really mattered, but this one had been only a minor irritant. However, one week later I received an email from a senior officer indicating that the whole matter had been looked into, personnel had been spoken to, and the terminology used when such matters arose was to be amended. A minor victory in a battle I had chosen not to fight.

As second in command of Prevent, my responsibilities now involved coordinating hundreds of officers seconded from forces up and down the country in an effort to identify and head off extremism, especially among young people. The task was similar to the one I'd been involved with during my time at the National Community Tension Scheme. Any time the police are alerted to concerns that a particular individual may be in the process of becoming radicalized, an operation goes into action in an attempt to head off the problem before it goes too far. Many thousands of individuals come to the attention of the Prevent teams, via schools, mosques, parents or members of the wider public; 65 per cent of them are Muslims, and the next biggest group are members of the far right. Once notified, the Prevent team coordinates a direct intervention designed to convince the individual that they're in danger of being misled. In the vast majority of cases, the person is a highly impressionable and vulnerable youth, and the intervention is successful.

The question of my possible promotion to chief superintendent was still on hold. I had missed the required pass mark in one of the relevant exams by a whisker. I'd complained about the use in the selection procedure of a particular psychometric test that had been deemed to be racist, and the result of my appeal was that the test would no longer be used, but nonetheless the decision stood.

Then, out of the blue, I was informed that I might, after all, be promoted to the rank of chief superintendent. I was, of course, thrilled to hear the news, and for a moment I hoped that some senior person had seen the injustice of holding me back when I was so obviously qualified and suitable. But not a bit of it. I quickly learned that when Bernard Hogan-Howe had retired as commissioner, he'd given a written undertaking to his staff officer – a man called Marcus Bennett – that he would be guaranteed three years 'acting up' at the rank of chief superintendent. This was unprecedented and left the Met in an awkward situation. Since there was now no role for Bennett, he would need to be promoted. The trouble was that he'd achieved a lower mark than me in the relevant exams – so, in order to fulfil the outgoing chief's commitment and promote Bennett, the Met would have to promote me as well. So they did, and in the process made history more or less by accident.

CHAPTER TWENTY-FIVE

Gross Misconduct

The day of 5 July 2018 should have been one of the proudest of my career. It was the first public event I'd attended since becoming the only BAME woman ever to be promoted to the rank of chief superintendent in the 189 years of the Met. The occasion was a gathering in New Scotland Yard in memory of Shafilea Ahmed from Warrington in Cheshire, who was murdered by her parents in a so-called honour killing. As the Met's lead police officer coordinating efforts to combat honour crimes, I'd been asked to chair the event, at which senior officers, volunteers and celebrities were present.

Shafilea Ahmed's story needs to be recounted not because it is unusual, but because it is sadly all too typical of an appalling crime that has become common here in Britain as elsewhere. It is emblematic because it is so tragically familiar.

It was in February 2004, five months after she'd gone missing from her home in Warrington, that Shafilea Ahmed's decomposed and partially dismembered body was found 70 miles away in the

River Kent in Cumbria. There were immediate suspicions that the girl had been killed because of her failure to conform to her parents' values, and specifically her unwillingness to agree to a marriage they had arranged for her in Pakistan. However, the police could find no proof, and an eventual coroner's inquest in January 2008 found that Shafilea had been the victim of a 'very vile murder', and delivered a verdict of unlawful killing.

There the matter might have rested, except that two and a half years later, in August 2010, Shafilea's younger sister Alesha arranged a burglary at her parents' house while she, her brother, sisters and parents were all at home. When questioned by the police, Alesha revealed that she had staged the robbery in order to give herself the opportunity to report to police what she knew about the death of her sister.

Alesha told police that Shafilea's refusal to accept an arranged marriage had brought perceived shame on the family, and so her father had put a plastic bag into the girl's mouth and suffocated her. She saw their mother in the kitchen 'sorting through a pile of blankets and sheets and holding a roll of black bin bags and two rolls of tape'. Later, Alesha looked out the window and saw her father carrying a large object wrapped in bin bags with brown tape around it. Later still, she saw him leaving in a car.

Shafilea's parents, Iftikhar and Farzana Ahmed, were charged with their daughter's murder. Both were found guilty and sentenced to life imprisonment with a minimum term of twenty-five years. Shafilea's death had been adopted as an example of the much wider problem of honour crimes, and the event at New Scotland Yard was designed to draw public attention to the need to stamp them out.

I did my best to remain composed and controlled throughout my brief summary of Shafilea's story, and most of the audience would, of course, have had no idea of the extent to which I could personally relate to the events I was describing. Like Shafilea, I had been put under enormous pressure by my parents to agree to a marriage I had no wish to accept. Also like the 17-year-old Shafilea, at 16 years old I had been part of a wider Asian community where no help or support seemed to be available. I had, of course, been forced to acquiesce and undergo the trauma and violence of a marriage arranged for me, while Shafilea had suffered the consequences of continuing to refuse.

Perhaps these were good reasons why I might have felt more than averagely moved by the occasion. However, what none of those present knew was that a few minutes before I'd taken the stage, I'd received a call which had nearly knocked me sideways. It was from the press office, to tell me that someone had leaked to the media that I was to be the subject of an internal investigation – a charge of gross misconduct, which, if I was found guilty, would mean a very ignominious end to my police career.

An accusation of gross misconduct is one of the most serious that can be made against a serving police officer. It covers matters such as assault on a colleague or a member of the public, giving or accepting bribes, racism, bullying, etc.

But the charge facing me didn't involve any of these. It was an allegation that I had lobbied on my own behalf for an award of a medal and, if proven, this might be a breach of internal police guidelines.

While struggling to concentrate on the important business at hand, rattling around in my head was the feeling of 'Here we go again'. What had emerged over three decades was a pattern of good news quickly being accompanied by bad news – and it seemed to be repeating itself. When, for example, all those years ago, I'd felt ready to take the sergeant's exam, suddenly there emerged the first suggestions that my performance had been below standard. When my experience and record seemed to make me a candidate for the High Potential Development Scheme, suddenly I was rejected and told 'never apply again'. When I'd been promoted to chief inspector, a minor domestic incident on the touchline of my son's football pitch had been turned into a national news story. When our house had been taken over and wrecked by cannabis farmers, someone informed the press that the house belonged to me, and not my husband Rod. When I was given an operational role as superintendent in Greenwich, someone tipped off the newspapers that I was a non-executive director of my husband's security firm, and that this might be in breach of the rules on outside interests. Time and time again, I had found myself hounded by journalists and photographers, which invariably led to outpourings of disgusting abuse directed at me on social media.

The inescapable pattern seemed to be: while very few people objected if a young Asian woman put on a police uniform, if we made the mistake of showing any ambition, or failed to know our place, or failed to play the game by the rules set by the brotherhood of white men dominating the highest ranks of the Met, then someone put a trip-wire in our path. Our little black or brown faces were OK if we kept quiet and stayed in the crowd, but as soon as any of us became 'uppity', we had to be reminded of where we stood.

And it wasn't necessary for everyone to subscribe to this ugly creed. Indeed, all it needed to achieve its aim was for good people to remain silent. With a few honourable exceptions, that's what they did.

But exactly what was the latest allegation? The action of mine that apparently justified the further derailing of my career was that I'd suggested to some friends and colleagues in the force that I could be a candidate to receive the Queen's Police Medal, which is awarded to just a few officers each year. Two colleagues had apparently been happy to recommend me, as a result of which they too were facing charges of misconduct.

Was it true? Had I done so? Yes, I had. Was it against the rules to have done so? That would be a matter of contention, but I knew immediately that I had made a mistake – I had given my enemies their opportunity, and I should have known better. While the British establishment scarcely has an honour which is not lobbied for, or asked for, or paid for, or awarded free of charge to someone from the right background, I should have known by now that such activities only apply to 'one of us'. What for most people would have been seen as a trivial transgression of an arcane rule, more honoured in the breach

than in the observance, provided an opportunity for my enemies
to strike another blow.

So why had I done it? Let me try to explain.

As a young Asian woman, I had joined – twenty-nine years
earlier – a police force that was totally controlled and run by
a close-knit coterie of white men. The culture and ethos of
so many of these men was to perpetuate their own hegemony
– sometimes via freemasonry, sometimes via the golf club,
sometimes via pubs and social clubs, and sometimes through
corrupt associations. They looked out for each other, tended to
associate together, to favour each other, and to promote each
other. It would have suited their agenda and the perpetuation
of the status quo if I, and a few others like me, had been
content to remain quiet, subservient, make the tea and have
our bums slapped. If only I had acquiesced to being turned
upside down at Chadwell Heath all those years ago and let
the men stamp the station logo onto my bottom. If I had done
that and remained silent while enduring countless indignities
in the meantime, no doubt I would still be standing behind a
reception desk in an outlying station, putting up with racist
and sexist comments and attitudes.

However, I am ambitious. It's a trait universally applauded
in men, but one which is frequently condemned when displayed
by women. Especially Asian women, who come from a culture
where 'getting above yourself' is criticized – sometimes viciously,
sometimes fatally. I have conducted my career in a context in
which everything I ever achieved had to be fought for. Had
I been a member of the white men's club, no doubt friends

and colleagues would have been quick to notice my possible eligibility for various rewards and honours, and would have lobbied behind the scenes for one of their own to be recognized. As it was, without some direct action on my part, I would be standing by and watching others receive recognition which perhaps might fairly have come my way.

I might or might not have been guilty of a technical breach of rules made up by those who don't have to lobby on their own behalf; a breach of a 'gentlemen's agreement'. But I am not a gentleman – I am a minority (Asian) within a minority (women), within the Met, and if I didn't shout for myself, I could be pretty sure that no-one else would.

If all this was not traumatic enough, worse was still to come. At the same time that I was being accused of gross misconduct, thirteen other officers of the same rank in the Met (of whom a disproportionate number – five – were BAME) were also facing disciplinary procedures. Charges in these other cases included assault and corruption – serious crimes – but of course the allegation against me didn't have to be fair, or true, or proportionate to achieve its objective. The allegation alone was enough.

Just ahead of the gathering of dignitaries at New Scotland Yard in honour of Shafilea Ahmed, I was told that, immediately following the event, I would be more or less confined to desk work. I was to have no further dealings with outside bodies, and no further use of social media. Despite the fact that the complaint against me had somehow been leaked to the press, I was to say nothing about the case, and nothing in my own defence. In the six months, or nine months, or entire year that this would take to be properly investigated, the smear would taint my career, the rumour and innuendo would spread, I would be unable to apply for a permanent position as chief superintendent, and what might be the last of a thirty-year career of loyal service would be marred.

The story was carried as a headline on BBC radio from first thing the next morning, and was subsequently picked up, repeated and further embellished by media sources as wide and various as the *Daily Mail*, the BBC South Asia Service, NDTV in India and the ironically named 'Clever News' on YouTube. As on every other occasion that my name had appeared in the media for any reason, I was quickly treated to the usual avalanche of social media comments of the 'go back to where you came from' variety.

How did it come about that a charge of a technical breach of internal regulations involving a woman of Asian background appeared on the radio, TV and throughout the press, while the far more serious allegations against multiple other officers of similar rank were not leaked and not published? How did a story of only passing interest to a few people find its way into the national and international headlines broadcast on BBC Radio 4, among other stories that included the PM 'seeing off' rebels over Brexit at Chequers and England taking on Sweden in the World Cup? Of course, the obvious answer is that the story was leaked, which raises the twin questions of by whom and with what motive?

To the first question, the BBC's home affairs correspondent

Danny Shaw, who 'scooped' the 'story', quite properly will not give an answer. He is satisfied, however, that he was not inadvertently used by those guilty of the institutional racism with which certain sections of the Met remain imbued. So then, why? What might be going through the mind of someone who picks up the phone to Danny Shaw to tell him about a disciplinary action against me, while presumably neglecting to put the charge in the context of the far more serious allegations against others of similar rank?

One can only speculate, and speculation is likely to remain the only means of enquiry, because the Met declined to take any other serious measures to investigate. This is in spite of a direct request from Janet Hills, Chair of the Met's Black Police Association, who wrote on my behalf to the Met on 20 July:

On 7th July 2018 a news article was mentioned on the BBC news website in relation to Temporary Chief Superintendent Parm Sandhu. This looked on the face of it, like a press release from DMC; however, I have subsequently found out that this is not the case and that the information was leaked.

At the time of the news article I was contacted by a number of people both internal and external to the organisation that asked, why the information had been put into the mainstream media as in their opinion it was not deemed newsworthy.

The position of the Met Black Police Association, is that if this information was leaked, we would like it investigated. Over the years officers and staff from African, Caribbean and Asian heritage are subjected to having their personal information leaked when they are investigated for misconduct matters. This has an adverse impact on them and their families.

In spite of this, and other protests on my behalf, no serious measures were ever taken to discover the source of the leak, and no senior officer took the opportunity to try to provide context for the charge, or to point out that even BAME officers should be presumed to be innocent until proven guilty. It was an opportunity not missed two weeks later when news reached the media that three (unnamed, white, male) officers had been charged with gross misconduct – this time of a far more serious nature involving corruption. On that occasion, the Met's assistant commissioner for professionalism, Helen Ball, interrupted her Sunday to issue a statement.

This morning, the *Sunday Times* reported that a number of MPS personnel were involved in an independent IOPC [Independent Office for Police Conduct] investigation into allegations of inappropriate interference in DPS [Directorate of Professional Standards] investigations and I know that this may have caused some colleagues concern.

Whilst it is true that there is currently an IOPC investigation into elements of decision making within DPS investigations, the article included unsubstantiated opinion and, as far as the Met is aware, inaccuracies. I think it is important to explain the situation as far as we are able to. Three officers have been served with gross misconduct notices. These are necessary processes which protect the rights of those subject to the IOPC investigation but do not in themselves imply anything more than that. One of these officers is subject to a criminal investigation. Assessments on the status of allegations concerning a number of other personnel remain ongoing. It is important to understand that the IOPC investigation is at an early stage and, as with any investigation, including others which have been high-profile recently, it is important to keep an open mind. No officers or staff have been suspended or restricted and those involved are being supported and kept informed.

Three white male officers accused of criminal activity and corruption had not been named and had not been put on restricted duties, while one female Asian officer accused of a technical breach of an internal regulation had. Yet senior staff in the Met are still vehemently rejecting the charge of institutional racism.

Now, digging deeper than I had ever had to in my career before, I attempted to rise above the humiliation of having been accused so publicly. I held my head up, took a deep breath and decided to attend the first annual conference of the Police Superintendents' Association since my promotion. It was held at the Leicester Marriott Hotel in mid-September 2018 and guest speakers included: the commissioner of the Met, Cressida Dick; Home Affairs Select Committee Chair, Yvette Cooper; and, of course, the then Home Secretary, Sajid Javid. The three-day conference is a useful chance to network and compare experiences with senior officers from other forces across the country. It also had a particular relevance for me this year because the issue of enforced marriages was on the agenda. However, what should have been an informative and enjoyable experience for a newly promoted chief superintendent turned into a trauma. From the moment I got there, I felt as though fingers were being pointed and tongues were wagging. It's not too much of an exaggeration to say I was made to feel like a criminal.

At the formal dinner on the first evening, I found myself quite literally rubbing shoulders with none other than the BBC reporter who'd received the unauthorized leak and broken the news of the latest accusation against me. Danny Shaw took the opportunity to offer me the chance to 'tell my side of the story', but, of course, even if I was inclined to do so, the restrictions placed upon me forbade me from discussing my case with anyone outside of the Met. Next, I found myself on the same table as Justin Davenport, crime editor of the London *Evening Standard*, and had to spend the evening avoiding being overheard. There were dozens of officers of my rank with outstanding accusations against them at the conference – some would turn out to be justified and others unjustified. But, being a woman, being non-white, and having been featured in the TV, radio and newspapers, it was me that people were pointing at.

I took some comfort when I learned that the Met's first ever female commissioner, Cressida Dick, had asked to see me. She listened to my side of the story and seemed sympathetic, and then she asked what she could do to help. I replied that she could speed up a process which could easily be dealt with in a day or two, but was instead due to take many months. I told her that I was being well paid to do a job with considerable responsibility, but was currently confined to a role with just five officers under my charge.

'I'm afraid I can't interfere with the appropriate authority,' said the commissioner.

'Then why did you ask what you could do for me?' I said. There was no answer.

I felt so gutted by the turn of events that when I got back to my desk the following week, I found myself contemplating resignation. For the first time in my career, I called the Met's Occupational Health Department, which is sub-contracted to an outside company and supposed to be independent. I told them I was feeling stressed. The woman was very nice and asked if the stress was a result of the disciplinary action against me. I said it was not.

'Then what's the cause?' asked the woman.

'Google me,' I said, and waited.

A minute passed before the woman spoke again. 'Oh my god,' she said. 'No wonder you're stressed. This is an outrage.'

Her search had thrown up a catalogue of headlines from all over the world about a 'top cop accused of gross misconduct', many of them taking the opportunity to roll out every calumny that had ever appeared in the press, including the 'assault on the touchline', the cannabis farm, and my 'scandalous' appointment as a director of my husband's company.

But I was not the only person paying a price for the manifest injustice being perpetrated against me. It has also had an unquantifiable impact on some of the most vulnerable people in the community. We had been making good progress in the campaign combating honour crimes and especially FGM, and as part of an ongoing programme of education, the government's inspectors at Ofsted had agreed to include some questions in a survey of schools. However, the deadline for agreeing everything was September, and the restrictions now placed on me made it impossible to get arrangements in place in time. The survey went to press without the inclusion of the questions about FGM.

Despite the fact that everything anyone needed to know in relation to my alleged transgression could have been ascertained in half a day, I resigned myself to an inevitable wait of several months. I was informed that any time I applied for a permanent role as chief superintendent, the interviewing officers would be told of the charges outstanding against me – which of course entirely stymied any chance I might have had of securing promotion. I got on with my daily duties as best I could, trying to keep up my spirits and setting an example to younger officers who might find themselves unjustly accused. Despite my best efforts to keep my focus on the job in hand, I couldn't help but wonder who had made the allegation in the first place. When eventually I received the background papers outlining the case against me, I realized that the answer should have been obvious all along.

In the period since I'd left Greenwich, DCS Richard Wood had been promoted to the rank of commander, and was now enjoying the exalted position of head of the murder squad. One day, he found himself deputizing on the committee which reviews recommendations for medals and honours. When examining the papers involving me, Wood had noticed that a citation from someone outside of the Met was written in language more usually used by a police officer – suggesting perhaps that they had been 'fed' the details by someone inside. Moreover, when he reviewed the stated reasons for the recommendation, he took issue with some of the claims being made on my behalf: specifically, he disputed my role in keeping tabs on the English Defence League (EDL) and calming community fears following the murder of Lee Rigby. He therefore objected to the recommendation, and referred it to a superior officer for further investigation. Had I not only exhorted others to recommend me for a medal, but then also falsified or exaggerated the justification for the award? All this from the very same officer with whom I'd been in dispute in the matter of the delegated authority.

While this might seem to some a rather minor disagreement between two colleagues – which any competent management could sort out in an hour – apparently, it did not seem that way to the Met. A team of officers was appointed to go back through the archives for six years to read my emails, with a view to determining whether I had or had not taken a leading role in controlling EDL demonstrations, and had or had not chaired community meetings as had been claimed.

While I remained confident that the operational claims made on my behalf were entirely justified and that the historic email traffic would prove them to be so, I came to the realization that something would need to be found, simply to justify all the fuss and expense of the investigation. And so it was. At a routine meeting with my line manager in September, I found myself served with notice of yet another charge against me. My crime this time? A breach of the data protection legislation.

It seems that officers trawling through emails about the murder of Lee Rigby and the EDL alighted on one from 2013 which I had sent to my private email address. These files should not have left the building, as it would be in breach of data protection laws. Unlike the alleged breach of internal guidelines in having encouraged others to support my eligibility for the medal, this offence was a matter of criminal law, which could therefore have far more serious consequences. Yet again I felt as though I had been kicked in the stomach. If it wasn't bad enough to already be publicly accused of dishonesty in relation to the alleged lobbying, now it was clear that any tiny administrative error I may have made in my twenty-nine years in the police force was to be investigated, just to drag my name through the mud.

On my way home that day, I wracked my brains for any

reason why I might have sent official files to my personal email address. When I arrived and was able to look at my in-box, I found that the files had indeed been sitting undisturbed in my hard drive for the past six years. Once more, I delved into my memory, seeking to recall why I would have sent the emails to myself. Then I remembered.

Around that time, we had been experiencing IT problems at work, and a number of important files had been lost or erased from the New Scotland Yard hard drive. Efforts were being made to fix the problem, but I was anxious that the files I was working on shouldn't be lost in the process. I'd sent them to myself at home, and as soon as the IT problem was resolved, I'd sent them back to the office. They'd never been opened or disclosed to anyone else. All I'd done was to keep them safe from being lost altogether. The action had been well intentioned and had brought about no harm to anyone, but nonetheless it was a technical breach of data protection laws, and now I was facing a criminal charge.

What was now happening to me was following a familiar pattern – one which BAME officers have been complaining about since the Bristol Seminars more than twenty years ago.

'Black officers are regularly accused of gross misconduct for allegations which would usually bring a charge of simple misconduct if alleged against a white officer,' says Janet Hills of the Black Police Association. 'BME officers are statistically far more likely to be accused of a misdemeanour than a white officer,' she adds, 'and far more likely to be dismissed from the force if found guilty.'

Exactly this had happened in recent memory to my friend Shab Chaudhri, to Leroy Logan, to Carol Howard, and to Gurpal Virdi, among others. Giving evidence to the House of Commons Home Affairs Select Committee in March 2019, John Azah, the chief executive of the Kingston Race and Equality Commission, reported that, of the total of six BAME officers at chief superintendent level in the Met, no fewer than five were facing disciplinary charges and were suspended or on restricted duties. He went on to report a recent conversation with a senior Met policeman, who was 'quite clear about how the process works. An officer complains about an issue; down the line this officer is accused of some other incident which is purported to be a criminal offence. The Home Office guidance says that the criminal offence has to be dealt with before the victim's complaint is dealt with. Therefore by the time the criminal offence is dealt with and protracted . . . the victim's complaint is lost in the system, and that confuses the issue.'

The pattern identified by John Azah found another uncomfortable echo in the case of Jennifer Izekor who, in 2012, had been invited by the then Home Secretary Theresa May to serve as commissioner of the Independent Police Complaints Committee (IPCC). Ms Izekor ruffled a few feathers within the Met by the thoroughness of her investigations into allegations of racial discrimination and, according to reports in *The Times*, she was warned by well-meaning officers that someone would 'do your legs' if she continued. Ms Izekor dismissed the suggestion, pointing out that she didn't work for the Met, but later found herself on the wrong side of a criminal allegation claiming that she had withheld evidence that would have exonerated officers who'd been accused of racism. Ms Izekor was obliged to stand down from her job during the investigation, which lasted for two and a half years and involved examining more than 700 documents. At the end of it, she was, of course, cleared of any wrongdoing.

Jennifer Izekor is completely clear that she was targeted with an entirely trumped up charge, and that this was the direct result of performing her role of investigating wrongdoing in the Met:

> If there are people at the heart of the Met where decisions are made, where power is held, who are so uncomfortable with being challenged on issues of racism and discrimination that they will do anything to take the challenge away instead of answering the questions they need to . . . then that raises very serious questions about what is changing and how much they are going to allow it to change.

Although now burning with a sense of personal injustice, I felt equally outraged by the waste of public money and resources. If your home is burgled tonight and you call the police for help, the chances are that no-one will even come out to see you. But the Met could apparently afford the manpower to be combing through my emails from six years ago in search of a technical breach that has never damaged anyone.

The point could scarcely have been more topical. An episode of Channel 4's *Dispatches* the following month reported that a quarter of all reported crimes nationally are not investigated at all, and that this was attributable to a reduction of 20,000 police officers in the eight years since 2010. A senior officer told the programme that police won't even attend the scene of a burglary 'unless we have CCTV, forensics, witnesses, likely suspects and identification'. A letter to *The Times* the following month reported: 'Three weeks ago my 16-year-old son and a friend of his were mugged in Norwood, South London, by a gang of seven youths who stole their phones, punched my son and threatened to stab him.' The incident had taken place in broad daylight and 'the whole incident was caught on CCTV . . . The police have footage of the boys, including face shots, but say they do not have the resources to go into schools to identify them.' Also in the same month, six young men were stabbed to death on six consecutive days on London streets. And just a few weeks later, a survey carried out by Her Majesty's Inspectorate of Constabulary found that one-third of people questioned claimed they had not seen a single police officer or community support officer in their area for the whole of the previous year.

Up until this point, the adverse publicity, the finger-pointing, the restrictions on my duties had been causing me stress and sleepless nights. Now, suddenly, this latest absurdity made something in my head go click. What had hitherto manifested as alarm and self-doubt suddenly morphed into a solid feeling of indignation, and the resolve and determination which had seen me through so many crises in the past kicked back in.

Ordinarily, someone in my position would look to the

Superintendents' Association for support, but by now this horror had been going on for four months and I hadn't even been asked to meet any of their people. Unsure where to turn for help and advice, I remembered running into a lawyer called Lawrence Davies from the firm Equal Justice. Davies had represented the former Met police firearms officer Carol Howard, and brought her complaint to an employment tribunal in 2014.

Exactly as in my own case, the Met's campaign of persecution against Carol Howard had begun only after she had made her initial complaint – in Carol's case for discrimination on grounds of race and gender. The Met had sought to discredit Carol Howard by leaking allegations against her to the newspapers ahead of the public hearing – just as had happened with me.

Lawrence Davies made a careful and painstaking examination of a sequence of events going back to my time at Greenwich, and advised me that I'd have a strong case for making a claim at an employment tribunal. My first reaction was very negative. I'd always advised people against going down that route in the past, because the Met would make your life hell, but now there was a more important motivation driving me. I was angry and I wanted to clear my name. I had dedicated my professional life to being an honest and committed police officer, and I didn't want to spend the rest of my career with colleagues looking at me as though I was a criminal. So, it was with a heavy heart that I began working with Davies to itemize the lengthy catalogue of snubs and slights, the grievances and the unfairness.

Ironically, my task was made easier by the fact that the ongoing investigation into my past had involved the inquiry team dredging up records and emails going back far further than would have been easily accessible. I was able to root out and give verbatim detail of scores of injustices, some relatively small and some significant, but which, when taken together, painted an ugly picture. It all added up to what seemed to be a persuasive case, and my confidence was given a further boost when my insurance company examined the evidence and agreed to underwrite my claim to the tune of £100,000.

So now I had the ordeal of a pending employment tribunal to add into the mix, alongside the investigation surrounding the Queen's Police Medal and the alleged criminal breach of data protection laws. In the event, the investigation into this last matter found its way to the front of the queue when I was summoned to be formally interviewed under caution on 1 February 2019. The venue was set for the Empress State Building in Earls Court, which is thirty-five miles from my home. Two days before the hearing, I received a document outlining the full extent of the prosecution case against me.

The day got off to an inauspicious start. I'd slept quite badly – unsurprisingly, because for the first time in my life I was now a suspect in a criminal investigation. It had snowed heavily, which added to my concern. If I got snowed in, it would be seen as intentionally not attending a pre-booked suspect interview.

Several trains were cancelled due to the bad weather and I arrived just before 9 a.m. to be met by my solicitor Rachel

Adamson, who'd travelled from Preston. I was also happy to see my police 'friend' Kim Warner, who is a superintendent from Norfolk, who was there to support me through the process. What followed was a un-nerving experience for a police officer who has spent twenty-nine years scrupulously sitting on the right side of the law, and on the right side of the interrogation desk.

At 10 a.m., I was taken into an interview room on the 21st floor, which was equipped with a telephone and video-recording facilities. The interview was taped. The criminal caution was read out to me, and I then had to explain what my understanding of that was. The whole situation felt surreal.

Detective Sergeant Paulette Rooke led the interview, and it was clear from the start that she felt uncomfortable. When we first entered the room, she asked how I would like to be addressed and said her first instinct was to call me ma'am. I said I was fine being called by my first name. She kept going red in the face, and during the interview she alternated between ma'am and Parm.

My solicitor then handed over a detailed statement we'd prepared in response to the charge, consisting of a series of itemized bullet points. The breach had occurred while I was trying to find ways to carry out my duties despite problems with the IT system; it had led to no harm or damage to anyone; the files had never been passed on or disclosed to anyone else; I had never made any material gain; and the whole thing had taken place six years earlier. Any objective person reading the statement would be mystified as to why it was worth wasting valuable police resources on this charge. Nonetheless, after a fifteen-minute break for Paulette to read and absorb the statement, the interrogation resumed.

'Did you share the emails?' My statement already made it clear that I had not. I declined to comment further.

'Did you know it was wrong?' Again, my statement already showed that I did indeed know it should not have happened, so I declined to comment further.

'Why did you do this?' My statement had already given her the reasons. For the past six years, until recently, I hadn't even remembered that I had. I declined to comment further.

'Have you been trained in managing data, etc?' Of course I had. There was no need to answer.

In short, after twenty-nine years of faithful and loyal service to the Metropolitan Police, I found myself in a position where I was obliged to heed legal advice and respond to a series of questions asked under caution, with 'no comment'.

When the tapes were switched off, Kim Warner remarked that he was amazed that ten months after the original allegations the investigation seemed to be no further forward. If any of his officers had proceeded so slowly, he would have wanted to know why, especially since during all that time I had been prevented from performing the highly responsible job for which I was being paid, and also prevented from applying for a permanent post as chief superintendent. My career was effectively in limbo, all for no apparent reason.

The waste of resource could scarcely have been made more poignant, because the hearing took place on the same day that the Met achieved our first ever successful conviction of a woman for the female genital mutilation of her own daughter. As the Met's lead officer on FGM over several years, I should have been out maximizing publicity for the development, appearing in the press, and perhaps even receiving a little of the credit. Instead, I was sitting on the wrong side of an interrogation table, searching my memory for information about an unintentional breach of data protection from six years earlier.

Whoever leaked the story about the charges against me to the press is in breach of regulations and has caused real harm, but there had not been any proper investigation. Meanwhile, my inadvertent breach of regulations from six years ago had caused no-one any harm, and I was being investigated like a common criminal. Little wonder, perhaps, that I was feeling aggrieved.

It might seem ironic that, while awaiting the outcome of my various disciplinary actions, I was attached to the Met's Directorate of Professional Standards, where I found myself in the unenviable position of having to mix with colleagues who were investigating the charges against me. The new posting put me in the front line of a series of incidents which, taken together, went some way to answering the question of whether Cressida Dick was right to describe the Metropolitan Police Service (MPS) as no longer institutionally racist. In one incident, a Somalian who had been arrested and taken to the cells for a strip search complained that one of the officers had described him, when naked, as a 'dancing monkey'. Of all the questions that might have arisen in the minds of the officers investigating the complaint, the one which apparently did occur was: Would a person of BAME background find it offensive to be called a dancing monkey? The question was asked of the Directorate of Professional Standards, and they asked me. 'Would you,' the question came, 'as a BAME person, find being described as a "dancing monkey" offensive?' This really happened.

In another incident, in an online discussion among MPS staff debating what had been learned since the murder of Stephen Lawrence, one officer commented that the killers were no doubt thugs. However, had police not secretly recorded their private conversations, it would not have been obvious that they were also racists, and therefore Stephen's murder would have been dealt with as an ordinary crime. In the course of his argument, he referred to Stephen using the 'n' word. I was obliged to react quickly to delete the reference from the online stream. I swallowed hard, and then invited the officer to join my own team for three weeks, in the hope that he might learn something.

Several weeks later, I was notified of the time and date of a second interrogation into the allegation that I had effectively nominated myself for the Queen's Police Medal, and that I had lied about the achievements that justified the medal. I took a deep breath and prepared myself for the ordeal. I was facing the prospect of being directly accused of having made up or exaggerated my participation in events that had been difficult and traumatic at the time, and the questions I'd be facing were coming indirectly from my previous boss, a man whose conduct I'd complained about years earlier.

It was only a few days before the examination was scheduled

to take place that I received the final and complete details of the case against me. It was with some apprehension that I opened the document and scanned the contents. It turned out that there was, after all, to be no accusation of dishonesty or exaggeration in the charge against me. I immediately made further enquiries, and was told that the investigating team had looked through something like 100,000 of my emails going back to 2013, and all they proved was that every one of the claims made in the nominations for the medal were justified. I had indeed chaired large-scale public meetings and had been in charge of policing public demonstrations involving the EDL and others. Everything claimed in the recommendation was borne out by the email traffic. So now all I had to do was to defend myself against a charge that I had transgressed what was said to be an internal police guideline against effectively nominating myself for the Queen's Police Medal.

Investigating officers had interviewed a number of people who nominated me for the medal. Each of them confirmed that they had felt under no pressure to do so. They all told detectives they believed that I deserved the honour and would nominate me again if given the opportunity. I was also able to produce a statement from the former chief constable of Derbyshire, Mick Creedon, in which he said he saw nothing wrong with officers nominating themselves. All this was unhelpful to the case for the prosecution. Less helpful still was the actual wording of the guidelines: 'Anyone can nominate anyone.'

I believe that any reasonable person reading the case for

and against me could only come to one conclusion and, five weeks later, that was the conclusion reached by the relevant disciplinary authority. After an ordeal lasting nearly eighteen months, in which I had been publicly humiliated and my career put on hold, on the afternoon of 17 June, I received a bland email declaring that, on the charge of nominating myself, there was 'no case to answer'. On the other charge, there had been a technical breach of data protection laws, but I was to receive words of advice and there would be no sanction against me.

I stared at the ten-line email for several minutes, breathing deeply and trying to take in the words. Of course, I had always known that the allegations against me were unjustified, but in the light of recent experience, I dared not hope that others would see things the same way. Now I felt a mix of relief and indignation – and sadness.

All those years ago, my mother warned me never to buy a house of my own because people would break my windows. I chose not to believe that. I bought my own house, and I forged my own way. I encouraged people from all backgrounds to join the police, and I made a life for myself. But, in the end, it turned out that my mother was right. If you come from where we come from, there are always people who want to break your windows.

My husband Rod was away on business that day, so I worked in the office until 7 p.m., and then took the train back to my empty home in Sevenoaks.

CHAPTER TWENTY-SIX

'You have personally failed!'

Wednesday 10 July 2019 would turn out to be a particularly long and stressful day for the first ever female commissioner of the Metropolitan Police. Cressida Dick was due that afternoon to give evidence to the House of Commons Home Affairs Select Committee investigation into progress made in the twenty years since the Macpherson report. Instead of spending the morning mugging up on any statistics which might prove helpful in sustaining her argument that institutional racism has disappeared from the Met, she had been obliged to attend one of her leadership conferences at New Scotland Yard.

After the conference, I was having a meeting in the corridor with Mark McEwan, who has the Orwellian title of commander responsible for inclusion. The commissioner came over to us and initially I thought she was going to ask if I was ok. Instead, she said: 'Oh, sorry, Parm, I just need to speak to Mark.'

I sat quietly while Cressida Dick told the commander that she was giving evidence to the Home Affairs Committee in an hour. She was anticipating a discussion on the merits of positive action (in which BAME candidates and officers are positively encouraged) versus positive discrimination (in which BAME candidates are given an actual advantage over their white counterparts). 'I'm going to argue for positive discrimination,' said Cressida, 'and I need three points from you.' Only then did it seem to occur to her that I might have something to contribute. 'Oh, Parm,' she said, 'maybe you can chip in?'

I admit to feeling a moment of indecision. On the one hand, this might be a good moment to toe the line and act the part of the obsequious junior, trotting out some respectful but essentially asinine platitudes. On the other hand, I was still angry about everything I had gone through over the past eighteen months – everything I felt that Cressida Dick could so easily have prevented. I felt my temper rising and took a deep breath.

'You haven't even used positive action and you could have done,' I said. Already I was jabbing my finger at her in a way which was clearly alarming both the commander and the commissioner. 'You have allowed targeted racial discrimination against me and others like me. Today you have five BAME females of superintendent rank, and by the end of the year you will have one. You have five BAME men at superintendent rank with a similar picture of discrimination.' Cressida looked stunned and McEwan's mouth was agape, but I was only just warming to my theme. 'You are not listening to us. I told you about this in September; you didn't listen then, you aren't listening now. I was a role model for the MPS and now my reputation is in tatters and people don't want to join us or go for promotion.'

Cressida tried to interrupt at this point and spluttered something about how I was still a role model. I'm afraid I jabbed my finger at her again and told her she was talking rubbish. I continued.

'I hold you personally responsible for taking us back twenty years and for destroying the MPS for me and people like me. Yes, go for positive action – because you personally have failed in everything else. You have personally led the organization, and just look at what you've done. You have personally failed.'

The commissioner was clearly taken aback but was only able to respond with, 'I have to go to the House of Commons now,' and with that she quickly retreated. McEwan sat in stunned silence. When eventually he spoke, his comment to me was brief and simple. 'Fair play to you.'

So, I like to think that my words were still ringing in her ears when Cressida Dick, one hour later, took her seat opposite a horse-shoe of MPs, chaired by Yvette Cooper.

There followed an excruciating two hours of interrogation in which the commissioner did her level best to persuade MPs that she had a zero-tolerance approach to racism in the Met and was 'passionate' about getting to grips with it. Unfortunately, just about every statistic she produced purporting to demonstrate progress was systematically unpacked and unpicked by Cooper and other MPs.

Her evidence got off to a poor start on the subject of whether the public believed the police are fair. When the commissioner stated that the gap in attitudes of BAME versus white people had narrowed, it was left to Yvette Cooper to point out that dissatisfaction among people of BAME background had increased by 13 per cent and that the gap had in fact widened.

Cressida then went on to admit that BAME police officers were twice as likely to be accused of misconduct than their white counterparts, but countered that outcomes were now more or less equal. Once again, it was left to the Chair to point out that outcomes for BAME officers were still worse than for white officers.

At the end of a bruising two hours, Yvette Cooper seemed incredulous that Cressida Dick still appeared to be maintaining that the Met was 'unrecognizable' from the organization so sorely criticized by Macpherson. Clearly beaten down and exhausted, the commissioner could only repeat that she found the accusation of institutional racism 'unhelpful'.

I entirely expected to receive a summons to the commissioner's office for a dressing down about my forthright verbal assault on my boss. At the very least, I thought she might be interested to hear more details of some of the facts I had thrown at her. Instead of which, the next official communication I received was an invitation to participate in a formal (and videotaped) interview about the serious allegations I'd made in my claim to the employment tribunal. Now heartily sick to death of the entire process, I declined.

Suddenly, I felt an irresistible need to take a breather before deciding how to proceed with my complaint. The Met had sought a postponement before responding to the details of my case, and the date was set for several months away, in September 2019. I resumed my role in the Directorate of Professional Standards, but far from enjoying some justifiable respite from the stresses of the past eighteen months, I found that my ordeal was a long way from being over.

Yet another unauthorized leak from someone in New Scotland Yard to the press led to journalists enquiring about the outcome of the charges against me. Although stories run by the *Daily Mail* and the BBC made it clear that I'd been exonerated, they still led to a cascade of the now familiar 'go home' and 'get back to your own country' comments on social media. The additional strain of further publicity was taking its toll.

Feeling increasingly desperate to find a way out of my immediate working environment, I applied for a job as a temporary commander. I didn't get it, and so I asked for routine feedback from Assistant Commissioner Nick Ephgrave. When I received the appointment for the meeting, I spotted a handwritten note in the margin – obviously accidentally forwarded on to me. The note advised Ephgrave that, before he saw me, he should acquaint himself with my 'complaint'.

This made it crystal clear that already 'my complaint' was a factor in assessing my career and future, rather than my skills and experience. Not for the first time, a BAME officer making a complaint about racial and gender issues was being further discriminated against by the Met.

This further slap in the face proved to be the last straw for me. On 29 July, I wrote to Assistant Commissioner Helen Ball:

I would like to make you aware that after thirty years of
service to the MPS, I have finally been driven to resign.
My last day of work for the MPS will be 22nd October
2019. The last few years, in which I have been subjected
to targeted racial and gender discrimination, have been
extremely difficult for me. In the past I have always felt
able to overcome such difficulties, but I have now been
forced into a position that has become untenable.

I went on to describe the most recent pressures which had driven
me to the brink and then over the edge, and then signed off:

It is with great sadness and a heavy heart that I concede
to the bullies and racists who belong to the MPS, more
than I have ever done.

Chief Superintendent Parm Sandhu

My final formal duty after thirty years in the Met was, perhaps
appropriately, to host a ceremony at the police training college
at Hendon, to dedicate a room to the memory of Stephen
Lawrence. Attending alongside the commissioner Cressida Dick
was Baroness Doreen Lawrence, as well as Stephen's brother
Stuart. John Azah, who had given such devastating evidence
about continuing racism in the force to the Home Affairs Select
Committee, was also present. On this occasion, and in front
of this audience, the commissioner was considerably more
restrained in the claims she made on progress in abolishing

institutional racism in the Met. While no-one hearing her could have doubted the sincerity of her tribute to Stephen and his parents, the Baroness was in no mood to let the force off lightly.

Doreen told the audience that when she'd first been informed that a room at Hendon was to be dedicated to her son, she'd had her doubts. She had come along today 'to make sure it wasn't a broom cupboard out the back somewhere'. She generously acknowledged that progress had been made, but then recalled a recent occasion when she'd visited New Scotland Yard with the radical lawyer Imran Khan; meanwhile, a friend waiting for them in the foyer overheard a stream of remarks about what a scandal it was that the two of them were being entertained in the building. There remain, she asserted, a number of racists still in senior positions in the Met. Cressida nodded politely. I have no doubt that she looks forward to the day when such occasions need bring no fear of similar embarrassment.

A few days later, at a small and low-key gathering at New Scotland Yard, the commissioner shook me warmly by the hand, and presented me with a framed certificate:

This is to certify that Chief Supt Parm Sandhu joined the Police Service as Constable on 20 August 1989 and retired on 22 October 2019. The Officer's conduct was Exemplary.

CHAPTER TWENTY-SEVEN

'Don't let the bastards grind you down'

I n January 2020, my mother was taken into hospital with a respiratory infection, and my newfound freedom meant that I was able to sit by her bedside every morning for two weeks, without having to explain to anyone where I was or what I was doing. That was a great blessing because it was to be her last illness.

The time together gave us the opportunity to talk, and she made it very clear that she was ready to die. In her own way, she had always been a fighter, and she told me over and over again that her last wish was that I should remain strong for this coming battle with the Met and that I would emerge with my professional reputation restored.

Against the odds, she seemed to be recovering from the condition that put her into hospital, but then she caught pneumonia from having been an in-patient, and died a few days later. No-one, including my mother, knew exactly how old she was; she'd been married at 10 years old and gave birth to her first child in her mid-teens. Jindo is now 72, so Mum was probably 88. Her death divided the family by continent of birth – I called it 'one body, two funerals' – as my three older siblings who were born in India followed Sikh traditions which involve ritual and conspicuous grief, while the three of us born in England celebrated her long and fruitful life.

Rod and I took some holidays and I started to adjust to life as a civilian after thirty years as a copper. There are a million odd little things that you come to take for granted as part of your life as a police officer. Being in uniform brings obvious restrictions, but even in plain clothes, as a police officer you're always wondering what's going on when you hear a distant siren, or bracing yourself for the possibility of having to intervene if there's a dispute in the street or on a train. Now all that was in the past. I think I'd probably still do something if I saw a crime being committed in a public place, but at least in those circumstances I'd be faced with the same choices as everyone else.

But, of course, I couldn't exactly relax because all the while there was the looming prospect of an acrimonious employment tribunal against the Met. The case had been scheduled for a hearing over three weeks in June 2020, and while my familiarity with courts and court proceedings meant that this held no particular fear for me, I'd be lying if I said it wasn't a dark cloud on my horizon.

The lines were drawn for what seemed sure to be an intense and bruising battle. In preparing its case, the Met had carried out an internal investigation into the officers named in my complaint, most notably my two senior colleagues at Greenwich, Richard Wood and Chris Hafford. I was not remotely surprised when the inquiry found absolutely no fault with the conduct of either of them – an outcome that would no doubt be used to resist my complaint at the tribunal. My allegations had been 'properly investigated', it would be said, and found to be without merit.

So I was amazed and initially bemused when my solicitor Lawrence Davies telephoned me to say that the Met was suggesting we take my case to a judicial mediation rather than the tribunal. This only happens when the Met would prefer to settle than to fight.

The call triggered a whole range of thoughts. If the Met was so sure of its ground, why would they prefer to agree a deal than defend themselves against my claims? If I agreed to a mediation, I would be denied my 'day in court', in which my complaints would be made public and my situation hopefully vindicated. On the other hand, I knew from long experience that courts and tribunals can be unpredictable; you never know what's going to happen on the day. The biggest considerations in my mind were the words of my mother, still ringing in my head. She wanted me to have my reputation restored.

Advice from my friends and family was to go along with the mediation to see where it led. If it gave me what I felt I needed, I could accept the findings and go about my business. If not, I could always take my chances and go on to fight the battle in a three-week public forum.

The mediation was set for Friday 6 March, and in preparation for the day, Lawrence and I set out the terms on which we would settle. The financial side was a simple and clinical calculation of income lost as a result of acts of discrimination, lost promotion, lost pensions and so on, plus an arbitrary figure in recognition of the stress caused to me by the Met's actions. More important to me was that the Met must write to all the people, inside and outside the force, who'd been asked to make statements against me. I wanted them to hear officially that there had been no case to answer and that the Met was apologizing for the distress caused by their inquiry.

The day of the mediation was coming up fast and, true to form, I received a phone call late on the previous evening to tell me that the venue had changed. Nonetheless, I felt confident as I approached the process – knowing that I was entirely ready to walk away if necessary.

My hopes of a successful outcome were given a further boost when I realized that the Met had sent Mark Simmons to represent them. Mark is a decent man who has always been supportive of me, and felt like a friendly face. It was a good sign.

The mediation process involves a form of shuttle diplomacy, in which the two parties sit in adjoining rooms and the judge shuttles between them, reporting 'he says this, she says that'. We set out the elements we needed if an agreement was to be reached and both sides took up positions. My initial optimism began to fail as the Met's opening gambit was so far away from what I felt they should be offering considering the thirty years of discrimination I had endured. After several hours, I asked to meet Mark on his own without lawyers. The judge said this was very unusual, but it was agreed.

'If this is the way you're going about it, I'm wasting my time,' I told him. I hadn't come for a nickel and dime back and forth. If the Met was serious, I would stay, if not I was going home and would see them again at the tribunal. Mark said he understood and the process began to make more serious progress and continued for the rest of the day.

I will not disclose the eventual agreement to settle my claim against the Met. I have no doubt at all that, just as with every other event in my recent career, the details will be leaked to the press and I will be invited to comment. I am content to leave the reader to judge whether I would have settled without the vindication I felt I needed.

When I left the mediation at the end of a long day, Rod and I went to the nearest bar. He bought me a glass of white wine and I took a single sip, and then I started to cry. I don't know why I did; I wasn't unhappy, but nothing could stop the tears from running down my face. After a few minutes, Rod was becoming anxious. Was I OK? Yes, I was OK, but I just couldn't stop crying. All the way home on the train, the tears flowed down my face. Other passengers looked at me, some showing concern, but there was nothing I could do. I slept all day the following day, and when I eventually awoke, my mind went over what had happened.

Finally, after years and years of stress and anxiety, my horizon was clear. Although, of course, I hadn't been thinking about all the negative aspects of my career for every single moment of my life, it was never far from my mind. On holidays, at Christmas, during family celebrations, in some corner of my brain, there was always this nagging feeling, inevitable when you find yourself in conflict with a powerful force. Unresolved business. Bad blood. Now, and only now, it was over. I was vindicated, my reputation was restored, and I felt properly free.

No doubt it's still far too soon for me to be able to sum up what I feel about my thirty years in the Metropolitan Police Service. Life dealt me more than my fair share of troubles in my early years, and I had seen a lot of hardship up close through my work in the Department of Health and Social Security before I joined the force. By then, I knew enough to realize that I was going to be an object of curiosity in an organization so dominated by middle-aged white men, and I was scarcely surprised when that sometimes turned into blatant sexism and racism. Time and time again, the agreement I'd reached with my friend Shab not to 'let the bastards grind you down' was put to the test, and time and time again we both came through. There were many highs and many lows, but I did my best to stay optimistic, and always took an opportunity to encourage anyone from a minority to join the police. Because only by producing a police service that properly reflects the community it's trying to serve will we eventually solve the problems of racism and sexism that remain institutional in the Met to this day.

So what, in the light of everything that happened to me in the last years of my service, would I say to a young BAME person considering joining the police today? With just a few reservations and warnings, I'd say go ahead and join. It won't be easy, and you'll see and bear witness to things you can scarcely imagine. You'll experience the best of people, and the worst of people, and you'll have to remain professional throughout. You'll be let down by some colleagues you should be able to rely on, but you'll also make friends for life. And if you can weather all the storms and troubles, you'll have the satisfaction that comes from providing a genuine and important service to your community.

As for me, I feel that, in the end, I didn't let the bastards grind me down – not totally or finally – and I'm ready for whatever the next chapter of life will bring. I'm free at last. Free to do what? Well, let's see. . .

Afterword to the Paperback Edition

'I want people who are going to be really strategic and forward thinking. I cannot forgive. If you fail me once I cannot trust you again.' I'm speaking these harsh words while standing on the landing dock of a remote Scottish island and flanked by two stony-faced former detectives. We're supervising the investigation into the brutal murder of a young woman who has been found bludgeoned to death in a country lane. In many ways it's familiar as the type of scene I've attended all too often in the last thirty years. This time though, there's an important difference, which is that we are surrounded by lights, cameras, make-up artists, a floor manager, producer and director. I've agreed to play the part of 'the boss' in a new series for Channel 4, in which the celebrated crime-writer Ian Rankin has invented a murder mystery, and members of the public have been invited to solve the crime. My opening words are designed to show what an uncompromising boss I'm intending to be.

As so often before, my life has taken a wholly unexpected turn. The publication of this book, and the publicity surrounding my departure from the Met, have led to me becoming the 'go to' retired senior officer for news media seeking comment on the frequent occasions when the Met is the story. The producers of *Murder Island* had been expecting to cast a typical Rebus-type white male detective for the role, but the mere fact that I am so unusual as a non-white and female senior officer for once has worked in my favour. I got the job, and we had an enjoyable two weeks of filming before the programmes went to air in October 2021.

Meanwhile events in the real world were proving to be far less enjoyable. Just a month earlier, the most senior police officer in the land seemed genuinely emotional as she commented on the conviction of a Metropolitan Police officer for the real-life rape and murder of 33-year-old Sarah Everard. Cressida Dick acknowledged that the Wayne Couzens case had shaken public confidence in the police and went on to promise that, 'As Commissioner, I will do everything in our power to learn any lessons… here in the Met, I commit to keep working with others to improve women's safety and reduce the fear of violence.'

There were so many questions to answer and lessons to learn. What did it say about the culture of the Met that a series of overt and abhorrent sexual acts by Couzens over several years had been treated as a source of humour rather than of concern? So flagrantly deviant was he, that Couzens was affectionately known by colleagues as 'the rapist', but no serious effort was made to curtail his behaviour.

While all this was going on, two police officers were awaiting trial for sharing selfies taken with the dead bodies of murder victims Nicole Smallman and Bibaa Henry, and were subsequently jailed. Meanwhile former Detective Superintendent Paige Kimberley was telling reporters that she had complained directly to Cressida Dick about a series of sexist comments being shared among officers in a WhatsApp group. She had received no reply, and instead of investigating Paige's complaint, the force withdrew an offer of work previously made to her.

Then the Independent Office for Police Conduct reported on a long-running WhatsApp correspondence involving fourteen officers at Charing Cross. The IOPC revealed a breath-taking litany of vile exchanges in which one officer wrote, 'I would happily rape you,' while another commented that, 'Getting a woman into bed is like spreading butter. It can be done with a credit card but it's quicker and easier to use a knife.' Another officer wrote, 'My dad kidnapped some African children and used them to make dog food.'

While I was unrestrained in my condemnation of these and other similar acts, I took the opportunity of every interview to emphasize that the vast majority of police officers are well-intentioned public servants in whom women and wider society can have confidence. I encouraged women from all backgrounds to join the police, and repeatedly offered to continue to work with the Met to bring about the radical changes which are so urgently needed. All the while, I have maintained my role as a mentor to some younger female officers.

My repeated offers of help went unanswered and, in the end, it was the Commissioner's consistent failure to listen to voices like mine, or to comprehend the real depth and scale of the problem, which led to her departure in February 2022. That evening on Channel 4 News I was asked by Krishnan Guru-Murthy if I thought Cressida had ultimately failed. I said she had, because women in particular had lost confidence in the Met: 'When you are sitting at home as a victim and thinking, "Shall I call the police… but if I call them, are they going to be sexist, misogynistic, homophobic or racist? Or are they going to be one of the good decent individuals who are working for the police service?" It's all hit and miss.'

Many months went by, and many names were put in the frame, before the then Home Secretary Priti Patel announced the appointment of Cressida's replacement. Sir Mark Rowley is a 58-year-old white man, a police-lifer; no doubt well-qualified but inevitably cast from more or less the same mould as just about every other senior officer in every police force in the land. The London mayor Sadiq Khan endorsed the appointment, commenting that 'Sir Mark has made clear to me that he is determined to be a reforming Commissioner, committed to implementing a robust plan to rebuild trust and confidence in the police and to drive through the urgent reforms and step change in culture and performance Londoners deserve.'

Let's all hope so. The task facing Cressida's successor is daunting. It remains to be seen whether our police service is perhaps the only public institution in which they still believe that it's acceptable to bully and intimidate women, require them to keep quiet about what's happened to them, and then to use the force of the law to keep them silent.

I hope that my account of what happened to me contributes to this important public debate – and that at long last somewhere in the Met, someone is listening.

Acknowledgements

Thanks go to Cathryn Summerhayes, Jess Molloy, Sophie Macaskill, Luke Speed, Alice Lutyens and Raneet Ahuja at Curtis Brown, to Dixie Linder at Cuba Pictures, and to James Nightingale, Sarah Chatwin and Karen Duffy at Atlantic Books. We also thank Emma Linch and Alex Wade for wise advice, as well as the former officers from the Met whose stories we've woven into our own.

Mostly our thanks to Satnam and the rest of the Sandhu family in London, Rod Jarman and Sam Richards for unwavering faith and support.

Illustration Credits